FACTS OF FAITH

FACTS of FAITH

BY

CHRISTIAN EDWARDSON

(*Revised*)

TEACH Services, Inc.
www.TEACHServices.com

World rights reserved. This book or any portion thereof may not be copied or reproduced in any form or manner whatever, except as provided by law, without the written permission of the publisher, except by a reviewer who may quote brief passages in a review.

The author assumes full responsibility for the accuracy of all facts and quotations as cited in this book. The opinions expressed in this book are the author's personal views and interpretation of the Bible and do not necessarily reflect those of TEACH Services, Inc.

Facsimile Reproduction

As this book played a formative role in the development of Christian thought and the publisher feels that this book, with its candor and depth, still holds significance for the church today. Therefore the publisher has chosen to reproduce this historical classic from an original copy. Frequent variations in the quality of the print are unavoidable due to the condition of the original. Thus the print may look darker or lighter or appear to be missing detail, more in some places than in others.

Copyright © 20013 TEACH Services, Inc.
ISBN-13: 978-1-57258-193-X
Library of Congress Control Number: 2001086715

Published by
TEACH Services, Inc.
www.TEACHServices.com

PREFACE

During forty years of caring for districts of churches and isolated believers, besides raising up new churches, by evangelistic effort, the author of this work became greatly impressed with the need of educating the people in the fundamental doctrines of the Holy Scriptures. He has found very few who could give from the word of God an intelligent reason for even its most prominent and important truths. This spiritual poverty any minister will discover by personal investigation.

When we add to this condition the fact that during the past twenty years new errors have been stealthily introduced among Christians generally—errors which undermine the very foundations of Bible truth and Christianity—it becomes evident that even professing Christians are unprepared for the crises they will be obliged to meet in the near future.

For several years many ministers and Bible students have urged that the author prepare the manuscript for this book, embodying numerous new quotations and references to works of great value. Limitations of space have permitted inclusion of only the choicest and most important selections from authentic historical and doctrinal works.

PUBLISHERS.

CONTENTS

THE PERFECT GUIDE	9
FORGING NEW WEAPONS	18
ROME UNDERMINES THE PROTESTANT FOUNDATIONS	26
THE PROPHETIC HISTORY OF THE WORLD	34
"A TIME, AND TIMES, AND HALF A TIME"	52
OTHER MARKS OF IDENTITY	61
CHRIST AND THE SABBATH	70
THE NEW TESTAMENT REST DAY	80
THE SABBATH IN HISTORY	83
SUNDAY IN THE EARLY CHURCH	88
INFLUENCES TOWARD APOSTASY	97
THE WALDENSES	118
CELTIC SABBATH-KEEPERS	134
WYCLIFFE, HUSS, AND ZINZENDORF	147
SABBATH-KEEPERS IN INDIA	153
THE REFORMATION	159
FINISHING THE REFORMATION	173
SABBATH REFORM IN SCANDINAVIA	178
THE TAIPING REVOLUTION	190
THE TWO MYSTERIES	193
THE ANTICHRIST	196
THE TIME OF THE END	212
A MESSAGE FOR OUR TIMES	216
THE UNITED STATES IN PROPHECY	234
MAKING AMERICA CATHOLIC	243
AMERICANISM VERSUS ROMANISM	256
THE JESUITS	273
THE MARK OF THE BEAST	288
THE IMAGE TO THE BEAST	302

The Perfect Guide

COULD it be thought possible that an all-wise Creator would bring so many millions of people into existence, as the inhabitants of this earth, and give them no information as to why they are here, or what His will is concerning them? No, that would be unreasonable. Just as surely as there is a judgment day coming, on which we all shall be called to account for our conduct, so surely He must have given us an infallible rule of life. But what is this "infallible rule"? The Roman Catholics say it is "The Church, with its traditions." But the Church has changed so greatly since its origin that if the apostles could arise from the dead they would not recognize it as the church they established. As for "tradition," it is like a story that grows and changes as it travels. No government would be satisfied with oral laws. In so important a matter as our eternal happiness we need a rule that is more stable and unchangeable, and this we have in God's infallible word, the Bible.

The Inspiration of the Bible

The Bible is not the product of man's thought and planning. "For the prophecy came not in old time by the will of man: but holy men of God spake as they were moved by the Holy Ghost." 2 Peter 1: 21. (Compare Isaiah 55: 8, 9; 2 Corinthians 3: 5.) Peter says: "The Holy Ghost by the mouth of David spake," and David himself declares: "The Spirit of the Lord spake by me." Acts 1: 16; 2 Samuel 23: 2. Of Jeremiah we read: "Then the Lord put forth His hand, and touched my mouth. And the Lord said unto me, Behold, I have put *My words in thy mouth.*" Jeremiah 1: 9. Thus the whole Bible is God's word, spoken through human instrumentality, for "*God hath spoken* by the mouth of all His holy prophets since the world began" (Acts 3: 21), and His hand guided them while they wrote. "All this," said David, "the Lord made me understand in writing by His hand upon me." 1 Chronicles 28: 19. And so, the prophets, after writing of Christ's coming, were "searching" their own writings to find out "what, or what manner of time the Spirit of Christ which was in them did signify, when it testified beforehand the sufferings of Christ, and the glory that should follow." 1 Peter 1: 11.

We have now presented the testimony of the Bible itself to the fact that "all Scripture is given by inspiration of God." 2 Timothy 3: 16. No consistent person can, therefore, receive one portion of it while he rejects another. Jesus says: "The Scripture cannot be broken." John 10: 35. He, the author of the Scriptures, displayed such implicit confidence in them, that even the devil did not dare to question their authority, when Christ faced him with the words: "It is written." Matthew 4: 4, 7, 10. Yes, "devils also believe, and tremble" (James 2: 19), for they know the Bible is true, while critics today doubt and ridicule (Jude 10). What has caused such terrible unbelief among men? We shall now briefly review the causes and the history of modern "Higher Criticism."

Rome Versus the Bible

After the Church had fallen from its apostolic purity of life and doctrine, it found that, where the Bible was read by the common people, they lost faith in the Church and opposed her worship as a species of idolatry. This was particularly true of the Waldenses, who had retained the Bible in their native language hundreds of years before the Reformation, and had copied and spread its pages over Catholic Christendom, wherever their missionaries traveled. It was natural, therefore, that the Roman church, instead of supplying the common people with the Scriptures in their native tongue, should oppose this. Cardinal Merry del Val says that on account of the activity of the Waldenses, and later of the Protestants, in spreading the Scriptures in the native language of the people, "the Pontiffs and the Councils were obliged on more than one occasion to control and

The Perfect Guide

sometimes even forbid the use of the Bible in the vernacular." He also says: "Those who would put the Scriptures indiscriminately into the hands of the people are the believers always in private interpretation—a fallacy both absurd in itself and pregnant with disastrous consequences. These counterfeit champions of the inspired book hold the Bible to be the sole source of Divine Revelation and cover with abuse and trite sarcasm the Catholic and Roman Church."—"*Index of Prohibited Books, revised and published by order of His Holiness Pope Pius XI*," "*Foreword*" *by Cardinal Merry del Val, pp. x, xi. Vatican Polyglot Press, 1930.*

These plain words from such an authentic source need no comment. Ever since the first "Index of Prohibited Books" was issued by Pope Paul IV, in 1599, the Bible has had a prominent place in these lists of forbidden books. And, before the invention of printing, it was comparatively easy for the Roman church to control what the people should, or should not, read; but shortly before the Reformation started, the Lord prepared the way for its rapid progress by the discovery of the art of printing. The name of Laurence Coster, of Holland, is often mentioned in connection with the story of the first production in Europe, in 1423, of movable type. In 1450 to 1455 John Gutenberg printed the Latin Bible at Mentz (Mainz), Germany. He endeavored for a time to keep his invention a secret, but Samuel Smiles relates:

"In the meanwhile, the printing establishments of Gutenberg and Schoeffer were for a time broken up by the sack and plunder of Mentz by the Archbishop Adolphus in 1462, when, their workmen becoming dispersed, and being no longer bound to secrecy, they shortly after carried with them the invention of the new art into nearly every country in Europe."—"*The Huguenots,*" *p. 7. London: John Murray, 1868.*

There being so few books to print, and there being a ready sale for Bibles, the printers risked all hazards from the opposition of the Church, and printed Bibles in Latin, Italian, Bohemian, Dutch, French, Spanish, and German. While these were so expensive that only the wealthy could afford to buy them, and their language was not adapted to the minds of the common people, yet they "seriously alarmed the Church; and in 1486 the Archbishop of Mentz placed the printers of that city, which had been the cradle of the printing-press, under strict censorship. Twenty-five years later, Pope Alexander VI issued a bull prohibiting the printers of Cologne, Mentz, Treves, and Magdeburg, from publishing any books without the express license of their archbishops. Although these measures were directed against the printing of religious works generally, they were more particularly directed against the publication of the Scriptures in the vulgar tongue."—*Id.*, *p. 8.*

THE REFORMATION AND THE BIBLE

The time had now come for the light to shine, and God's word could no longer be kept from the people. Prophecy states that in spite of captivity, fire, and sword, "they shall be holpen with a *little help.*" Daniel 11: 33, 34. But the people had been kept in darkness so long that they could not endure the glaring light of all the Bible truths at once. They had to come gradually, and the hour had struck for the Reformation to begin.

In preparing for the Reformation, the Lord had worked in marvelous ways to provide protection for the Reformers. The night before Martin Luther nailed his ninety-five theses on the door of the castle church at Wittenberg, the Elector Frederick of Saxony had a remarkable dream. In relating it to Duke John the next morning he said:

"'I must tell you a dream which I had last night. . . . For I dreamed it thrice, and each time with new circumstances. . . . I fell asleep, . . . I then awoke. . . . I prayed . . . God to guide me, my counsels, and my people according to truth. I again fell asleep, and then dreamed that Almighty God sent me a monk. . . . All the saints accompanied him by order of God, in order to bear testimony before me, and to declare that he did not come to contrive any plot. . . . They asked me to have the goodness graciously to permit him to write something on the door of the church of the Castle of Wittenberg. This I granted through my chancellor. Thereupon the monk went to the church, and began to write in such large characters that I could read the writing at Schweinitz. The pen which he used was so large that its end reached as far as Rome, where it pierced the ears of a lion that was crouching there, and caused the triple crown upon the head of the Pope to shake. All the cardinals and princes, running hastily up, tried to prevent it from falling. . . . I awoke, . . . it was only a dream. [Again he fell asleep.]

"'Then I dreamed that all the princes of the Empire, and we among them, hastened to Rome, and strove, one after another, to break the pen; but the more we tried the stiffer it became, sounding as if it had been made of iron. We at length desisted. . . . Suddenly I heard a loud noise—a large number of other pens had sprung out of the long pen of the monk. I awoke a third time: it was daylight.' . . .

"So passed the morning of the 31st October, 1517, in the royal castle of Schweinitz. . . . The elector has hardly made an end of telling his dream when the monk comes with the hammer to interpret it."—*"History of Protestantism," J. A. Wylie, LL.D., Vol. I, pp. 263-266.*

One can hardly wonder that the Elector of Saxony became Luther's protector during his long struggle with the Papacy. The greatest work that was accomplished by these "pens" of the Reformation was the translation of the Bible into the language of the common people. True, there had been some attempts made before this time to produce the Scriptures in the vernacular, but without much success, as the language was almost unintelligible to the common people, and the price prohibitive.

After Martin Luther had spent much time in the homes and company of the people that he might acquire their language, he, with his co-workers, translated the Bible into a language that, while it was dignified and beautiful, was so natural and easy to be understood by the ordinary mind that it made the Bible at once "the people's book." The New Testament was translated in 1521, and fifty-eight editions of it were printed between 1522 and 1533: seventeen editions at Wittenberg, thirteen at Augsburg, twelve at Basel, one at Erfurt, one at Grimma, one at Leipzig, and thirteen at Strassburg. The Old Testament was first printed in four parts, 1523 to 1533, and finally the entire Bible was published in one volume in 1534.

In 1522, Jacques Lefevre translated the New Testament into French, and Collin, at Meaux, printed it in 1524. In 1525, William Tyndale translated the New Testament into English. All these New Testaments were translated from the original Greek, and not from the imperfect Latin Vulgate, used by the papal church.

Printing presses were kept busy printing the Scriptures, while colporteurs and booksellers sold them to the eager public. The effect was tremendous.

"Every honest intellect was at once struck with the strange discrepancy between the teaching of the Sacred Volume and that of the church of Rome."—*"Historical Studies," Eugene Lawrence, p. 255. New York: Harper Brothers., 1876.*

In the Book of God there were found no purgatory, no infallible pope, no masses for the dead, no sale of indulgences, no relics working miracles, no prayers for the dead, no worship of the Virgin Mary or of saints! But there the people found a loving Saviour with open arms welcoming the poorest and vilest of sinners to come and receive forgiveness full and free. Love filled their hearts and broke the shackles of sin and superstition. Profanity, coarse jests, drunkenness, vice, and disorder disappeared. The blessed Book was read by young and old, and became the talk in home and shop, while the Church with its Latin mass lost its attraction.

Rome's Fight

Rome was awake to the inevitable result of allowing the common people to read the Bible, and the Vicar of Croydon declared in a speech at St. Paul's Cross, London: "We must destroy the printing press, or it will destroy us."—*"The Printing Press and*

The Perfect Guide 15

the Gospel," by E. R. Palmer, p. 24. The papal machinery was therefore set in motion for the destruction of the Bible.

"There now began a remarkable contest between the Romish Church and the Bible—between the printers and the popes. . . . "To the Bible the popes at once declared a deathless hostility. To read the Scriptures was in their eyes the grossest of crimes. . . . The Inquisition was invested with new terrors, and was forced upon France and Holland by papal armies. The Jesuits were everywhere distinguished by their hatred for the Bible. In the Netherlands they led the persecutions of Alva and Philip II; they rejoiced with a dreadful joy when Antwerp, Bruges, and Ghent, the fairest cities of the workingmen, were reduced to pauperism and ruin by the Spanish arms; for the Bible had perished with its defenders. . . .

"To burn Bibles was the favorite employment of zealous Catholics. Wherever they were found the heretical volumes were destroyed by active Inquisitors, and thousands of Bibles and Testaments perished in every part of France."—*"Historical Studies," Eugene Lawrence, pp. 254-257.*

In Spain, not only were the common people forbidden to read the Bible, but also university professors were forbidden by the "Supreme Council" of the Inquisition to possess their valuable Bible manuscripts.

"The council, in consequence, decreed that those theologians in the university who had studied the original languages, should be obliged, as well as other persons, to give up their Hebrew and Greek Bibles to the commissaries of the holy office, on pain of excommunication."—*"History of the Inquisition of Spain," D. J. A. Llorente, Secretary of the Inquisition, p. 105. London, 1827.*

"In 1490, Torquemada [the Inquisitor-General] caused many Hebrew Bibles and more than six thousand volumes to be burnt in an *Auto da fe* at Salamanca."—*"Literary Policy of the Church of Rome," Joseph Mendham, M. A., p. 97. London, 1830.*

How many thousands of invaluable manuscripts thus perished in the flames of the Inquisition, eternity alone will reveal.

It is exceedingly difficult for a Protestant in our days to fathom the extent of this fear of and enmity against the Bible, manifested by the Roman church. With her it was actually a life or death struggle! A person must read the history of the Inquisition, and examine the Roman Indexes of Forbidden Books, to understand her viewpoint. Inquisitor General Perez del Prado gave expression to her feelings and her bitter lament when he declared in horror "'that some individuals had carried their audacity to the execrable extremity of demanding permission to read the Holy Scriptures in the vulgar tongue, without fearing to encounter mortal poison therein.'"—"*History of the Inquisition of Spain,*" *D. Juan Antonio Llorente, p. 111.*

The funeral piles were lit all over Europe. Samuel Smiles says of France:

"Bibles and New Testaments were seized wherever found, and burnt; but more Bibles and Testaments seemed to rise, as if by magic, from their ashes. The printers who were convicted of printing Bibles were next seized and burnt. The *Bourgeois de Paris* [a Roman Catholic paper] gives a detailed account of the human sacrifices offered up to ignorance and intolerance in that city during the six months ending June, 1534, from which it appears that twenty men and one woman were burnt alive. . . . In the beginning of the following year, the Sorbonne obtained from the king an ordinance, which was promulgated on the 26th of February, 1535, for the suppression of printing!"—"*The Huguenots,*" *Samuel Smiles, pp. 20, 21, and first footnote.*

"Further attempts continued to be made by Rome to check the progress of printing. In 1599 [1559] Pope Paul IV issued the first *Index Expurgatorius,* containing a list of the books expressly prohibited by the Church. It included all Bibles printed in modern languages, of which forty-eight editions were enumerated; while sixty-one printers were put under a general ban."—*Id., p. 23.*

"Paul IV, in 1559, put it [Sully's name] in the first papal *Index Expurgatorium.*"—"*History of the Inquisition of the Middle Ages,*" *Henry Charles Lea, Vol. III, p. 587.*

The Perfect Guide

"The first Roman 'Index of Prohibited Books' (*Index librorum prohibitorum*), published in 1559 under Paul IV, was very severe and was therefore mitigated under that pontiff by decree of the Holy Office of 14 June of the same year."— *Catholic Encyclopedia, Vol. VII, p. 722, art. "Index."*

Persecution raged more or less all over Europe: "In 1545, the massacre of the Vaudois of Province was perpetrated"; the 24th of August, 1572, the St. Bartholomew Massacre commenced, and continued until between 70,000 and 100,000 innocent and unsuspecting persons were murdered in cold blood for being Protestants. The massacre was secretly planned by the leaders of the Roman church.

"Sully says 70,000 were slain, though other writers estimate the victims at 100,000."—*"The Huguenots," Samuel Smiles, pp. 71, 72.*

"Catherine de Medicis wrote in triumph to Alva, to Philip II, and to the Pope. . . . Rome was thrown into a delirium of joy at the news. The cannon were fired at St. Angelo; Gregory XIII and his cardinals went in procession from sanctuary to sanctuary to give God thanks for the massacre. The subject was ordered to be painted, and a medal was struck, with the Pope's image on one side, and the destroying angel on the other immolating the Huguenots."—*Id., 71, 72.*

New Lines of Attack

Finally, however, the papal church discovered that her opposition to the Bible only betrayed the sad fact that, instead of being the divinely instituted church of the Bible, she and the Scriptures were deadly enemies, and that her open fight was furnishing the world with the clearest evidences to justify the Reformation. Her relentless persecution was making martyrs, but not loyal Catholics. She must halt her course and forge new weapons against Protestantism, if she ever hoped to win the battle. But what were these weapons to be? These we shall consider in the next two chapters.

Forging New Weapons

THE Roman church had discovered that the root of her troubles lay in the reading of the Bible by the laity, and had opposed it with all the power at her command. But she finally realized that her open war on the Scriptures had aroused suspicion that her life and doctrines were out of harmony with God's word, and could not endure the light of an open Bible.

To allay such feelings she must make it appear that she was not opposed to the Scriptures, but only to the "erroneous Protestant Bible." But how could such an impression be made, when that Bible was a faithful translation of the Hebrew and Greek texts, in which the Scriptures were originally written? Then, too, the Protestants had, at that time, some of the most able Hebrew and Greek scholars in all Christendom.

Providence had brought the Reformers in contact with some of the best sources of Bible manuscripts: (1) When the Turks captured Constantinople in 1453, many of the Greek scholars fled to the West, bringing with them their valuable manuscripts from the East where Christianity originated, and then Greek and Hebrew learning revived in the West.* (2) With this influx from the East came also the Syrian Bible, used by the early church at Antioch in Syria (Acts 11:26), which was translated directly from the Hebrew and Greek manuscripts long before the Massoretic (O.T.) text, and is the oldest known Bible manuscript (unless it should be the one lately discovered by Chester Beatty.† (3) During their severe persecutions the Waldenses came into contact with the Reformers at Geneva, and thus their

---
* See "History of the English Bible," by W. F. Moulton, pp. 34-36.
† Copies of the Syriac Bible were later found among the Syrian Christians at Malabar, South India, with all the earmarks of the old Syrian manuscripts. See "The Old Documents and the New Bible," by J. P. Smyth, pp. 166, 167; "Indian Church History," by Thomas Yates, p. 167; "Christian Researches in Asia," by Claudius Buchannan, pp. 80, 143.

Bible, which had been preserved in its apostolic purity, was brought to the Reformers.*

Translations direct from the original languages in which the Holy Scriptures were written, and comparisons with ancient sources, by men of high scholarly ability and sterling integrity, gave the Protestants a perfectly reliable Bible.* In spite of these plain facts, the Catholic authorities had to do something to turn the minds of their people away from the Protestant Bible, so widely distributed. They therefore advanced the claim that Jerome's Latin Vulgate translation was more correct than any copy we now have of the original Hebrew and Greek texts. We shall now examine this claim.

THE LATIN VULGATE BIBLE

At the Council of Trent (1545-1563), in the fourth session, the second Decree, in 1546, they decided that the Latin Vulgate should be the standard Bible for the Roman church. But then they discovered a curious fact, that during the 1050 years from the time Jerome brought out his Latin Vulgate Bible in 405 A.D., until John Gutenberg printed it in 1455, it had been copied so many times, mostly by monks, and so many errors had crept in, that no one knew just what was the actual rendering of the original Vulgate. The learned Roman Catholic professor, Dr. Johann Jahn says of it:

"The universal admission of this version throughout the vast extent of the Latin church multiplied the copies of it, in the transcription of which it became corrupted with many errors. . . . Cardinal Nicholas, about the middle of the twelfth century, found '*tot exemplaria quot codices*' (as many copies as

---

* An illustration of how some learned Roman Catholics have estimated the Protestant Greek New Testament can be seen when we read of the Catholic legislation on forbidden books. A commentator says:
"In diocesan seminaries the textbook prescribed in Greek was very often some portion of the original text of the New Testament, and Protestant editions were selected, as they contained a more ample vocabulary, and, perhaps, better grammatical annotations than Catholic editions. Such an act would appear quite pardonable and excusable, as the text was entire and pure. . . . But according to the present rule . . . bishops have no power to select such works."—"*A Commentary on the Present Index Legislation,*" *Rev. T. Hurley, D. D., p. 70. New York: Benziger Brothers, 1908.*
With their feelings against Protestant books, such permits could not have been given, unless the superiority of the book demanded it.

manuscripts)."—"*Introduction to the Old Testament,*" *Sec. 62, 63.* (Quoted in "*History of Romanism,*" *Dr. John Dowling, ed. of 1871, p. 486.*)

The Catholic Encyclopedia says of the Latin Vulgate:

"From an early day the text of the Vulgate began to suffer corruptions, mostly through the copyists who introduced familiar readings of the Old Latin or inserted the marginal glosses of MSS. which they were transcribing."—*Vol. XV, p. 370, art.* "*Versions,*" "*The Vulgate.*"

The Council of Trent having made Jerome's Latin "Vulgate the standard text,"* it must now determine which of the hundreds of copies (all differing) was the correct "Vulgate." A commission was therefore appointed to gather materials so as to "restore St. Jerome's text," but its members were "not to amend it by any new translations of their own from the original Hebrew and Greek."†) They "were merely to collect manuscripts and prepare the evidence for and against certain readings in the text, after which the Pope himself, by reason not of his scholarship, but of his gift of infallibility, decided straight off which were the genuine words!"—"*The Old Documents and the New Bible,*" *J. Paterson Smyth, B.D., LL.D., pp. 174, 175. London and New York: 1907.*

Pope Sixtus V undertook this work of revision, and to make sure of its being correct, he read the proofs himself. This edition was printed at Rome in 1590, accompanied by a bull forbidding the least alteration in this infallible text. "But alas! . . . The book was full of mistakes. The scholarship of Sixtus was by no means great, and his infallibility somehow failed to make up for this defect."—*Id., p. 175.*

The Catholic Encyclopedia comments:

"But Sixtus V, though unskilled in this branch of criticism, had introduced alterations of his own, all for the worse. . . . His immediate successors at once proceeded to remove the blunders and call in the defective impression."—*Vol. II, p. 412.*

---

* See Cardinal Gasquet's article in the *Forum* for August, 1926, p. 203.

† "History of the Council of Trent," T. A. Buckley, Part II, chap. 16, p. 127.

All available copies of the Bible of Pope Sixtus were called in and burnt as were the heretics. Pope Clement VIII, in 1592, ordered a better edition to be made, accompanying it with a similar bull. Dr. James, keeper of the Bodleian Library at Oxford, where one of Pope Sixtus's Bibles remained, compared it with that of Pope Clement, and found two thousand glaring variations in them. He published his findings in a book called: "Bellum Papale, i.e. the Papal War." ("History of Romanism," Dr. J. Dowling, p. 487. New York: 1871.)

Dr. Thomas James, in the following statement, gives valuable information on the Vulgate Bible:

"Isidorus Clarius hath noted eight thousand places erroneous in the vulgar bible, the divines of Louvaine, and Joannes Benedictus have observed above twice as many differences, from the original Hebrew and Greek fountains. If Paulus V., the now pope, will take the pains to reform these also; in my judgment, he shall do a work very acceptable unto the whole Christian world, both Protestant and papist."—*"A Treatise of the Corruptions of Scripture, Councils, and Fathers," p. 208. London: 1843.*

The Catholic Encyclopedia says of the latest revision of the Vulgate by Pope Clement:

"This revision is now the officially recognized version of the Latin Rite and contains the only authorized text of the Vulgate. That it has numerous defects has never been denied."—*Vol. XV, p. 370.*

That the Roman church is not satisfied with the present Vulgate text is seen by the fact that in 1907 Pope Pius X, according to the *Forum*, commissioned H. E. Francis Aidan Cardinal Gasquet, with his Benedictine Order, to reproduce the true Latin text of St. Jerome by a new revision. Cardinal Gasquet says of the former attempt made by Pope Clement VIII, in 1592:

"The commission labored for some forty years, and strange to say, many of the changes proposed by them were never inserted in the final revision. From the notes of this commission it may be safely said that had they been accepted we should have had a much better critical text than we now possess." *"Forum," August, 1926, p. 203.*

The Catholic Encyclopedia points out a fact often overlooked by scholars today, that "the Hebrew text used by St. Jerome was comparatively late, being practically that of the Masoretes. For this reason his version, for textual criticism, has less value than the Peshito and the Septuagint. As a translation it holds a place between these two."—*Vol. XV, p. 370.*

E. S. Buchanan, M. A., B. Sc., says of Jerome's translation:

"Jerome, to the great loss of posterity, did not dig deep into the history of the text. He did not revise on the Latin and Greek texts of the second century; but solely on the Greek text of the fourth century, and that was a text too late and too limited in range and attestation on which to base an enduring fabric. . . . He was not bidden to search for the earliest MSS. He was not bidden to bring together the versions of the East and the West. He was not bidden to make inquiry for the lost autographs with a view to the reconstruction of the Apostolic text. He was only bidden to prepare a suitable text for ecclesiastical usage. And this he has done; but it is painful to think of all he left undone, that with his position of vantage he might have done."
—*"The Records Unrolled," p. 20. London: John Ouseley, Ltd.*

From these considerations we see, that, even if the original text of Jerome's translation could be reconstructed, it would not be of as much textual value as is sometimes supposed. We are not depreciating the Catholic Bible. We wish Catholics would read it more than they do. All we are here aiming at is this: When leading Catholic authorities admit that their Bible is of so little value as a *"Standard Text,"* then why do they so relentlessly oppose the circulation of the authorized Protestant Bible, which is translated from the best *original* sources? Henry Guppy, M. A., D. Ph. et Litt., Librarian of the John Rylands Library, England, says:

"The Church of Rome has always bitterly opposed any attempt to circulate the Bible in the language of the people, and license to read the Scriptures, even when

Forging New Weapons 23

truly and catholicly translated, was but sparingly granted. "In spite, however, of the denunciations uttered by the Roman Catholic priests against what they were pleased to term the incorrect and untruthful translations which were in circulation, the Bible continued to be read by increasing numbers of people. Indeed, the attempts to suppress it created a prejudice against the Roman Catholic Church; and, as time wore on, it was felt by many Catholics that something more must be done than a mere denunciation of the corrupt translations in the direction of providing a new version which the Roman Church could warrant to be authentic and genuine."—"*A Brief Sketch of History of the Translation of the Bible,*" *p. 54. London: University Press, 1926.*

After the Jesuits had been expelled from England in 1579, they settled at Rheims, France, where they translated the New Testament from the Latin Vulgate into English. This was printed in 1582. Later they moved to Douay, where they printed the Old Testament in 1609. We have seen that the learned Catholic doctors, Johann Jahn and Isidor Clarius, acknowledged that there were 8,000 errors in the Vulgate Bible, and as a stream cannot be expected to rise higher than its fountain, we must conclude that the errors are carried over into the Douay Version. We shall take the space to mention only two of them:

1. The Douay Bible uses the word "adore" where the Protestant Bible has "worship." (Compare Matthew 4: 10 in both Bibles.) While the Protestant Bible says that Jacob "worshiped, *leaning upon* the top of his staff," the Douay Version says that he "adored the top of his rod." Hebrews 11: 21. "The Approved Holy Catholic Bible," with "Annotations by the Rev. Dr. Challoner," and approved by Pius VI, says: "Jacob . . . worshiped the top of his rod." Thus Catholics have proof for worshiping relics.

2. Our Protestant Bible more correctly translates 2 Timothy 3: 16 to read, "All Scripture is given by inspiration of God," but the Douay Version reads: "All scripture, inspired of God, is profitable." As can be readily seen, this latter rendering gives

no assurance that the Bible is inspired, but simply makes the superfluous statement that what is inspired is profitable. And so it is left with the church to say what is inspired.*

In full view of all the foregoing facts, how can Roman Catholic authors shut their eyes to it all, and brazenly declare that their church alone has the true and correct Bible? They say:

"She alone possesses the true Bible and the whole Bible, and the copies of the Scriptures existing outside of her pale, are partly incorrect and partly defective.

"This Bible was the celebrated Vulgate, the official text in the Catholic Church, the value of which all scholars admit to be simply inestimable. . . . The Council of Trent in 1546 issued a decree, stamping it as the only recognized and authoritative Version allowed to Catholics. . . . It was revised under Pope Sixtus V in 1590, and again under Pope Clement VIII in 1593, who is responsible for the present standard text. It is from the Vulgate that our English Douai Version comes."—*"Where We Got the Bible," Right Rev. Henry G. Graham, pp. 7, 16, 17. London: Eighth Impression, 1936.*

Do these men actually believe that Protestants have no access to the facts of history, but are dependent on such misstatements! Or are they vainly hoping that the public will have no opportunity to read the Protestant side of the story?

The interesting part of it all is the fact that the Catholic Church, after proclaiming so loudly since 1546 that the Latin Vulgate is "the only recognized and authoritative version," and crying out against the Protestant Bibles (translated from the original Hebrew and Greek text) as "heretical," is herself at last driven, by facts long known within her own circle, to translate the Bible "from the original text," Hebrew and Greek. What a complete somersault! This late Catholic version is called "The Westminster Version" (printed by Longmans, Green and Co., London). But, as the work is intrusted mostly to the Jesuits, we can expect very little change from their former Douay Version, except that it will be more carefully

---

*The new Catholic version of 1941 renders it: "All Scripture is inspired by God."

written to conform to the Roman viewpoint (judging from the portions that have already been published). For instance, the correct note under Revelation 13:18 is entirely changed, but Revelation 22:14 reads the same as in the Douay Version: "Blessed are they that wash their robes." In our Authorized Protestant Version (King James') it reads: "Blessed are they that do His commandments."

Inspired by Revelation 22:14, P. P. Bliss, musician assisting D. L. Moody, wrote the hymn:

"Hear the words our Saviour hath spoken,
Words of life unfailing and true:
Careless one, prayerless one, hear and remember,
Jesus says, 'Blessed are they that do.'
Blessed are they that do His commandments,
Blessed, blessed, blessed are they."

Later Mr. Bliss went to Rome, where he learned that "Blessed are they that wash their robes," "must be the correct" rendering. And "during his last week in Rome," he told his brother-in-law that he was sorry he had written that hymn. He declared: "I see so clearly its contradiction of the gospel that I have no liberty in singing it." Then he wrote the hymn: "Free from the law, oh, happy condition."—"*Memories of Philip P. Bliss,*" *D. W. Whittle, pp. 131, 132. New York: A. S. Barnes and Co., 1877.* It is deplorable that this good Christian man should get such impressions at Rome. But, sad to say, P. P. Bliss is not the only beloved Protestant that has been in touch with Rome, and lost his desire and *liberty* to teach the good old truths of the Protestant Bible.

Some follow the Roman Catholic translation of Revelation 22:14, because the Vatican possesses one of the three oldest Bible manuscripts (Codex Vaticanus). But that manuscript ends with Hebrews 9:14, so that it could not give Catholics the proper rendering of Revelation 22:14.*

---
* For further light on this point see "A Brief Sketch of the History of the Translation of the Bible," H. Guppy, p. 7, and "The Records Unrolled" by E. S. Buchanan, p. 50.

Rome Undermines the Protestant Foundations

THE second, and more effective, weapon Rome used against the Reformation was "higher criticism," in an effort to undermine the very foundation of Protestantism.

The strongest appeal of the Roman Catholic Church lies in its claim to "apostolic succession," that is, that its popes descended in direct line from the apostles. Protestants, originating in the sixteenth century, have no such appeal. Their strong argument lies in their exact conformity with the Bible in faith and morals. "The Bible, and the Bible only" is their battle cry. The Bible reveals man's utter inability to attain justification by his own works, and offers it as a "free gift," obtained by faith in the merits of Jesus Christ alone. The Bible presents good works only as the natural fruit of genuine faith. On this foundation was Protestantism built. Before going further we shall let Catholics and Protestants state their foundations.

Catholic Foundation

"Like two sacred rivers flowing from paradise, the Bible and divine Tradition contain the Word of God, the precious gems of revealed truths. Though these two divine streams are in themselves, on account of their divine origin, of equal sacredness, and are both full of revealed truths, still, of the two, Tradition is to us more clear and safe."—"*Catholic Belief,*" *Joseph Faa di Bruno, D.D., p. 33. New York: Benziger Brothers., 1912.*

"But since Divine revelation is contained in the written books and the unwritten traditions (Vatican Council, I, II), the Bible and Divine tradition must be the rule of our faith; since, however, these are only silent witnesses, . . . we must look for some proximate rule which shall be animate or living. . . .

The Bible could not be left to interpret itself." Therefore Catholics declare the "Church to be its acknowledged interpreter." And under the heading: "The Catholic Doctrine Touching the Church as the Rule of Faith," we read: "Now the teaching Church is the Apostolic body continuing to the end of time." But of the teachers of this body, they say: "Unless they be united with the Vicar of Christ [the Pope], it is futile to appeal to the episcopate in general as the rule of faith." They then sum up their rule of faith thus: "'Hence we must stand rather by the decisions which the pope judicially pronounces than by the opinions of men, however learned they may be in Holy Scripture.'"—"*Catholic Encyclopedia,*" *Vol. V, pp. 766-768, art. "Faith, Rule of."* The teaching Church, with the pope at its head, is therefore the Catholic "rule of faith."

Thus we see that the Roman Catholic Church places tradition above the Bible as more safe, and substitutes the pope for the Holy Spirit as the guide. Christ promised His followers: "Howbeit when He, the Spirit of truth, is come, He will guide you into all truth." "He shall teach you all things, and bring all things to your remembrance." John 16: 13; 14: 26. That these promises are not confined to the leaders of the church, is made plain by John, who applies them to all Christians: "But the anointing which ye have received of Him abideth in you, and ye need not that any man teach you: but as the same anointing teacheth you of all things, . . . ye shall abide in Him." 1 John 2: 27. In answer to these Scriptures the Catholic writers say:

"Nor can it be said that being a divinely inspired book, its prime Author, the Holy Ghost, will guide the reader to the right meaning."—"*Things Catholics Are Asked About,*" *M. J. Scott, S. J., p. 119. New York: 1927.*

Protestant Foundation

Protestants have announced as their rule of faith: "The Bible, and the Bible only," with the Holy Spirit as its sole Interpreter. William Chillingworth, M. A., says:

"The Bible, I say, the Bible only, is the religion of Prot-

estants! . . . I for my part, after a long and (as I verily believe and hope) impartial search of 'the true way to eternal happiness,' do profess plainly that I cannot find any rest for the sole of my foot but upon this rock only. I see plainly and with my own eyes, that there are popes against popes, councils against councils, some fathers against others, the same fathers against themselves, a consent of fathers of one age against a consent of fathers of another age, the church of one age against the church of another age. . . . In a word, there is no sufficient certainty but of Scripture only for any considering man to build upon."
—"*The Religion of Protestants,*" *William Chillingworth, M. A.,* p. 463. London: 1866.

"'The Bible, I say, the Bible only, is the religion of Protestants!' Nor is it of any account in the estimation of the genuine Protestant, *how early* a doctrine originated, if it is not found in the Bible. . . .

"He who receives a single doctrine upon the mere authority of tradition, let him be called by what name he will, by so doing, steps down from the Protestant rock, passes over the line which separates Protestantism from Popery, and can give no valid reason why he should not receive all the earlier doctrines and ceremonies of Romanism, upon the same authority."—"*History of Romanism,*" *John Dowling, D. D., pp. 67, 68. New York: 1871.*

This childlike faith in the Bible as God's infallible word carried the Reformers above all opposition, and swept over Europe with an irresistible force which threatened to engulf the old, decaying structure of the Roman church. This unabated force could be broken only by robbing Protestants of their implicit faith in the Bible. They would then lose their power as surely as did Samson, when he was shorn of his locks. (Judges 16: 19, 20.)

Rome Undermining Protestant Foundations

Richard Simon, a Roman Catholic priest, called the "Father of Higher Criticism," in 1678 wrote "A Critical History of the Old Testament" in three books, laying down the rules for a

Rome Undermines the Protestant Foundations 29

more exact translation. He advanced the new theory that only the ordinances and commands of the books of Moses were written by him, while the historical parts were the product of various other writers. Simon's declared purpose was to show that the Protestants had no assured principle for their religion. (See edition of 1782.) "This work led to a very extended controversy and the first edition was suppressed."* So vigorous was the opposition of the learned, that his theory lay dormant for seventy-five years. The Catholic Encyclopedia says:

"A French priest, Richard Simon (1638-1712), was the first who subjected the general questions concerning the Bible to a treatment which was at once comprehensive in scope and scientific in method. Simon is the forerunner of modern Biblical criticism. . . . A reaction against the rigid view of the Bible [was one of] the factors which produced Simon's first great work, the '*Histoire critique du Vieux Testament*' ['Critical History of the Old Testament'] which was published in 1678. . . . It entitles him to be called the father of Biblical criticism."—*Vol. IV, p. 492.*

"In 1753 Jean Astruc, a French Catholic physician of considerable note, published a little book, '*Conjectures sur les memoires originaux dont il parait que Moyse s'est servi pour composer le livre de la Genese* (Conjectures on the original records from which it appears that Moses composed the book of Genesis).'"—*Id., same page.* (See also *New Schaff-Herzog Encyclopedia of Religious Knowledge, Vol. I, p. 336, art, "Jean Astruc."*)

His book is rightly named, for in it he *conjectured* that the book of Genesis must have been written by two different authors, because the Creator is there called "God" ("Elohim") in some places, and "Lord" ("Jehovah") in other places. Such a line of reasoning would be as inconsistent as to claim that Paul's Epistle to the Philippians, for instance, must have been written by two different apostles, because our Saviour is there called "Jesus" in some places, and "Christ" in others. But what about the places where He is called "Jesus Christ"? And so in Gene-

---
* Catalogue of R. D. Dickinson, 1935, No. 462, p. 10, book No. 167.

sis. Who wrote the five passages where He is called "Lord God" ("Jehovah Elohim")? In 1792, Dr. Alexander Geddes, a Roman Catholic priest of Scottish origin, carried this "fragmentary hypothesis" still further. Absurd as this theory was, the Protestants fell into the trap set for them, and Germany, the seat of the Reformation, became the seat of this destructive "higher criticism." Today this inconsistent criticism of the Bible has invaded the seminaries, colleges, and universities of practically all Protestant denominations, and few ministers are free from its blighting influence. Edwin Cone Bissell, Professor in McCormick Theological Seminary, Chicago, carried out this "fragmentary" theory in his book, "Genesis Printed in Colors, Showing the Original Sources from Which It Is Supposed to Have Been Compiled" (Hartford, 1892), displaying the seven colors of the rainbow in shorter or longer fragments, each representing a different author or editor.

Harold Bolce spent two years investigating American colleges from Maine to California, and wrote his astounding findings in the *Cosmopolitan Magazine,* May to August, 1909. Here are a few expressions culled from his report:

"In hundreds of classrooms it is being taught daily that the Decalogue is no more sacred than a syllabus; that the home as an institution is doomed; that there are no absolute evils; that immorality is simply an act in contravention of society's accepted standards; . . . *and that the daring who defy the code* [the moral law] *do not offend any Deity, but simply arouse the venom of the majority*—the majority that has not yet grasped the new idea; . . . and that the highest ethical life consists at all times in the breaking of rules which have grown too narrow for the actual case. . . .

"*There can be and are holier alliances without the marriage bond than within it.* . . . *Anything tolerated by the world in general is right.* . . . The notion, . . . that there is anything fundamentally correct implies the existence of a standard outside and above usage, and no such standard exists."—*Pp. 665, 666, 674, 675, 676.*

Can anyone wonder at what Dr. Charles Jefferson declares? He says:

"A theological student at the end of the first year of his seminary course is the most demoralized individual to be found on this earth. His early conception of the Bible has been torn down all the way to the cellar, and he is obliged to build up a new conception from the foundations."—"*Things Fundamental,*" *pp. 120, 121.*

In regard to the inevitable result of teaching the rising generation such revolutionary ideas, and of undermining completely their moral standards, and their belief in God, the editor of the *Cosmopolitan Magazine* says in a note to Mr. Bolce's articles:

"These are some of the revolutionary and sensational teachings submitted with academic warrant to the minds of hundreds of thousands of students in the United States. It is time that the public realized what is being taught to the youth of this country. 'The social question of to-day,' said Disraeli, 'is only a zephyr which rustles the leaves, but will soon become a hurricane.' It is a dull ear that cannot hear the mutterings of the coming storm."—"*Cosmopolitan Magazine,*" *May, 1909, p. 665.*

The Bible declares: "They have sown the wind, and they shall reap the whirlwind." "There is no truth, nor mercy, nor knowledge of God in the land. By swearing, and lying, and killing, and stealing, and committing adultery, *they break out,* and blood toucheth blood." Hosea 8: 7; 4: 1, 2. (Compare 2 Timothy 3: 1-5.) Yes, the saying is true, that "whatsoever a man soweth, that shall he also reap." Galatians 6: 7.

The Christian Register for June 18, 1891, page 389, commenting favorably on the work of higher criticism, says:

"Thomas Paine, though stigmatized and set aside as an infidel, finds reincarnation in the modern scientific Biblical critic. . . . He lived too far in advance of his age. The spirit of modern scientific criticism had not yet come. . . . And now it is interesting to find that, in a different spirit and with different tools, and bound by certain traditions, . . . the professors in our orthodox seminaries are doing again the work which Paine did."

As long as these men domineered over the Old Testament, most of the Christian teachers remained silent. But the work did not stop there. The Lutheran Pastor Storjohan of Oslo, Norway, says of Wellhausen:

"After they have permitted him to domineer over the Old Testament for more than twenty-five years, it is not more than reasonable, and a just punishment, that he in his presumption has now undertaken his war on the Gospels."—*"Bibelen paa Pinebaenk [The Bible on the Inquisitorial Rack]," p. 7. Christiania, 1907.*

In closing let us briefly point out the road which higher criticism had to travel, after it had taken the first step: When critics had denied the historicity of the books of Moses (the Pentateuch), they discovered that the Psalms referred to them as acknowledged history. (Psalms 33: 6, 9; 29: 10; 77: 20; 103: 7; 105: 6-45; 106: 7-33.) To be consistent, the Psalms had to be rejected. They also found that the books of Joshua, Samuel, Kings, Chronicles, and Nehemiah, and the prophets acknowledged the Pentateuch as the inspired work of Moses (Joshua 23: 6; 1 Kings 2: 3; 2 Chronicles 35: 6; Nehemiah 8: 1, 8; Daniel 9: 11, 13; Malachi 4: 4), so these books had to be rejected.

But then they found that the New Testament repeatedly referred to the Old Testament as inspired authority (about eight hundred twenty-four times), and to their consternation they discovered that Jesus declared the first five books in the Bible were written by Moses (Mark 12: 26; Luke 24: 25, 44, 45), and that He asked: "If ye believe not his [Moses'] writings, how shall ye believe My words?" John 5: 46, 47. The critics had declared that the account of the Flood was only a myth, which no intelligent person could believe. But Jesus said: "Noe entered into the ark," and "the Flood came, and took them all away." Matthew 24: 38, 39. He even believed the truthfulness of the account of Jonah's being in the great fish for three days, and of his preaching in Nineveh afterwards. (Matthew 12: 40, 41.) There was, therefore, no way of reconciling Jesus to higher criticism, so they rejected Him as the divine Son of God.

Rome Undermines the Protestant Foundations

For if Jesus did not know that those Old Testament stories were only myths, He was deceived. If He knew this, and yet taught them, He was a deceiver. In either case He could not be divine, they reasoned.

"If in the dawning of the fortieth century, it shall be found that the law and the prophets are obsolete, the Gospels and Epistles discarded, Moses forgotten, and Paul and his writings set aside to make room for the inerrant productions of [higher critics], . . . if it shall then appear that the hunted prophets who wandered in sheepskins and goatskins, and were destitute, afflicted, and tormented, 'of whom the world was not worthy,' have gone down before the onslaught of the learned and well-salaried professors of modern universities; if it shall appear that the word of the Lord which they uttered at the loss of all things and at the peril of life itself has paled its ineffectual fires before the rising radiance of oracular higher criticism; if it shall then be learned that God hath chosen the rich in this world, poor in faith, and heirs of the kingdom—who can tell how welcome this information may prove to those who suppose that gain is godliness, and that it is easier for a camel to go through the eye of a needle than for a poor man to enter the kingdom of heaven?"
—"*The Anti-Infidel Library*," *H. L. Hastings*, "*More Bricks from the Babel of the Higher Critics*," *pp. 172, 173. Boston: Scriptural Tract Repository, 1895.*

Some might properly ask how Romanists dared to start higher criticism. Would not this menace be equally dangerous to their church? Absolutely not! The Roman church rests on an entirely different foundation. The Church, and not the Bible, is her authority. She flourishes best where the Bible is least circulated, as history amply shows. But Protestantism that rejects the inspiration of the Bible, has abandoned its foundation, and stands helpless. It is like a ship that has lost its mooring, thrown away its chart and compass, and is drifting toward—Rome.

The Prophetic History of the World

THE prophecies of the Bible are not difficult to understand, if we follow the rules laid down in Scripture for interpreting prophecy. These rules are few in number, and they are not complicated. When used in connection with prophetic symbols, "sea," or "waters," stand for "multitudes" of people (Revelation 17: 15; Isaiah 8: 7; 17: 12; Jeremiah 6: 23); "wind" stands for "war" (Jeremiah 4: 12, 13; 25: 31, 32); "beasts" stand for "kingdoms" (Daniel 7: 23); and "days" for "years" (Ezekiel 4: 6).

The prophet Daniel saw in vision four winds of war, which strove upon the great sea of people, and four great beasts, or kingdoms, came up one after the other. "The first was like a lion, and had eagle's wings." Daniel 7: 2-4. In Jeremiah 49: 19, 22, 28, a lion is used to symbolize the kingdom of Babylon (606-538 B. C.). The second beast was like a bear (Daniel 7: 5), and denoted Medo-Persia, the next world empire (538-331 B. C.). The "three ribs in the mouth of it" were the three chief countries which it conquered, Lydia, Babylon, and Egypt.

He next saw a leopard having four heads and four wings (v. 6), symbolizing the Grecian Empire (331-168 B. C.). A leopard is very alert, and adding to this symbol four wings would indicate that Grecia would make rapid conquest, which was true. Alexander the Great marched his army 5,100 miles in eight years and conquered the then known civilized world. The four heads on the leopard denote the four divisions into which that empire was split up after the death of Alexander.

"The fourth beast," the angel explained, "shall be the fourth kingdom upon earth." V. 23. The fourth empire from Babylon was Rome (168 B. C. to 476 A. D.). The angel also informs us that "the ten horns out of this kingdom are ten kings that shall arise." V. 24. The Roman Empire was split up into just ten

The Prophetic History of the World 35

smaller kingdoms between the years 351 and 476 A. D. The following are their ancient and modern names:
1. Alemanni—Germany. 2. Franks—France. 3. Anglo-Saxons—England. 4. Burgundians—Switzerland. 5. Visigoths—Spain. 6. Suevi—Portugal. 7. Lombards—Italy. 8. Heruli. 9. Vandals. 10. Ostrogoths.

This prophecy is so plain, and the explanation so natural and easy to understand, that all commentators, both Protestant and Catholic, fully agree on it. (See Sir Isaac Newton's "Observations upon the Prophecies," pp. 157-159; Bishop Thomas Newton, "Dissertations on the Prophecies," pp. 201-221; Joseph Tanner on "Daniel and the Revelation," pp. 165-174; Martin Luther's "Introduction," pp. 32, 33, Frederikshald, 1853.)

The Douay, or Catholic, version of the Bible has the following notes on Daniel 7: 3, 7, 8. "*Four great beasts.* Viz., the Chaldean, Persian, Grecian, and Roman empires." "*Ten horns.* That is, ten kingdoms, (as Apoc. 17. 12,) among which the empire of the fourth beast shall be parcelled." "*Another little horn.* This is commonly understood of Antichrist."

In regard to these ten kingdoms, Sir Isaac Newton says: "Whatever was their number afterwards, they are still called the Ten Kings from their first number."—"*Daniel and the Apocalypse*," *p. 187; first printed, 1733; reprinted, London: 1922.*

The Little Horn

"I considered the horns, and, behold, there came up *among them* another little horn." Daniel 7: 8. Let us now consider all the characteristics this prophecy gives to the little horn, and we shall be forced by weight of evidence to settle on just one power as the fulfillment of these predictions.

(1) It was to come up "among" the ten European kingdoms into which the Roman Empire was split. (V. 8.) (2) It "shall rise" to power "*after them.*" (V. 24.) (3) "And he shall be *diverse* from the first" ten kingdoms; that is, different from ordinary, secular kingdoms. (V. 24.) Any one acquainted with history knows that the Papacy is the only power that answers to

all these specifications. It rose "among" the kingdoms of Western Rome, "after" they were established in A. D. 476, and it differed from a purely civil power. But the angel gives still another mark of identity to the little horn. (4) Before it "there were *three of the first horns plucked up by the roots.*" (V. 8.) That is, in coming up it pushed out before it three of the former horns by the roots. Thus three kingdoms were to be plucked up to give place for the Papacy. This prediction found its exact fulfillment in the destruction of the three Arian kingdoms: the Heruli, the Vandals, and the Ostrogoths, as we now shall see. Rev. E. B. Elliott, M.A., says:

"I might cite *three* that were eradicated from before the Pope out of the list *first* given; viz., the *Heruli* under Odoacer, the *Vandals,* and the *Ostrogoths.*"—"*Horœ Apocalypticœ,*" *Vol. III, p. 168, Note 1. London: 1862.*

In former days crowns of conquered kings were placed on the head of the conqueror. (2 Samuel 12:30.) It is symbolically fitting, therefore, that the pope wears a triple crown. Bishop Thomas Newton, speaking of the power that destroyed the three horns, says: "And the pope hath in a manner pointed himself out for the person by wearing *the triple crown.*"—"*Dissertations on the Prophecies,*" *p. 220. London.*

A brief statement of the political and religious conditions in the Roman world is necessary here in order that the reader may better grasp the real situation in which these three Arian kingdoms found themselves. After Constantine had removed the seat of the empire from Rome to Constantinople, the Roman people were (at intervals) ruled from that Eastern capital, until the pope had grown to power in Rome. While the Papacy was gradually gaining control over the people of the West, the Eastern emperors were courting the good will of the popes in order to hold their Western subjects.

From the time of Constantine to that of Justinian there was a deadly struggle between the two largest factions of the Church, the Catholics and the Arians. Often there was terrible strife, and even bloodshed. "The streets of Alexandria and of Constantinople were deluged with blood by the partisans of rival bishops."—"*History of Christianity*," *H. H. Milman, Book III, chap. 5, par. 2, p. 410. New York: 2-vol. ed., 1881.* Most of the barbarian nations into which the Roman Empire was now split had accepted the Catholic faith. But the Heruli, the Vandals, and the Ostrogoths were Arians.

While the emperors courted the help of the popes for political reasons, the popes sought the assistance of the emperors to destroy the Arians. Theodosius, the Emperor of the East, had already (380-395 A. D.) given "fifteen stern edicts against heresy, one on the average for every year of his reign. . . . So began the campaign which ended in the virtual extinction of Arianism in the Roman world."—"*Italy and her Invaders," Thomas Hodgkin, Vol. I, pp. 368, 369. Oxford: Clarendon Press, 8-vol. ed. of 1899.*

In A. D. 380, the Emperor Theodosius issued an edict which said: "We order those who follow this law to assume the name of Catholic Christians: we pronounce all others to be mad and foolish, and we order that they bear the ignominious name of heretics. . . . These are to be visited . . . by the stroke of our own authority."—"*Italy and her Invaders," T. Hodgkin, Vol. I, p. 183. Two-vol. ed. of 1880.*

"Thus did the reign and legislation of Theodosius mark out the lines of future relationship between Pope and Emperor." —*Id., p. 187.*

Embassies passed continually between the pope of Rome and the emperor of Constantinople, and in 381 A. D. Theodosius arranged for a general council of the clergy at Constantinople, which finally established the Catholic doctrine. "To him also, at least as much as to Constantine, must be attributed the permanent alliance between the Church and the State."—*Id., pp. 182, 183.*

The Heruli

The Heruli under Odoacer had established themselves in Italy, 476 A. D.; and while this Arian king ruled all his subjects impartially, he endeavored to shield his people from the persecution inaugurated by the combined efforts of the pope and the emperor. Pasquale Villari, writing of the period between 468 and 483 A. D., says:

"At that time the Pope was morally, and even more than morally speaking, the most powerful personage in Italy. If Odovacar [Odoacer], as an Arian, had openly opposed him, Simplicius [the Pope] could have easily roused the whole country against him, and made it impossible for him to maintain his position in Italy."—"*The Barbarian Invasion of Italy,*" *Vol. I, pp. 145, 146. New York: Charles Scribner's Sons, 1902.*

And just such an opportunity soon presented itself:

"Pope Simplicius died on the 2nd of March, 483, whereupon Odovacar made a false move, of which he felt the consequences before long. Undoubtedly it was very important for him to control the choice of a new Pontiff. He sought not only to prevent the riots which had often caused bloodshed in the streets of Rome on similar occasions, but also desired a Pope well disposed to himself. Thus when the preliminary assembly failed to agree in the choice of a candidate, the Pretorian Prefect, Cecina Basilius, suddenly intervened in Odovacar's name, and declared that no election would be valid without the King's voice. . . . A decree was likewise issued prohibiting the alienation of Church property and threatening anathema on all who failed to respect it. After this the Assembly was summoned to sanction the decree and decide the election, which resulted in favor of Felix II (483-492), the candidate recommended by Odovacar."
—*Id., p. 146.*

"His interference in the Papal election has cast into the Roman Church the seed of a deep and threatening distrust towards him."—*Id., p. 147.*

Rome could never forgive such an affront, and through its faithful ally, the emperor, another barbarian nation, the Ostrogoths, were called in to destroy the hated Heruli. Niccolo Machiavelli relates how the popes used such a method. He says:

"Nearly all the wars which the northern barbarians carried

on in Italy, it may be here remarked, were occasioned by the pontiffs; and the hordes, with which the country was inundated, were generally called in by them. The same mode of proceeding still continued, and kept Italy weak and unsettled."—"*History of Florence,*" *p. 13. Washington and London: Universal Classics Library, 1901.*

Villari says that Theodoric at the head of the Ostrogothic hordes entered Italy in the autumn of 488, backed by the authority of the emperor and the Church. Because the discord that had now broken out between Odovacar and the pope had weakened the former and consequently made him less formidable, after two disastrous battles he retreated toward the city of Rome for safety from the Ostrogoths, but "the gates of Rome were shut in his face, and the inhabitants of Italy began to show him marked hostility; partly on account of his recent conflict with the Church, partly for the increased deeds of spoliation. . . . The Church had taken advantage of all these causes of discontent in order to excite the populace against him; and before long it was openly said that the clergy had organized a general conspiracy against him somewhat, it would seem, in the style of the Sicilian Vespers."—"*The Barbarian Invasion of Italy,*" *2-vol. ed. of 1880. Vol. I, pp. 153-156.*

John Henry Cardinal Newman, D. D., says:

"Odoacer was sinking before Theodoric, and the Pope was changing one Arian master for another."—"*An Essay on the Development of Christian Doctrine,*" *Part II, p. 320. London: 1878.*

Villari continues: "On the 5th of March, 493, Theodoric entered Ravenna in triumph, all the clergy coming forth to meet him, chanting Psalms, and with the Archbishop at the head of the procession."—"*The Barbarian Invasion of Italy,*" *Vol. I, p. 158.* Ten days later Odoacer was murdered in cold blood.

Hodgkin points out that this coming of the archbishop to meet the Ostrogoths was staged so as to "impress vividly on the minds both of Italians and Ostrogoths that Theodoric came as the friend of the Catholic Church."—"*Italy and Her Invaders,*"

8-vol. ed., *Vol. III, book 4, pp. 234, 235.* Hodgkin further states that the Roman clergy were privy to a terrible secret plot of murdering the followers of Odovacar all over Italy. (Id., pp. 225, 226.)

The Heruli disappeared from history. Thus the first of the three horns of Daniel 7: 8 was "plucked up by the roots," and history leaves no room for doubt but that the Papacy through its allies engineered this act because of its opposition to Arianism.

The Emperor Justinian

Before passing to the next power destroyed by the Papacy we shall briefly state the condition of the Roman Empire at this time. Justinian had finally ascended the throne of Constantinople as the Emperor of the East, 527 A. D. He was a shrewd politician, and in his effort to extend his rule over the whole of the Roman Empire he realized his need of securing the cooperation of the highly organized Catholic Church, for it was directed by a single head (the pope), and worked as a unit all over the empire, while the Arian nations stood separately, without any central organization, and hence they were weak. Then too, the Arians were very wealthy, and if Justinian could conquer them in the name of "the true Church," he could confiscate their property and thus secure means to carry on his many wars. We read:

"Justinian (527) . . . already meditated . . . the conquest of Italy and Africa."—*"Decline and Fall," Edward Gibbon, chap. 39, par. 17.*

"Justinian felt that the support of the Pope was necessary in his reconquering of the West."—*"History of Medieval Europe," L. Thorndike, Ph. D., p. 133. Cambridge, Mass.: 1918.*

"Justinian spared nothing in his efforts to conciliate the Roman Church, and we find inserted with evident satisfaction in Justinian's *Code* pontifical letters, which praised his efforts to maintain 'the peace of the church and the unity of religion.'"— *"Cambridge Medieval History," Bury, Gwatkin, and Whitney, Vol. II, p. 44. New York: 1913.*

Procopius, the historian who followed Justinian's armies, says:

"In his zeal to gather all men into one Christian doctrine, he recklessly killed all who dissented, and this too he did in the name of piety. For he did not call it homicide, when those who perished happened to be of a belief that was different from his own."—"*Secret History of the Court of Justinian*," *pp. 138, 139. Chicago: P. Covici, 1927.*

"Now the churches of these so-called heretics, especially those belonging to the Arian dissenters, were almost incredibly wealthy."—*Id., p. 121.*

"Agents were sent everywhere to force whomever they chanced upon to renounce the faith of their fathers. . . . Thus many perished at the hands of the persecuting faction; . . . but most of them by far quitted the land of their fathers, and fled the country . . . and thenceforth the whole Roman Empire was a scene of massacre and flight."—*Id., p. 122.*

Dom John Chapman (Roman Catholic) says of Justinian:

"He felt himself to be the Vicegerent of the Almighty to rule the world and bring it all to the service of Christ. His wars were holy wars. In later centuries a Byzantine battle began like a church ceremony. Even in the sixth century every enterprise was consecrated by religion.

"He was well aware that judicious persecution is a great help towards conversion! . . . He strengthened the existing laws against pagans, Jews, and heretics. . . . Many were burnt at Constantinople after the Emperor had made vain attempts to convert them. John of Ephesus . . . was employed in this apostolate. He boasts that in 546 he gained 70,000 pagans in Asia Minor, including nobles and rhetoricians and physicians, and many in Constantinople. Tortures discovered these men, and scourgings and imprisonment induced them to accept instruction and baptism. A Patricius, named Phocus, hearing that he had been denounced, took poison. The Emperor ordered that he should be buried as an ass is buried. The pious Emperor paid all the expenses of this Christian mission, and gave to each of the 70,000 Asiatics the white garments for their baptism and a piece of money."

"Other heretics were given three months grace. All magistrates and soldiers had to swear that they were Catholics."—*"Studies in the Early Papacy," Dom John Chapman, p. 222. London: Sheed and Ward, 1928. New York: Benziger Brothers.*

The Vandals

"Justinian's cherished aim was the reconquest of Italy by the Empire; but in order to succeed in this it was necessary to secure his rear by overthrowing the Vandals and resuming possession of Africa."—*"The Barbarian Invasion of Italy," P. Villari, Vol. I, p. 197.*

A pretext for breaking his oath of peace with the Arian Vandals soon presented itself. The Vandal government had oppressed the Roman Catholics just as the emperor, under the influence of the Papacy, had oppressed the Arians. But when Hilderic came to the Vandal throne he, through the influence of his Catholic wife, had restored the Roman clergy to their ancient privileges, and this had so displeased the Vandal leaders that Gelimer, a zealous Arian, had dethroned and imprisoned him, and reigned in his place. "A strong appeal was thus made to the piety [?] of the Emperor to deliver the true Catholic Church of the West out of the hands of the barbarian heretics."—*"Medieval and Modern History," P. V. N. Myers, p. 62. Boston: 1897.*

Justinian wavered for a time, fearing to attack these warlike Vandals, but a Catholic bishop assured him of victory, claiming "he had seen a vision, in which God commanded that the war should be immediately undertaken. 'It is the will of Heaven, O Emperor!' exclaimed the bishop."—*Id., p. 63.*

Treachery, which with Rome and her allies has always been a justifiable weapon, was here used in the service of the church by her dutiful son. Justinian sent an army of 200,000 trained men under the leadership of Belisarius to conquer the Vandals, without declaring war, and unbeknown to Gelimer, their king. Villari says:

"Belisarius landed on the African coast at nine days' march from Carthage [the Vandal capital]. He did not assume the attitude of a conqueror, but came, he said, as the deliverer of the Catholics and Romans, the clergy and lay proprietors, who were all equally oppressed by those foreign barbarians, the heretic Vandals."—"*The Barbarian Invasion of Italy,*" *Vol. I, p. 198.*

Thus Belisarius won the enthusiastic support of a large part of the population. To undermine the zeal of the Vandal leaders for their king he sent the "leading men of the Vandals" a letter from Justinian, stating that he intended only to dethrone the usurping king, who was tyrannizing over them, and to give them back their liberty. The letter reads:

"'It is not our purpose to go to war with the Vandals, nor are we breaking our treaty with Gaiseric. We are only attempting to overthrow your tyrant, who making light of Gaiseric's testament keeps your king a prisoner. . . . Therefore join us in freeing yourselves from a tyranny so wicked, that you may enjoy peace and liberty. We give you pledge in the name of God that we will give you these blessings.' . . . The overseer of the public post deserted and delivered all the horses to Belisarius."—"*History of the Later Roman Empire,*" *J. B. Bury, Vol. II, p. 130. London: The Macmillan Co., 1925.*

But Justinian never intended to keep his solemn oath to grant them liberty, and the people soon found Rome the severest of tyrants.

"In 533 the Byzantine general, Belisarius (q.v.) landed in Africa. The Vandals were several times defeated, and Carthage was entered on Sept. 15, 533. . . . In the next year Africa, Sardinia, and Corsica were restored to the Roman Empire. As a nation, the Vandals soon ceased to exist."—*Nelson's Encyclopedia, Vol. XII, art. "Vandals," pp. 380, 381. New York: 1907.*

"Religious intolerance accompanied the imperial restoration in the West. In Africa, as in Italy, Arians were spoiled for the benefit of Catholics, their churches were destroyed or ruined, and their lands confiscated."—"*Cambridge Medieval History,*" *Bury, Gwatkin, and Whitney, Vol. II, p. 44. New York: 1913.*

"The Arian heresy was proscribed, and the race of these remarkable conquerors was in a short time exterminated. . . . There are few instances in history of a nation disappearing so rapidly and so completely as the Vandals of Africa."—"*A History of Greece Under the Romans*," George Finlay, p. 234. London and New York: J. M. Dent, ed., 1856.

"Africa, subdued by the arms of Belisarius, returned at once under the dominion of the empire and of Catholicism. . . . One imperial edict was sufficient (A. D. 533) to restore all the churches to the Catholic worship."—"*Latin Christianity*," H. H. Milman, Book 3, chap. 4, p. 455. New York: Crowell & Co., 1881. Thus the second horn of Daniel 7:8 was "plucked up by the roots."

Here we have one sample out of many in history as to what kind of religious liberty Rome grants wherever she obtains the power.

The Ostrogoths

Theodoric, king of the Ostrogothic nation of Italy, maintained complete religious liberty for all classes and creeds. He wrote to Justin, Emperor of the East, who was persecuting the Arians:

"'To pretend to a domination over the conscience, is to usurp the prerogative of God; by the nature of things the power of sovereigns is confined to political government; they have no right of punishment but over those who disturb the public peace; the most dangerous heresy is that of a sovereign who separates himself from part of his subjects, because they believe not according to his belief.'"—"*History of Latin Christianity*," H. H. Milman, Vol. I, Book III, chap. 3, p. 439. New York: 1860.

The wars of the migrating barbarians on the one side, and the persecutions of heathen, Jews, and Arians by the Catholic Church on the other, had kept Italy in constant turmoil. Agricultural pursuits were neglected, people crowded into the cities, and want and starvation faced the population. But Theodoric's wise and firm rule, and the strict religious liberty he established in Italy, brought peace, prosperity, and happiness to all classes. J. G. Sheppard, D. D., says:

"'Theodoric deserves the highest praise; for, during the thirty-eight years he reigned in Italy, he brought the country to such a state of greatness, that her previous sufferings were no longer recognizable.' . . . What then prevented this man, with so great a genius for government, and so splendid an opportunity for its exercise, from organizing a Germanic empire, equal in extent and power to that which obeyed the sceptre of the old Roman Cæsars? Or why did he fail, when Charlemagne, with a greater complication of interests to deal with, for a time at least, succeeded?

"The causes were mainly these; causes . . . very similar, at all times, in their operation. In the first place, Theodoric was an Arian, and there was a power antagonistic to Arianism growing up already on the banks of the Tiber, stronger than the statesmen's policy or the soldier's sword—the spiritual power of the church of Rome. . . . Such a power was necessarily altogether incompatible with the existence of an Arian empire. And it proved mightier than its rival."—"*Fall of Rome,*" *John G. Sheppard, D. D., pp. 301, 302. London: 1861.*

In order to give the reader a better understanding of the means used by the Papacy to destroy these Arian kingdoms, we shall quote from Thomas Hodgkin a few brief statements. He states that Theodoric, the Ostrogothic king, endeavored to have "a close league for mutual defence formed between the four great Arian and Teutonic monarchies, the Visigothic, the Burgundian, the Ostrogothic, and the Vandal." But "diplomatists were wanting [who could act] as their skillful and eloquent representatives, traveling like Epiphanius from court to court, and bringing the barbarian sovereigns to understand each other, to sink their petty grievances, and to work together harmoniously for one common end. Precisely these men were the Catholic prelates of the Mediterranean lands to whom it was all-important that no such Arian league should be formed. . . . All over the Roman world there was a serried array of Catholic bishops and presbyters, taking their orders from a single centre, Rome, feeling the interest of each one to be the interests of all, in lively and constant intercourse with one another, quick to discover, quick to disclose the slightest weak place in the organization of the new heretical kingdoms. Of all this there was not the slightest trace on the other side. The Arian bishops . . . stood apart from one another in stupid and ignorant isolation."— *"Italy and Her Invaders," Thomas Hodgkin, (8-vol. ed.) Vol. III, Book 4, pp. 381-383. Oxford: 1899.*

This same principle was clearly stated by the Catholic bishop Avitus, when the Arian king Gundobad appealed to him not to allow the Catholic king Clovis to overrun his country. Avitus answered: "If Gundobad would reconcile himself to the Church, the Church would guarantee his safety from the attacks of Clovis."—*Id., p. 384.*

The religious liberty, with its attendant blessings to the country, which Theodoric had inaugurated, did not satisfy the Catholic bishops; for Rome does not want religious liberty for other churches, but sole domination for herself.

"The religious toleration which Theodoric had the glory of introducing into the Christian world, was painful and offensive to the orthodox zeal of the Italian."—*"Decline and Fall," Edward Gibbon, chap. 39, par. 17.*

"Theodoric, . . . being an Arian, could not long remain on harmonious terms with a Pope and [an] Emperor of the Orthodox creed, [who were] necessarily bound to combine against him sooner or later."—*"The Barbarian Invasion of Italy," P. Villari, Vol. I, p. 178. London: 1913; New York: Scribner, 1902.*

This was only natural. The fundamental principles of the church of Rome are such that she can never concede to any other denomination the equal right to exist and to carry on its worship. Urged on by the pope and his bishops, Emperor Justin had enacted severe laws against Arians (524 A. D.), and Justinian began his reign in 527 by making laws still more severe.

"Theodoric, the King of Italy, at first maintained something of his usual calm moderation; he declined all retaliation, to which he had been incessantly urged, on the orthodox of the West."—"*Latin Christianity,*" *H. H. Milman, D. D., Vol. I, Book III, chap. 3, p. 440.*

But the concerted efforts of pope and emperor, by fire, sword, and exile, to exterminate "Arianism" at last "awakened the just resentment of Theodoric, who claimed for his distressed brethren of the East the same indulgence which he had so long granted to the Catholics of his dominions. . . . And a mandate was prepared in Italy, to prohibit, after a stated day, the exercise of the Catholic worship. By the bigotry of his subjects and enemies, the most tolerant of princes was driven to the brink of persecution."—"*Decline and Fall,*" *chap. 39, par. 17.*

"In Italy, Theodoric's prolonged toleration had reconciled no one to him, and his ultimate severity exasperated his Roman subjects. A dumb agitation held sway in the West, and the coming of the Emperor's soldiers was eagerly awaited and desired."
—"*Cambridge Medieval History,*" *Bury, Gwatkin, and Whitney, Vol. II, p. 10. Chicago: The Macmillan Company, 1913.*

"And truly the chief men of Rome were suspected, at this very time, of carrying on a treasonable correspondence with the Court of Constantinople, and machinating the ruin of the Gothic empire in Italy."—"*History of the Popes,*" *A. Bower, Vol. II, p. 421. Dublin: 1749.*

In the summer of 535 Belisarius started with 7,500 men besides his own guards to conquer Italy and destroy the Arian heretics. This he could do only by the assistance of the Roman Catholics.

"But with great shrewdness he had quickly won their good will, by announcing that he came to deliver them from the barbarian yoke, and from the Arian persecution, and also for the purpose of restoring Rome to her ancient grandeur."—"*The Barbarian Invasion of Italy,*" *P. Villari, Vol. I, p. 201.*

Witigis [Vitiges] was now the king of the Ostrogoths, and Rome was continuing its usual policy. Professor J. B. Bury says:

"In the meantime Belisarius had left Naples and was marching northward. The Romans, warned by the experiences of Naples, and urged by the Pope, who had no scruples in breaking his oath with Witigis, sent a messenger inviting him to come. He . . . entered Rome on December 9, A. D. 536."—"*History of the Later Roman Empire,*" Vol. II, pp. 179, 180.

"Such, then, was the Pope Silverius . . . who, having sworn a solemn oath of fealty to Witigis, now, near the end of 536, sent messengers to Belisarius to offer the peaceful surrender of the city of Rome."—"*Italy and Her Invaders,*" T. Hodgkin (8-vol. ed.), Vol. IV, Book 5, p. 93. 1885.

"Rome betrayed. The Catholics, on the first approach of the emperor's army, boldly raised the cry that the apostolic throne (!) should no longer be profaned by the triumph or toleration of Arianism, nor the tombs of the Cæsars trampled by the savages of the North; and deputies of the pope and clergy, and of what is called the senate and people, waited upon the approaching army to whom they threw open the gates of the city; and the Catholics were rewarded for their treason by the apparent respect of Belisarius for the pope."—"*History of the Christian Church,*" N. Summerbell, page 340, third edition. Cincinnati: 1873.

Witigis then besieged the city of Rome from March, 537, to March, 538, when he raised the siege, after losing the flower of his army, and retired to Ravenna, his capital. T. Hodgkin says:

"With heavy hearts the barbarians must have thought, as they turned them northwards, upon the many graves of gallant men which they were leaving on that fatal plain. Some of them must have suspected the melancholy truth that they had dug one grave, deeper and wider than all, the grave of the Gothic monarchy in Italy."—"*Italy and Her Invaders,*" (8-vol. ed.) Vol. IV, p. 285.

A deathblow was thus given to the Ostrogoths in 538 A. D., and their attempts to re-establish themselves after this were but the last flicker of a lamp being extinguished. Belisarius followed them this same year to their "last stronghold of power. Ravenna was soon entered by the troops of the empire, and with it fell the great kingdom of the Ostrogoths."—"*Fall of Rome,*" *J. G. Sheppard, p. 306. London: 1892.*

"Then occurred a singular phenomenon,—the annihilation and disappearance of a great and powerful people from the world's history."—*Id., p. 307.*

But let all remember, that "the success of Justinian's invasion was due to the clergy; in the ruin they brought upon their country, and the relentless tyranny they drew upon themselves, they had their reward."—"*History of the Intellectual Development of Europe,*" *J. W. Draper, M. D., LL. D., Vol. I, p. 355. New York: Harper Brothers., 1889.*

The last of the three Arian "horns" of Daniel 7: 8 had passed away, and with it passed also the liberty of the common people. Dr. N. Summerbell truthfully says:

"The Dark Ages, introduced by the persecution of an enlightened Church in the sanguinary wars of Justinian to exalt the Catholics, continued up to the fourteenth century. It was a long, dark night, when ignorance, bigotry, and cruelty reigned, and truth, purity, and justice were crushed out."—"*History of the Christian Church,*" *p. 342.*

THE LOMBARDS

It has been claimed by some that the Lombard nation was one of the three horns of Daniel 7: 8, which were rooted up by the Papacy. We shall therefore investigate this claim carefully before leaving this subject. It is true that the Lombards, who settled in Italy, 568 A. D., were at first Arians, but they soon became converted to the Roman Catholic faith (615 A. D.). Professor J. B. Bury says:

"In the century which intervened between the death of Gregory I [604 A. D.] and the accession of Gregory II [715] the Lombards had been transformed from Arian heretics into devout Catholics, so that the religious difficulty which parted Roman from Lombard had disappeared."—"*The Cambridge Medieval*

History," Vol. II, p. 694. New York: The Macmillan Company, 1913.

That the Lombards were not subdued on account of any opposition to the papal church is also witnessed by the following quotation:

"Slowly however the light of faith made way among them and the Church won their respect and obedience. This meant protection for the conquered."—*The Catholic Encyclopedia, Vol. IX, art. "Lombards," p. 338.*

Even though the Lombards were subdued by Pepin (755 A. D.), and later by Charlemagne (774), yet they were not destroyed. The Lombard kingdom in Italy had long been divided into smaller "duchies," and Charlemagne allowed several of these to continue, while they nominally recognized him as emperor (such an arrangement became common for centuries in Italy).

"The Lombards, having now been two hundred and thirty-two years in the country, were strangers only in name; and Charles, wishing to reorganize the states of Italy, consented that they should occupy the places in which they had been brought up, and call the province after their own name, Lombardy. . . .

"In the meantime, the Emperor Charles died and was succeeded by Lewis, . . . [and] at the time of his grandchildren, the house of France lost the empire, which then came to the Germans. [During these changes] the Lombards [were] gathering strength."—*"The History of Florence," N. Machiavelli, pp. 15, 16. Washington and London: Universal Classics Library, 1901.*

In 1167 A. D., the different Lombard cities were organized into separate republics, and combined into the famous Lombard League. Being devoted to the pope they fought the excommunicated German emperor, Frederick Barbarossa, who would subjugate them, and who "endeavored to force upon the church an anti-pope in the place of Alexander III."

Finally in 1176 A. D., the combined armies of the Lombard

League met the emperor's forces in a decisive battle on the plains of Legnano. "The imperial army was so utterly overthrown and dispersed, that for some time the fate of the emperor was uncertain. Three days after the battle he appeared in Pavia, alone, and in . . . disguise. . . . For twenty-one years Frederick had been struggling against the independence of Lombardy. With seven armies he had swept their doomed territory, inflicting atrocities the recital of which sickens humanity. The fatal battle of Legnano left him for a time powerless, and he was compelled to assent to a truce for six years. At the expiration of this truce, in the year 1183, by the peace of Constance, the comparative independence of Lombardy was secured; a general supremacy of dignity rather than of power being conceded to the emperor." —"*Italy from the Earliest Period to the Present Day*," *John S. C. Abbott, pp. 438, 439. New York: 1860.*

Not only had the kingdom of Lombardy maintained its independence, but "the generous resistance of the Lombards, during a war of thirty years, had conquered from the emperors political liberty for all the towns in the kingdom of Italy."—"*A History of the Italian Republics*," *J. C. S. de Sismondi, p. 61. New York: 1904.*

If space permitted, we could trace the kingdom of Lombardy for nearly two centuries more, but this will suffice to prove that the Lombards were not destroyed by Charlemagne, when subdued by him in 774, neither could they be one of the three powers plucked up by the roots to give place for the Papacy. (Daniel 7:8.) A people plucked up by the roots in 774 would hardly fight so heroically for four hundred years afterwards to maintain their independence till mighty emperors had to yield. But even if the Lombards had been destroyed by Charlemagne in 774, they could not be reckoned as one of the three nations plucked up to give place to the Papacy; for, if we reckon the 1260 years of papal supremacy from 774, they would end in 2034 A. D., which would entirely dislocate the prophetic reckoning, as we shall see in the next chapter.

"A Time, and Times, and Half a Time"

THE little horn of Daniel 7: 8, 25, was to reign for "a time and times and the dividing of time." This same "time, and times, and half a time" is also mentioned in Revelation 12: 14, and in the sixth verse it is said to be "a thousand two hundred and threescore days." In prophecy a day always stands for a year. (Ezekiel 4: 6.) This prophetic period is therefore 1260 literal years. We shall now show that these 1260 years began in 538 A. D., and invite the reader to notice the four great changes that took place that year:

1. We have already seen that the little horn symbolized the Papacy, and that three Arian kingdoms, which stood in its way, were plucked up by the roots, and that the last of these received its deathblow in 538 A. D. through the efforts of Justinian, the faithful son of the church of Rome.

2. History states that the work of Justin and Justinian in elevating the Papacy to power brought on a new era, introducing the Middle Ages:

"Accordingly, the religious and political tendencies of the Empire now took so different a direction as to positively constitute the dawn of a new era. . . . Thus at last Rome had triumphed, after fighting so long with unflinching vigour and without yielding a single point."—"*The Barbarian Invasion of Italy,*" *P. Villari, Vol. I, pp. 177, 178.*

"The reign of Justinian is more remarkable as a portion of the history of mankind, than as a chapter in the annals of the Roman Empire or of the Greek nation. The changes of centuries pass in rapid succession before the eyes of one generation. . . .

"With the conquest of Rome by Belisarius, the history of the ancient city may be considered as terminating; and with his defence against Witigis [A. D. 538], commences the history of the

"A Time, and Times, and Half a Time"   53

Middle Ages."—"*Greece Under the Romans,*" *George Finlay, pp. 198, 240, Dent edition, revised by author, 1877.*

3. Even the Papacy itself changed, so there was *a new order of popes* after 538 A. D. History relates:

"Down to the sixth century all popes are declared saints in the martyrologies. Vigillius (537-555) is the first of a series of popes who no longer bear this title, which is henceforth sparingly conferred. From this time on the popes, more and more enveloped in worldly events, no longer belong solely to the church; they are men of the state, and then rulers of the state."—"*Medieval Europe,*" *Belmont and Monod (revised by George Burton Adams), p. 120. New York: H. Holt & Co., 1902.*

In the foregoing quotation the date of Vigillius should be 538 instead of 537 for the following reason:

"Vigillius having been thus ordained in the year 537, . . . and the death of Silverius having been certainly not earlier than 20 June, A. D. 538, it is evident that for at least seven months his position was that of an unlawful anti-pope, his predecessor never having been canonically deposed."—*Dictionary of Christian Biography, Drs. Smith and Wace, Vol. IV, art. "Vigillius," p. 1144. London: 1887.*

For this reason A. Bower says:

"From the death of Silverius the Roman Catholic writers date the Episcopacy of Vigillius, reckoning him thenceforth among the lawful popes."—"*History of the Popes,*" *Vol. II, p. 488, under the year "538." Dublin: 1751.*

"His [Silverius'] death happened on the 20th of June . . . 538."—*Id., p. 488.*

Dr. Philip Schaff says:

"Vigillius, a pliant creature of Theodora, ascended the papal chair under the military protection of Belisarius (538-555)."—"*History of the Christian Church*" *(7-vol. ed.), Vol. III, p. 327. New York: Scribner's, 1893.* See also "*General History of the Catholic Church,*" M. l'Abbe J. E. Darras, Vol. II, pp. 146, 147 (New York: 1866), and "The Official Catholic Directory" for 1933, "List of Roman Pontiffs" on page 7.

4. Dr. Summerbell gives still another reason why we should date the beginning of the papal supremacy from 538. He says: "Justinian . . . enriched himself with the property of all 'heretics'—that is non-Catholics, and gave all their churches to the Catholics; published edicts in 538 compelling all to join the Catholic Church in ninety days or leave the empire, and confiscated all their goods."—"*History of the Christian Church,*" *pp. 310, 311. Cincinnati: 1873.* The same is stated by Samuel Chandler in "History of Persecution," pp. 142, 143; and by Edward Gibbon, in "Decline and Fall," chap. 47, par. 24.

THE STATE RELIGION

Thus we see that Roman Catholicism was made the state religion in 538, and all other religions were forbidden. What gave special significance to these edicts of Justinian was the fact that he had already in 533 declared the bishop of Rome to be the head of the universal church, and had subjected all the priests even of the East under the see of Rome. This fact he wrote to Pope John II on March 15, 533, in the following language:

"With honor to the Apostolic See, . . . We hasten to bring to the knowledge of Your Holiness everything relating to the condition of the Church, as we have always had great desire to preserve the unity of your Apostolic See, and the condition of the Holy Churches of God, as they exist at the present time, that they may remain without disturbance or opposition. Therefore, We have exerted Ourselves to unite all the priests of the East and subject them to the See of Your Holiness. . . . For we do not suffer anything which has reference to the state of the Church, even though what causes the difficulty may be clear and free from doubt, to be discussed without being brought to the notice of Your Holiness, because you are the head of all Holy Churches, for we shall exert Ourselves in every way (as has already been stated), to increase the honor and authority of your see. . . .

"Therefore we request your paternal affection, that you, by your letters, inform Us and the Most Holy Bishop of this Fair

City, and your brother the Patriarch, who himself has written by the same messengers to Your Holiness, eager in all things to follow the Apostolic See of your Blessedness, in order that you may make it clear to Us that Your Holiness acknowledges all the matters which have been set forth above."—"*The Civil Law of Justinian,*" *translated by S. P. Scott, A. M. (in 17 volumes), Book 12, pp. 11-13.*

To this letter Pope John II answered:

"John, Bishop of the City of Rome, to his most Illustrious and Merciful Son Justinian.

"Among the conspicuous reasons for praising your wisdom and gentleness, Most Christian of Emperors, and one which radiates light as a star, is the fact that through love of the Faith, and actuated by zeal for charity, you, learned in ecclesiastical discipline, have preserved reverence for the See of Rome, and have subjected all things to his authority, and have given it unity. . . .

"This See is indeed the head of all Churches, as the rules of the Fathers and the decrees of Emperors assert, and the words of your most reverent piety testify. . . .

"We have received with all due respect the evidences of your serenity, through Hypatius and Demetrius, most holy men, my brothers and fellow bishops, from whose statements we have learned that you have promulgated an Edict addressed to your faithful people, and dictated by your love of the faith, for the purpose of overthrowing the designs of heretics, which is in accordance with the evangelical tenets, and which we have confirmed by our authority with the consent of our brethren and fellow bishops, for the reason that it is in conformity with the apostolic doctrine. . . .

"Therefore, it is opportune to cry out with a prophetic voice, 'Heaven will rejoice with You, and pour out its blessing upon You, and the mountains will rejoice, and the hills be glad with exceeding joy.' . . .

"The favor of Our Lord . . . remain forever with you, Most Pious Son, Amen. . . .

"Given at Rome, on the eighth of the Kalends of April, during the Consulate of Emperor Justinian, Consul for the fourth time."—*Id., pp. 10-15.*

Both of these letters appear in the "Code of Justinian," as well as the following law:

"Concerning the Precedence of Patriarchs:

"Hence, in accordance with the provisions of those Councils, we order that the Most Holy Pope of Ancient Rome shall hold the first rank of all the Pontiffs, but the Most Blessed Archbishop of Constantinople, or New Rome, shall occupy the second place after the Holy Apostolic See of Ancient Rome, which shall take precedence over all other sees."—*Id., Vol. XVII, p. 125.* (*"Constitutions of Justinian," Vol. XVII, 9th Collection, Title 14, chapter 2.*)

Under date of March 25, 533, Justinian, writing to Epiphanius, Patriarch of Constantinople, stating that he had written the above letter to the pope, "repeats his decision, that all affairs touching the Church shall be referred to the Pope, 'Head of all bishops, and the true and effective corrector of heretics.'"—*"The Apocalypse of St. John," George Croly, A. M., p. 170, second edition. London: 1828.*

"The epistle which was addressed to the Pope, and another to the Patriarch of Constantinople, were inserted in the volume of the civil law; thus the sentiments contained in them obtained the sanction of the supreme legislative authority of the empire. . . .

"The answer of the Pope to the imperial epistle was also published with the other documents; and it is equally important, inasmuch as it shows that he understood the reference that had been made to him, as being a formal recognition of the supremacy of the see of Rome."—*"A Dissertation on the Seals and Trumpets of the Apocalypse," William Cuninghame, pp. 185, 186. London: 1843; cited in "Source Book," pp. 383, 384, ed. of 1922.*

"The recognition of the Roman see as the highest ecclesiastical authority (cf. *Novellæ*, cxxxi) remained the cornerstone of his [Justinian's] policy in relation to the West."—*New*

Schaff-Herzog Encyclopedia, Vol. VI, art. "Justinian," p. 286. Thus we see that the way had been prepared in 533, in anticipation of the three final acts which were to occur in 538, when the Arian powers were destroyed, Catholicism made the state religion, and the Papacy placed under the protection of the state, which gave rise to the long struggle between church and state as to which should be supreme.

CLOSE OF THE 1260 YEARS

Having now seen that the 1260 years of papal supremacy began in 538 A. D., it is an easy matter to find their close. Adding the 1260 years to 538 brings us to the year 1798. And if we have given the right application to this prophecy, history must record an event in 1798 that would appear like a death stroke to the Papacy. Turning to history we find just such an event recorded:

The official Swedish newspaper, *Stockholms Posttidning*, for March 29, 1798, has the following news item:

"Rome, the 21st of Feb. [1798], Pope Pius VI, has occupied the papal chair for all of twenty-eight years, but the 15th inst. his government in the Papal States was abolished, and five days later, guarded by one hundred French soldiers, he was taken away from his palace and his capital. . . .

"His . . . property was sold by the French, and among it were seven hundred head of cattle, one hundred fifty horses, and eight hundred cords of wood. . . .

"Poor Pius! He must have felt very sad as he left Rome to go into captivity. When he departed his tear-filled eyes were turned heavenward."

Rev. E. B. Elliott, A. M., says of these events:

"In the years 1796, 1797, French dominion being established by Bonaparte's victories in *Northern Italy*, . . . the French armies [urged] their march onward to the Papal Capital. . . . The aged Pope himself, now left mere nominal master of some few remaining shreds of the Patrimony of Peter, experienced soon after *in person* the bitterness of the prevailing anti-papal spirit. . . .

"On pretence of an insult to the French Ambassador there, a French corps d'armee under Berthier, having in February, 1798, crossed the Apennines from Ancona, and entered Rome, the tricolour flag was displayed from the Capitol, amidst the shouts of the populace, the Pope's temporal reign declared at an end, and the Roman Republic proclaimed, in strict alliance fraternization with the French. Then, in the Sistine Chapel of the Vatican, the ante-hall to which has a fresco painted by Papal order commemorative of the Protestant massacre on St. Bartholomew's day, (might not the scene have served as a memento of God's retributive justice?) there, while seated on his throne, and receiving the gratulations of his cardinals on the anniversary of his election to the Popedom, he was arrested by the French military, the ring of his marriage with the Church Catholic torn from his finger, his palace rifled, and himself carried prisoner into France, only to die there in exile shortly after."—"*Horæ Apocalypticæ*," Rev. E. B. Elliott, A. M., Vol. III, pp. 400, 401. London: 1862.

Arthur R. Pennington, M. A., F. R. Hist. Soc., says of this event:

"One day the Pope was sitting on his throne in a chapel of the Vatican, surrounded by his cardinals who had assembled for the purpose of offering him their congratulations on his elevation to his high dignity. On a sudden, the shouts of an angry multitude penetrated to the conclave, intermingled with the strokes of axes and hammers on the doors. Very soon a band of soldiers burst into the hall, who tore away from his finger his pontifical ring, and hurried him off, a prisoner, through a hall, the walls of which were adorned with a fresco, representing the armed satellites of the Papacy, on St. Bartholomew's day, as bathing their swords in the blood of unoffending women and helpless children. Thus it might seem as if he were to be reminded that the same God who visits the iniquities of the fathers upon the children unto the third and fourth generation, had made him the victim of His retributive justice for a deed of atrocity which had long been crying aloud to Him for ven-

"A Time, and Times, and Half a Time"   59

geance."—"*Epochs of the Papacy*," pp. 449, 450. London: 1881.

Rev. Joseph Rickaby, an English Jesuit, writes:

"When, in 1797, Pope Pius VI fell grievously ill, Napoleon gave orders that in the event of his death no successor should be elected to his office, and that the Papacy should be discontinued.

"But the Pope recovered. The peace was soon broken; Berthier entered Rome on the 10th February, 1798, and proclaimed a republic. The aged Pontiff refused to violate his oath by recognizing it, and was hurried from prison to prison in France. . . . No wonder that half Europe thought Napoleon's veto would be obeyed, and that with the Pope the Papacy was dead."—"*The Modern Papacy*," p. 1. London: Catholic Truth Society.

Rev. George Trevor, Canon of York, writes of this eventful year:

"The object of the French Directory was the destruction of the pontifical government, as the irreconcilable enemy of the republic. . . . The aged pope was summoned to surrender the temporal government; on his refusal, he was dragged from the altar. . . . His rings were torn from his fingers, and finally, after declaring the temporal power abolished, the victors carried the pope prisoner into Tuscany, whence he never returned (1798).

"The Papal States, converted into the *Roman Republic*, were declared to be in perpetual alliance with France, but the French general was the real master of Rome. . . . The territorial possessions of the clergy and monks were declared national property, and their former owners cast into prison. The Papacy was extinct: not a vestige of its existence remained; and among all the Roman Catholic powers not a finger was stirred in its defence. The Eternal City had no longer prince or pontiff; its bishop was a dying captive in foreign lands; and the decree was already announced that no successor would be allowed in his place."—"*Rome: From the Fall of the Western Empire*," pp. 439, 440. London: 1868.

An English secular writer, John Adolphus, says of 1798:

"The downfall of the papal government, by whatever means effected, excited perhaps less sympathy than that of any other in Europe: the errors, the oppressions, the tyranny of Rome over the whole Christian world, were remembered with bitterness; many rejoiced, through religious antipathy, in the overthrow of a church which they considered as idolatrous, though attended with the immediate triumph of infidelity; and many saw in these events the accomplishment of prophecies, and the exhibition of signs promised in the most mystical parts of the Holy Scriptures."—"*History of France from 1790-1802,*" *Vol. II, p. 379. London: 1803.*

God's prophetic clock had set the year 1798 as the end of the papal supremacy, and when that hour struck, the mighty ruler on the Tiber, before whose anathemas the kings and emperors of Europe had so long trembled, went "into captivity" (Revelation 13: 10), and his government in the Papal States was abolished. Thus the historical events fit exactly into the mold of prophecy, and establish the fact that "we have also a more sure word of prophecy; whereunto ye do well that ye take heed, as unto a light that shineth in a dark place, until the day dawn." 2 Peter 1: 19. But prophecy foretells that this "deadly wound" would be healed, and that the world once more, for a brief moment, would follow the papal power. (Revelation 13: 3.) In the following chapter we shall consider the other specifications of this remarkable prophecy.

Other Marks of Identity

"He Shall Speak Great Words"

THE little horn was to "speak great words against the Most High." Daniel 7:25. We shall now quote a few extracts from authentic Roman Catholic sources showing the fulfillment of this prophetic utterance: Pope Leo XIII in his "Great Encyclical Letters" says: "We hold upon this earth the place of God Almighty."—*P. 304.* In this encyclical the pope has capitalized all pronouns referring to himself and to God.

In a large, authentic work by F. Lucii Ferraris, called "Prompta Bibliotheca Canonica Juridica Moralis Theologica," printed at Rome, 1890, and sanctioned by the Catholic Encyclopedia (Vol. VI, p. 48), we find the following statements regarding the power of the pope:

"The Pope is of so great dignity and so exalted that he is not a mere man, but as it were God, and the vicar of God. . . .

"Hence the Pope is crowned with a triple crown, as king of heaven and of earth and of the lower regions. . . .

"So that if it were possible that the angels might err in the faith, or might think contrary to the faith, they could be judged and excommunicated by the Pope. . . .

"The Pope is as it were God on earth, sole sovereign of the faithful of Christ, chief king of kings, having plenitude of power, to whom has been entrusted by the omnipotent God direction not only of the earthly but also of the heavenly kingdom."—*Quoted in "Source Book," (Revised Edition) pp. 409, 410. Washington, D. C.: 1927.*

The Catholic Encyclopedia says of the pope:

"The sentences which he gives are to be forthwith ratified in heaven."—*Vol. XII, art. "Pope," p. 265.*

Pope Leo XIII says:

"But the supreme teacher in the Church is the Roman Pontiff. Union of minds, therefore, requires, together with a perfect accord in the one faith, complete submission and obedience of will to the Church and to the Roman Pontiff, as to God Himself."—"*The Great Encyclical Letters,*" *p. 193.*

We leave it with the reader to decide whether or not these are "great words." St. Alphonsus de Liguori, a sainted doctor of the Roman church, claims the same power for the Roman priests. He says:

"The priest has the power of the keys, or the power of delivering sinners from hell, of making them worthy of paradise, and of changing them from the slaves of Satan into the children of God. And God himself is obliged to abide by the judgment of his priests. . . . The Sovereign Master of the universe only follows the servant by confirming in heaven all that the latter decides upon earth."—"*Dignity and Duties of the Priest,*" *pp. 27, 28. New York: Benziger Brothers., Printers to the Holy Apostolic See, 1888.*

"Innocent III has written: 'Indeed, it is not too much to say that in view of the sublimity of their offices the priests are so many gods.'"—*Id., p. 36.*

These must truly be called "great words"!

A Persecuting Power

The little horn was also to "wear out the saints of the Most High." Daniel 7: 25. That is, it was to persecute them till they were literally worn out. Has the Papacy fulfilled this part of the prophecy? In order to do Roman Catholics no injustice, we shall quote from unquestioned authorities among them. And, since they persecute people for "heresy," we must first let them define what they mean by "heresy." In the New Catholic Dictionary, published by the Universal Knowledge Foundation, a Roman Catholic institution, New York, 1929, we read:

"Heresy (Gr., *hairesis*, choice), deciding for oneself what one shall believe and practise."—*Art. "Heresy," p. 440.*

According to this definition any one who will not blindly submit to papal authority, but will read the Bible, deciding for himself what he shall believe, is a "heretic." What official stand has the Catholic Church taken in regard to such heretics? This we find stated in the Catholic Encyclopedia in the following words:

"In the Bull 'Ad exstirpanda' (1252) Innocent IV says: 'When those adjudged guilty of heresy have been given up to the civil power by the bishop or his representative, or the Inquisition, the *podesta* or chief magistrate of the city shall take them at once, and shall, within five days at the most, execute the laws made against them.' . . . Nor could any doubt remain as to what civil regulations were meant, for the passages which ordered the burning of impenitent heretics were inserted in the papal decretals from the imperial constitutions 'Commissis nobis' and 'Inconsutibilem tunicam.' The aforesaid Bull 'Ad exstirpanda' remained thenceforth a fundamental document of the Inquisition, renewed or reinforced by several popes, Alexander IV (1254-61), Clement IV (1265-68), Nicolas IV (1288-92), Boniface VIII (1294-1303), and others. The civil authorities, therefore, were enjoined by the popes, under pain of excommunication to execute the legal sentences that condemned impenitent heretics to the stake. It is to be noted that excommunication itself was no trifle, for, if the person excommunicated did not free himself from excommunication within a year, he was held by the legislation of that period to be a heretic, and incurred all the penalties that affected heresy."—*Vol. VIII, p. 34.**

This Encyclopedia was printed in 1910, and bears the sanction of the Catholic authorities, and of their "censor," so that here is up-to-date authority showing that the Roman church sanctions persecution. The Roman church here acknowledges, that, when she was in power, she forced the civil government to burn those whom she termed heretics, and the government officials who failed to execute her laws, became

---

* See also "Dictionary of the Inquisition," in "Illustrations of Popery," J. P. Challender, pp. 377-386, New York, 1838; and "History of the Inquisition of the Middle Ages," H. C. Lea, Vol. I, pp. 337 338, New York, 1888.

heretics by that neglect, and suffered the punishment of heretics. Professor Alfred Baudrillart, a Roman Catholic scholar in France, who is now a Catholic Cardinal, says:

"The Catholic Church is a respecter of conscience and of liberty. . . . She has, and she *loudly proclaims that she has*, a 'horror of blood.' Nevertheless when confronted by heresy she does not content herself with persuasion; arguments of an intellectual and moral order appear to her insufficient, and she has recourse to force, to corporal punishment, to torture. She creates tribunals like those of the Inquisition, she calls the laws of the State to her aid, if necessary she encourages a crusade, or a religious war and all her 'horror of blood' practically culminates into urging the secular power to shed it, which proceeding is almost more odious—for it is less frank—than shedding it herself. Especially did she act thus in the sixteenth century with regard to Protestants. Not content to reform morally, to preach by example, to convert people by eloquent and holy missionaries, she lit in Italy, in the Low Countries, and above all in Spain the funeral piles of the Inquisition. In France under Francis I and Henry II, in England under Mary Tudor, she tortured the heretics, whilst both in France and Germany during the second half of the sixteenth and the first half of the seventeenth century if she did not actually begin, at any rate she encouraged and actively aided, the religious wars. No one will deny that we have here a great scandal to our contemporaries. . . .

"Indeed, even among our friends and our brothers we find those who dare not look this problem in the face. They ask permission from the Church to ignore or even deny all those acts and institutions in the past which have made orthodoxy compulsory."*—"*The Catholic Church, the Renaissance, and Protestantism,*" *pp. 182-184. London: 1908.* This book bears the sanction of the Roman Catholic authorities, and of their "censor."

Andrew Steinmetz says:

"Catholics easily account for their devotion to the Holy See,

---

* This explains why some Catholic authors deny that their church ever persecuted.

in spite of its historical abominations, which, however, very few of them are aware of—their accredited histories in common use, 'with permission of authority,' veiling the subject with painful dexterity."—"*History of the Jesuits,*" *Vol. I, p. 13. London: 1848.*

Dr. C. H. Lea says:

"In view of the unvarying policy of the Church during the three centuries under consideration, and for a century and a half later, there is a typical instance of the manner in which history is written to order, in the quiet assertion of the latest Catholic historian of the Inquisition that 'the Church took no part in the corporal punishment of heretics.'"—"*History of the Inquisition of the Middle Ages,*" *Vol. I, p. 540. New York: Harper and Brothers, 1888.*

Pope Gregory IX (1227-1241) made the following decree for the destruction of all heretics, which is binding on civil rulers:

"Temporal princes shall be reminded and exhorted, and if needs be, compelled by spiritual censures, to discharge every one of their functions: and that, as they desire to be reckoned and held faithful, so, for the defence of the faith, let them publicly make oath that they will endeavor, *bona fide* with all their might, to extirpate from their territories all heretics marked by the Church; so that when anyone is about to assume any authority, whether spiritual or temporal, he shall be held bound to confirm his title by this oath. And if a temporal prince, being required and admonished by the Church, shall neglect to purge his kingdom from this heretical pravity, the metropolitan and other provincial bishops shall bind him in fetters of excommunication; and if he obstinately refuse to make satisfaction this shall be notified within a year to the Supreme Pontiff, that then he may declare his subjects absolved from their allegiance, and leave their lands to be occupied by Catholics, who, the heretics being exterminated, may possess them unchallenged, and preserve them in the purity of the faith."—"*Decretalium Gregorii Papae Noni Conpilatio,*" *Liber V, Titulus VII, Capitulum XIII,*

(*A Collection of the Decretals of Gregory IX, Book 5, Title 7, Chapter 13*), dated *April 20, 1619*.

The sainted Catholic doctor, Thomas Aquinas, says:

"If counterfeiters of money or other criminals are justly delivered over to death forthwith by the secular authorities, much more can heretics, after they are convicted of heresy, be not only forthwith excommunicated, but as surely put to death."—"*Summa Theologica*," *2a, 2ae, qu. xi, art. iii.*

That this principle is sanctioned by modern Catholic priests, we can see from the following statement:

"The church has persecuted. Only a tyro in church history will deny that. . . . Protestants were persecuted in France and Spain with the full approval of the church authorities. We have always defended the persecution of the Huguenots, and the Spanish Inquisition."—"*Western Watchman*," *official organ of Father Phelan. St. Louis, Mo.: Dec. 24, 1908.*

We have now seen from the "decretals" of popes, from sainted doctors of the Roman church, and from authentic Catholic books, that they sanction and defend persecution, and history amply bears out the fact. Dr. J. Dowling says:

"From the birth of Popery in 606, to the present time, it is estimated by careful and credible historians, that more than *fifty millions* of the human family, have been slaughtered for the crime of heresy by popish persecutors, an average of more than *forty thousand religious murders* for every year of the existence of Popery."—"*History of Romanism*," *pp. 541, 542. New York: 1871.*

W. E. H. Lecky says:

"That the Church of Rome has shed more innocent blood than any other institution that has ever existed among mankind, will be questioned by no Protestant who has a competent knowledge of history. The memorials, indeed, of many of her persecutions are now so scanty, that it is impossible to form a complete conception of the multitude of her victims, and it is quite certain that no power of imagination can adequately realize their sufferings."—"*History of the Rise and Influence of the Spirit of Ration-*

Other Marks of Identity 67

alism in Europe," *Vol. II, p. 32. London: Longmans, Green, and Co., 1910.*

John Lothrop Motley, speaking of papal persecution in the Netherlands, says:

"Upon February 16, 1568, a sentence of the Holy Office [the Inquisition] condemned *all the inhabitants* of the Netherlands *to death* as heretics. . . . A proclamation of the king, dated ten days later, confirmed this decree of the Inquisition, and ordered it to be carried into instant execution. . . . This is probably the most concise death warrant that was ever framed. Three millions of people, men, women, and children, were sentenced to the scaffold in three lines."—"*The Rise of the Dutch Republic," (2-vol. ed.) Vol. I, p. 626. New York.*

Many Roman Catholic authors today have tried to prove that their church does not sanction persecution, but facts of history are too plain to be denied. Eternity alone will reveal what God's dear children suffered during the Dark Ages. Accordingly as the Papacy attained to power, the common people became more oppressed, until "the noon of the Papacy was the midnight of the world."—"*History of Protestantism," J. A. Wylie, LL.D., Vol. I, p. 16. London.*

"THINK TO CHANGE TIMES AND LAWS"

But Daniel 7: 25 has still another prediction concerning the "little horn"; namely, that it should "think to change times and laws," or as the Revised Version has it: "times and the law." James Moffatt's translation reads: "He shall plan to alter the sacred seasons and the law." Now, as the two preceding statements in this verse depict what the Papacy should do against the Most High, we must conclude that it is also the "times and the law" of the Most High which the Papacy should attempt to *change.* This could not refer to the ceremonial laws of the Jews, which were abolished at the cross (Ephesians 2: 15; Hebrews 9: 9, 10), but to the Ten Commandments, which are binding in the Christian era, to which dispensation this prophecy applies. (Matthew 5: 17-19; 19: 16-19; Luke 16: 17; Romans 3: 31; 7: 7,

12, 14; James 2: 10, 11.) From the prophecy of Daniel 7: 25 it is therefore evident that the Papacy would attempt to make some changes in the moral law.

After the worship of images had crept into the church during the fourth to the sixth centuries, its leaders finally removed the second commandment from their doctrinal books, because it forbids us to bow down to images (Exodus 20: 4, 5), and they *divided the tenth*, so as to retain ten in number. Thus the Catholic Church has two commandments against coveting, while Paul six times speaks of it as only *one* "commandment." (Romans 7: 7-13.) Then, too, the Lord has purposely reversed the order of the supposed ninth and tenth commandments in Deuteronomy 5: 21 to what they are in Exodus 20: 17, so that the Catholics, following Deuteronomy 5: 21, have "Thou shalt not covet thy neighbor's wife" as their ninth commandment, while the Lutherans, following Exodus 20: 17, have it as part of their tenth commandment, and their ninth command is: "Thou shalt not covet thy neighbor's house." Thus we see how people get themselves into trouble when they attempt to change the law of God.

The Papacy was also to change times. But the only commandment of the ten that has to do with *time* is the fourth, which commands us to keep holy the seventh day, on which God rested at creation. (Exodus 20: 10, 11; Genesis 2: 1-3.) It is a remarkable fact that Christ, His apostles, and their followers kept the seventh day in common with the Jews (Mark 6: 2, 3; Luke 4: 16, 31; 23: 52-56; Acts 13: 42, 44; 16: 12, 13; 17: 2; 18: 1-4), and that the New Testament is entirely silent in regard to any change of the Sabbath from the seventh to the first day of the week. This would be natural enough if the original Sabbath, which they were then keeping, should continue. But if a new day was to take its place in the Christian church, its Founder would certainly have given explicit directions for its observance. Yet not a word was spoken by Christ or His apostles, either before or after His resurrection, as to such a change.

It is another remarkable fact that Sunday is never called by any sacred title in the New Testament, but always referred to as

a *weekday*, never as a holy day. It is classed as one of the weekdays, being called "the first day of the *week*."
And yet we find the Christian world generally keeping it. Who made this change, when it is not recorded in the Bible? When, how, and why was it made? Who dared to lay hands on Jehovah's law, and change His Holy Sabbath, without any warrant of Scripture?
All Protestant denominations disclaim any part in this crime. But the Roman Catholic Church boasts of having made this change, and even points to it as an evidence of its authority to act in Christ's stead upon earth. We shall therefore ask her two pointed questions: 1. When did you change the Sabbath? 2. Why did you do it? Here are her answers:
"The first proposition needs little proof. The Catholic Church for over one thousand years before the existence of a Protestant, by virtue of her Divine mission changed the day from Saturday to Sunday."—"*The Christian Sabbath,*" *p. 29. Baltimore, Md.: "Catholic Mirror," Sept. 23, 1893.*
"*Ques.*—Which is the Sabbath day? *Ans.*—Saturday is the Sabbath day.
"*Ques.*—Why do we observe Sunday instead of Saturday?
"*Ans.*—We observe Sunday instead of Saturday because the Catholic Church, in the council of Laodicea (A. D. 336), transferred the solemnity from Saturday to Sunday. . . .
"The Church substituted Sunday for Saturday by the plenitude of that divine power which Jesus Christ bestowed upon her."—"*The Convert's Catechism of Christian Doctrine,*" *Rev. Peter Geiermann, C. SS. R., p. 50. St. Louis, Mo.: 1934.* (This work received the "apostolic blessing" of Pope Pius X, Jan. 25, 1910.)
"The Church . . . took the pagan Sunday and made it the Christian Sunday. . . . And thus the pagan Sunday, dedicated to Balder, became the Christian Sunday, sacred to Jesus."— "*Catholic World,*" *(New York), March, 1894, p. 809.*
We shall enter into this subject more thoroughly in the following chapters.

Christ and the Sabbath

THOSE who oppose the Bible Sabbath center their attack on three points, claiming (1) that the Sabbath was not instituted at creation, and hence is not an original law for the whole human family; (2) that the Sabbath commandment is not a moral command as the other nine, but was a part of the Jewish ceremonial law; (3) that Christ or the apostles abolished the Sabbath, and gradually substituted the first day of the week in its place. We shall now test these propositions one by one.

THE SABBATH AN EDENIC INSTITUTION

God the Father has always worked through His Son, both in creation and in redemption. (Genesis 1: 26; Hebrews 1: 1, 2, 8-10; John 3: 16.) Therefore it was Christ who created the world in six days and rested on the seventh day. "All things were made by Him; and without Him was not any thing made that was made. . . . He was in the world, and the world was made by Him, and the world knew Him not." John 1: 3, 10. (Compare Colossians 1: 14-18.) It is a great comfort to a poor, weak sinner to know that our Saviour is "the Mighty God" (Isaiah 9: 6) who spoke the worlds into existence (Psalm 33: 6, 9), and who is "upholding all things by the word of His power" (Hebrews 1: 3). His word has creative power, and if we receive it by faith, it will change our hearts and lives, and give us victory over sin. (John 1: 12; Genesis 1: 3; 2 Corinthians 4: 5, 6; Matthew 5: 16; Isaiah 60: 1.)

As the crowning act on the sixth day, the Lord made man in His own image, and then He "rested on the seventh day" from a "finished" work. (Genesis 1: 27, 31; 2: 1-3.) Thus the seventh day stood as a memorial and reminder of a *finished* work in Christ. And when man lost the image of God through sin,

Christ came to restore in man that divine image by a new creation. (Colossians 3: 10; Ephesians 4: 24; 2: 10; 2 Corinthians 5: 17.) On the cross He cried out: "It is finished." John 19: 30. (See Hebrews 10: 14.) This was on Friday evening, and He rested the Sabbath day from the work of redemption, just as He had originally rested on it from the work of creation. (Luke 23: 52-56.) Thus the seventh-day Sabbath is Christ's memorial of redemption as well as of the creation. (Ezekiel 20: 12; Hebrews 13: 8. See "The Great Controversy," p. 769.) And both events were for the whole human race, and not for the Jews only.

Christ says: "The Sabbath was made for *man*." Mark 2: 27. And therefore it was made when man was created. "So God created man in His own image. . . . And the evening and the morning were the sixth day. . . . And He rested on the seventh day. . . . And God blessed the seventh day, and sanctified it." Genesis 1: 27, 31; 2: 2, 3. This was two thousand years before Abraham (the first Jew) was born, therefore the Sabbath could not be Jewish. But, as Christ says, it was "made for *man*," and the term "man" is not confined to any one race, but embraces all *mankind*.

We are not alone in believing that the Sabbath was instituted at creation, as the following quotations from leading men in different denominations show:

F. C. Cook, M. A., Canon of Exeter, says:

"'And God blessed the seventh day.' The natural interpretation of these words is that the blessing of the Sabbath was immediately consequent on the first creation of man, for whom the Sabbath was made (Mark 2: 27). It has been urged from the silence concerning its observance by the patriarchs, that no Sabbatic ordinance was really given until the promulgation of the law, and that this passage in Genesis is not historical but anticipatory. There are several objections, which seem fatal to this theory."—"*The Holy Bible, with an Explanatory and Critical Commentary by Bishops and Clergy of the Anglican Church," Vol. I, p. 37. New York: 1875.*

Thomas Hamilton, D. D., in his Five-Hundred-Dollar

Prize Essay, meets this objection to the historicity of Genesis in the following forceful way:

"Paley . . . says: 'The words [of Genesis 2: 1-3] do not assert that God *then* blessed and sanctified the seventh day.' . . . But such an interpretation really amounts to an interpolation. It alters the passage. . . . Once admit such a mode of dealing with Scripture, or of dealing with any other book, and we may bid farewell to certainty regarding any author's meaning. . . . No history could stand if subjected to such treatment. The plainest and most unvarnished statements might be so twisted and distorted as to bear a meaning the exact contrary to that intended by its author. . . .

"It is not only said God 'rested,' but He 'blessed,' the day and 'sanctified' it. . . . If all this do [sic.] not amount to the institution of a weekly Sabbath for man in all time coming, . . . we fail to see what intelligible meaning or purpose is to be extracted from the narrative."—"*Our Rest Day,*" *pp. 10-15, New edition. Edinburgh: 1888.*

Dr. Martin Luther says on this text:

"God blessed the Sabbath and sanctified it to Himself. It is moreover to be remarked that God did this to no other creature. God did not sanctify to Himself the heaven nor the earth nor any other creature. But God did sanctify to Himself the seventh day. This was especially designed of God, to cause us to understand that the 'seventh day' is to be especially devoted to divine worship. . . .

"It follows therefore from this passage, that if Adam had stood in his innocence and had not fallen he would yet have observed the 'seventh day' as sanctified, holy and sacred. . . . Nay, even after the fall he held the 'seventh day' sacred; that is, he taught on that day his own family. This is testified by the offerings made by his two sons, Cain and Abel. The Sabbath therefore has, from the beginning of the world, been set apart for the worship of God. . . . For all these things are implied and signified in the expression 'sanctified.'

"Although therefore man lost the knowledge of God by sin,

yet God willed that this command concerning the sanctifying of the Sabbath should remain. He willed that on the seventh day both the word should be preached, and also those other parts of His worship performed which He Himself instituted."—"*Commentary on Genesis,*" *Vol. I, pp. 138-140, translation by Professor J. N. Lenker, D. D., Minneapolis: 1904; and also "Copious Explanation of Genesis," Vol. I, pp. 62, 63. Christiania: 1863.*

The following words from a distinguished Hebrew scholar are worthy of note here:

"'*Finished.*' To finish a work, in Hebrew conception, is to cease from it, to have done with it. *On the seventh day.* The seventh day is distinguished from all the preceding days by being itself the subject of the narrative. In the absence of any work on this day, the Eternal is occupied with the day itself, and does four things in reference to it. *First,* He ceased from His work which He had made. *Secondly,* He rested. . . . *Thirdly,* He blessed the seventh day. . . . *In the fourth place,* He hallowed it or set it apart to a holy rest. . . .

"The present record is a sufficient proof that the original institution was never forgotten by man. . . .

"Incidental traces of the keeping of the Sabbath are found in the record of the Deluge, when the sacred writer has occasion to notice short intervals of time. The measurement of time by weeks then appears (Genesis 8: 10, 12). The same division of time again comes up in the history of Jacob (Genesis 29: 27, 28). This unit of measure is traceable to nothing but the institution of the seventh-day rest."—"*A Critical and Exegetical Commentary on the Book of Genesis with a New Translation,*" *J. G. Murphy, D. D., T. C. D. (Professor of Hebrew, Belfast), pp. 70, 71. Andover: 1866.*

Dr. J. P. Lange says: "The expression, He hallowed it, must be for man, for all men who were to be on the earth.

"If we had no other passage than this of Genesis 2: 3 there would be no difficulty in deducing from it a precept for the universal observance of a Sabbath, or the seventh day, to be devoted to God, as holy time, by all of that race for whom the earth and its nature were especially prepared. The first man must have known it. The words 'He hallowed it,' can have no meaning otherwise. They would be a blank unless in reference to some who were required to keep it holy."—*Commentary on the Holy Scriptures, John Peter Lange, D. D., Vol. I, pp. 196, 197. New York: 1884.*

Dr. M. W. Jacobus, Professor George Bush, and C. O. Rosenius, and others forcefully emphasize the same facts. The preceding statements taken from leading men in different denominations need no comment. They state the plain facts of the Bible narrative in their most natural setting.

Another remarkable thing in this connection is the fact that the heathen nations for centuries after the days of Noah retained the seventh-day Sabbath. The learned Dr. John Kitto says:

"We find from time immemorial the knowledge of a week of seven days among all nations—Egyptians, Arabians, Indians—in a word, all the nations of the East, have in all ages made use of this week of seven days, for which it is difficult to account without admitting that this knowledge was derived from the common ancestors of the human race."—*Encyclopedia of Biblical Literature, Vol. II, art. "Sabbath," p. 655.*

Professor A. H. Sayce declares:

"The Sabbath-rest was a Babylonian, as well as a Hebrew, institution. Its origin went back to pre-Semitic days. . . . In the cuneiform tablets the *Sabattu* is described as 'a day of rest for the soul,' . . . it was derived by the Assyrian scribes from two Sumerian or pre-Semitic words, *sa* and *bat*, which meant respectively 'heart' and 'ceasing.' . . . The rest enjoined on the Sabbath was thus as complete as it was among the Jews." —*"Higher Criticism and the Monuments," pp. 74, 75.*

During their servitude in Egypt, the majority of the Jews evidently worked on the Sabbath, just as the rank and file of the Jews do today, but the knowledge of it was retained then as now, and it was kept holy by a faithful few. Besides other evidences, we see this from the fact that, thirty days after they left

Christ and the Sabbath

Egypt, and more than two weeks *before the law was given on Sinai*, God *tested* the people on Sabbath-keeping (Exodus 16: 4, 27, 28), which He certainly could not have done, if the Sabbath had not been known among them till the law was given on Sinai. Then, too, God speaks of it as a familiar institution. (Compare Exodus 16:28 with Genesis 26:5 and 2:3.) The fourth commandment itself points back to creation and commands us to *"remember* the Sabbath day" on which He rested at the close of creation week. (Exodus 20: 8, 11.) No human logic can therefore explain away the historical facts that the Sabbath was set apart for man at creation.

THE SABBATH MORAL OR TYPICAL?

Some claim that the Sabbath commandment does not enforce the observance of *the seventh day of the week*, but only the seventh part of our time, the particular day being left to our choice. But nothing could be more contradictory to the plain wording of the commandment. If God's commands and promises are to be so construed as to mean the very opposite of what they state, then we may bid farewell to all certainty and comfort derived from the Scriptures. God commands us to keep, not *a* seventh, but *the* seventh, day, on which He rested, the day He blessed and sanctified. (Exodus 20: 10, 11.) The Sabbath rests on a historical event that cannot be changed to another day, any more than our birthday can be changed.

In regard to the claim that the Sabbath commandment is not moral as the other nine, but ceremonial, it needs only to be said that there is no statement to that effect in the whole Bible, and it would involve its advocates in the most serious difficulty. All through the Bible a clear distinction is maintained between the two laws, the moral and the ceremonial. God spoke the Ten Commandments to the people directly, "and He added no more" (Deuteronomy 5: 22); He engraved them on two *tables of stone* (Exodus 32: 16; Deuteronomy 9: 10); and had them laid "in the ark" (Deuteronomy 10: 5; 1 Kings 8: 9). But the ceremonial law of ordinances was spoken to the people by

Moses, was written by him "in a book," and laid beside the ark. (Exodus 21: 1; 24: 3, 4, 7; Deuteronomy 31: 24-26.*) Now we respectfully ask: Would any one claim that God did not understand the difference between moral and ceremonial laws, and hence wrote a ceremonial command into the very bosom of His moral law, the Decalogue? Such an accusation of God would be preposterous, and yet, this is what the above claim necessarily implies! We must therefore conclude that all the Ten Commandments are moral, which practically all the leading religious denominations teach in their confessions of faith.

Did Christ Change the Sabbath?

Christ came to lift people out of the degradation of sin, not to leave them in sin. He received the name "JESUS: for He shall save His people from their sins." Matthew 1: 21. And "sin is the transgression of the law." 1 John 3: 4. The law here referred to is the moral law of the Ten Commandments. (Romans 7: 7, 12; James 2: 10, 11.) Christ firmly refuted the idea that He was to abolish any part of God's law. He says: "Think not that I am come to destroy the law. . . . For verily I say unto you, Till heaven and earth pass, one jot or one tittle shall in no wise pass from the law." Matthew 5: 17, 18. Christ was to "magnify the law, and make it honorable." Isaiah 42: 21. And this He did, for He freed it from all the traditions and additions of men. (Matthew 15: 3, 6, 9, 13.) The Pharisees had burdened down the Sabbath with hundreds of man-made regulations. All these Jesus swept away, and restored it to its original purpose, that it should be a blessing, a sacred "delight" to God's people. (Isaiah 58: 13.) But He never made any change in the day. He kept it Himself, and taught His followers to do the same. (Luke 4: 16, 31; Matthew 24: 20; 12: 11, 12.)

Satan's Hatred of the Sabbath

The Lord gave His Sabbath to man as a weekly reminder of Christ's sanctifying and keeping power, because man needed this

---

* The English and American Revised Versions, the Jewish, Danish, Norwegian, and Swedish versions render Deuteronomy 31: 26, "*by the side* of the ark." Others render it "*at* the side of the ark," and "*beside* the ark."

reminder. (Ezekiel 20: 12.) But Satan has always tried to blot out all memory of the true God from the earth, and to draw man's allegiance and worship to himself through idolatry. (1 Corinthians 10: 20.) He has therefore made relentless efforts to pull down God's Sabbatic flag, and to trample it in the mire. We have seen that for a long time after the descendants of Noah had dispersed over the earth they retained the knowledge of the Sabbath. This was true even after they went into idolatry. Egypt was the first among the heathen nations to attempt to suppress the seventh-day Sabbath, and influenced other nations to regard the first day as the weekly holiday of their sun-god. Truels Lund gives us the following information on this important and interesting subject of the week in Egypt, in his extensive work:

"According to the Assyrian-Babylonian conception, the particular stress lay necessarily upon the number seven. . . . The whole week pointed prominently towards the seventh day, the feast day, the rest day, in this day it collected, in this it also consummated. 'Sabbath' is derived from both 'rest' and 'seven.' With the Egyptians it was the reverse. . . . For them on the contrary the sun-god was the beginning and origin of all things. The day of the Sun, Sunday, therefore, became necessarily for them the feast day. . . . The holiday was transferred from the last to the first day of the week."—"*Daglige Liv i Norden,*" *Vol. XIII, pp. 54, 55.*

"The seven planetary names of the days were at the close of the second century A. D., prevailing everywhere in the Roman Empire. . . . This astrology originated in Egypt, where Alexandria now so loudly proclaimed it to all. . . . 'The day of the Sun' was the Lord's day, the chiefest and first of the week. The evil and fatal Saturn's day was the last of the week, on which none could celebrate a feast. . . .

"From Rome, through the Roman legionaries, the seven planetary days pressed farther north to Gaul, Britain, and Germany. Everywhere . . . people yielded respectfully to the astrology in its popular form: the doctrine concerning the

Sun-day with its fortune, the Moon-day with its alternative play, and the filthy, unlucky Saturday. . . . As a concentrated troop the planetary appellations and names of heathen deities stood on guard, when later Christianity reached Europe, and attempted to displace them. . . .

"For the Christians the lot was cast by the reception of the . . . day of the sun. Not till they themselves had later gained power were they awakened to doubt. . . . And the heathen names of the days seemed at variance with Christian faith."—*Id.*, *pp. 91, 92, 110.*

The London Anglican rector, T. H. Morer, says of Sunday: "It is not to be denied but we borrow the name of this day from the ancient Greeks and Romans, and we allow that the old Egyptians worshiped the sun, and as a standing *memorial* of their veneration, dedicated this day to him. And we find by the influence of their example, *other* nations, and among them the Jews themselves, doing him homage."—"*Six Dialogues on the Lord's Day,*" *p. 22. London: 1701.*

Thus we see how Satan, through heathenism, tried to stigmatize the Sabbath of Jehovah and to elevate Sunday as a joyful day. The Egyptians worshiped their sun-god under the name of Osiris, and the Apis bull (the golden calf made at Horeb) was a representation of him. This worship was conducted by turning to the rising sun. (Ezekiel 8: 16.) Therefore the Lord ordered the tabernacle always to be pitched with the front toward the east, so that the people, worshiping before it, had to turn their backs upon sun worship. (Numbers 3: 23. See also Exodus 26: 22; 36: 27, 32 in American Revised Version, and Jeremiah 32: 33.) Talbot W. Chambers, D. D., says that sun worship was "the oldest, the most widespread, and the most enduring of al forms of idolatry known to man."

"The universality of this form of idolatry is something remarkable. It seems to have prevailed everywhere. The chief object of worship among the Syrians was Baal—the sun. . . . In Egypt the sun was the kernel of the state religion."—"*The Old Testament Student,*" *pp. 193, 194. January, 1886.*

Christ and the Sabbath

In Babylon the sun-god was called Bel, in Phœnicia and Palestine, Baal, and Sun-day was "the wild solar holiday of all pagan times."—"*North British Review,*" *Vol. XVIII, p. 409.*

Rev. W. H. Poole says:

"The first and principal idol was the sun—the glorious luminary of the day. . . . Baal was the great sun-god of all the East. With our Israelitish ancestors the sun-god came west. His day is our Sunday. Every time you name our Sabbath-day Sunday you are reminded of our great, great, great grandfathers' principal deity."—"*Anglo-Israel in Nine Lectures,*" *pp. 389, 390. Detroit, Mich.: 1889.*

The Encyclopedia Britannica says of the worship of Baal:

"As the sun-god he is conceived as the male principle of life and reproduction in nature, and thus in some forms of his worship is the patron of the grossest sensuality, and even of systematic prostitution. An example of this is found in the worship of Baal-Peor (Numbers 25)."—*Vol. III, (New American ed., Werner Co.), art. "Baal," p. 175.*

This sun worship was the greatest of all abominations to God (Ezekiel 8: 13-16), and the warnings to Israel have great significance to us today: "I will visit upon her the '*days of Baalim,* wherein she burned incense to them, and she decked herself with her earrings and her jewels, and she went after her lovers, and forgat Me, saith the Lord." Hosea 2: 13. (See also 1 Corinthians 10: 11.)

When we remember that it was Christ who took Israel out of Egypt (Hebrews 11: 26, 27; 1 Corinthians 10: 4), and who labored so earnestly to turn them away from sun worship and Sunday-keeping, and that it was Satan who always led them into this idolatry, we ask with all candor: Could any one suppose that Christ, in the New Testament, has exchanged places with Satan, so that He is now leading people to keep Sunday, while the devil is leading them to keep the Sabbath of Jehovah? Every thoughtful person must say with the Apostle Paul: "God forbid." Romans 3: 31.

The New Testament Rest Day

CHRIST is "the way, the truth, and the life." John 14: 6. He has gone all the way before us, "leaving us an example, that ye should follow His steps" (1 Peter 2: 21), and "he that saith he abideth in Him ought himself also so to walk, even as He walked" (1 John 2: 6), and all will admit that the footsteps of Jesus cannot lead any one astray. Let us therefore agree to follow His steps in regard to Sabbath observance. He worked as a "carpenter" at Nazareth during "the six working days," but rested on the seventh-day Sabbath. (Mark 6: 2, 3; Ezekiel 46: 1; Luke 4: 16.) And after He began His ministry, He faithfully continued His Sabbath-keeping. (V. 31.)

While He taught His disciples that such necessary work as eating, healing the sick, or lifting a sheep out of a pit, was *lawful* to do on the Sabbath days (Matthew 12: 1-12), He thereby acknowledged the claims of the Sabbath *law*, which makes ordinary work not *lawful* on that day. It was "the Spirit of Christ" in the prophets (1 Peter 1: 10, 11) who instructed His people to "bear no burden on the Sabbath day" through the gates of Jerusalem (Jeremiah 17: 21, 22, 27). And when foretelling the destruction of that city (which took place A. D. 70) Jesus warned His disciples saying: "But pray ye that your flight be not . . . on the Sabbath day." Matthew 24: 20. This warning was not, as some would have us believe, on account of the gates being closed on that day, for in the same connection Jesus says: "Let him which is on the housetop not come down." V. 17. But how could he flee without coming down from the housetop? There can be only one answer. There was an elevated road from one flat roof to another on which they could flee till they reached the wall, where they could be let down. (See Acts 9: 25; Joshua 2: 15; 1 Samuel 19: 12.) In such a case closed gates could hardly come into consideration. This instruction shows Christ's sacred regard for the Sabbath, and His anxiety that His church should keep it properly. A Lutheran minister says: "When God gave the third [fourth] commandment, . . . He designated definitely the seventh day, which already had been sanctified by Him at creation, as this rest day. And as Christ says that He had not come to destroy the law (Matthew 5: 17), so He has also in the words of His last prophetic speech (Matthew 24: 20), which has reference to the destruction of Jerusalem, and the flight of the Christian church from the doomed city, expressly emphasized the Sabbath, or Saturday, as the still valid rest day, by saying: 'Pray, that your flight be not on the Sabbath' (on which day ye according to the third [fourth] commandment should rest, and not undertake any long journey). For this reason many godly Christians have solemnly upbraided the Christian church for keeping Sunday instead of Saturday: it [the church] can have no right to change God's commandment, and, if in the catechism the whole commandment had been embodied verbatim in its entire wording from Exodus 20: 8-11, as has been done in the Heidelberg Catechism, then we should still keep the Saturday holy, and not the Sunday."—*"Opbyggelig Katekismus undervisning," ("Edifying Instruction in the Catechism,")* K. A. Dachsel, *pp. 23, 24.* Bergen: *1887.*

"'Neither on the Sabbath day.' The Jewish Christians might entertain scruples against traveling on the Sabbath beyond the legal distance, which was about five furlongs."—"*A Commentary on the Gospels of Matthew and Mark,*" John J. Owen, D. D., LL. D., *p. 314.* New York: Scribner and Co., *1868.*

Christ had so carefully instructed His followers about proper Sabbath-keeping, that they would not even anoint His sacred body on the Sabbath. They "prepared spices and ointments" on Friday, "and rested the *Sabbath day* according to the *commandment,*" but early the next morning, "the first day of the week," they came to the grave to anoint Him. (Luke 23: 52-56; 24: 1.) They left their work unfinished from Friday evening until Sunday morning, because they "rested the Sabbath day according to the commandment." Luke wrote this thirty-five years after the resurrection. Some claim that the Sabbath was abolished at the cross, and that therefore the Sabbath commandment is not mentioned in the New Testament. But here we find the Sabbath commandment in the New Testament, and we find that it enjoins the keeping of the "Sabbath" which comes between Friday and the "first day of the week" and that Christ's followers were keeping it.

The apostles are entirely silent in regard to any change of the day of rest from the seventh to the first day of the week. Paul, while working among the Gentiles, knew of no change. At Antioch he preached on the Sabbath, and when asked by the Gentiles to preach the same sermon again, he did not suggest a meeting on Sunday, but waited till "the next Sabbath day." (Acts 13: 14, 42, 44.) He knew of no other weekly rest day than the Sabbath, for he worked at his trade as tent maker during the "six working days" (Ezekiel 46: 1), but "he reasoned in the synagogue every Sabbath, and persuaded the Jews and the Greeks" (Acts 18: 1-4). And this was his custom. (Acts 17: 2.) When he came where there were no Jewish synagogues, he did not stay in the hustling, bustling, heathen city on God's holy day, but the record says: "And on the Sabbath we went out of the city by a river side, where prayer was wont to be made." Acts 16: 12, 13. This shows it was a matter of conscience with him to keep the Sabbath. He says: "Do we then make void the law through faith? God forbid: yea, we establish the law." Romans 3: 31.

If Christ or the apostles had changed the Sabbath from the seventh to the first day of the week, does it not seem strange that they never informed us about it in the New Testament, which is the only record they left us? Could they have neglected to inform us regarding so important a matter? Paul declares emphatically: "I kept back nothing that was profitable unto you." Acts 20: 20. History reveals that most of the Christian church kept the seventh-day Sabbath till the seventh century.

The Sabbath in History

AS WE continue our study of the Sabbath question, we shall first consult an eyewitness, who had traveled over the greater part of Christendom: Socrates, the Greek historian, who was born about 380 A. D. M'Clintock and Strong's Cyclopedia says of him: "He is generally considered the most exact and judicious of the three continuators of the history of Eusebius, being less florid in his style and more careful in his statements than Sozomen, and less credulous than Theodoret. 'His impartiality is so strikingly displayed,' says Waddington, 'as to make his orthodoxy questionable to Baronius, the celebrated Roman Catholic historian; but Valesius, in his life, has shown that there is no reason for such suspicion.'"—*Vol. IX, art. "Socrates," p. 854.*

Socrates says of the year 391 A. D.:

"For although almost all Churches throughout the world celebrate the sacred mysteries [the Lord's Supper] on the Sabbath of every week, yet the Christians of Alexandria and at Rome, on account of some ancient tradition, refuse to do this. The Egyptians in the neighborhood of Alexandria, and the inhabitants of Thebais, hold their religious meetings on the Sabbath, but do not participate of the mysteries in the manner usual among Christians in general: for . . . in the evening . . . they partake of the mysteries."—*"Ecclesiastical History," Book 5, chap. 22, page 289. London: G. Bell and Sons, 1892.*

The footnote which accompanies the foregoing quotation explains the use of the word "Sabbath." It says:

"That is, upon the Saturday. It should be observed, that Sunday is never called 'the *Sabbath*' (τὸ σάββατον) by the ancient Fathers and historians. . . . The Latins kept the Sabbath as a fast, the Greeks as a feast; and the 64th of the Apostolical Canons forbids any of the clergy to fast on the Sabbath (Saturday) under pain of being deposed, and likewise a layman under the penalty of excommunication." — *Id., p. 289.*

This shows that all the churches throughout the world kept Saturday as the Sabbath in 391, but that some did not have the Lord's Supper till in the evening. There had sprung up a hot controversy in regard to fasting on the Sabbath. Who was it that urged this Sabbath fasting against the will of the churches in general? Pope Sylvester (314-335) was the first to order the churches to fast on Saturday, and Pope Innocent (402-417) made it a binding law in the churches that obeyed him.

Dr. Peter Heylyn says:

"Innocentius did ordaine the Saturday or Sabbath to be alwayes fasted. . . . It was by him intended for a binding law. [Most of the churches refused, however, to obey him.] And in this difference it stood a long time together, till in the end the *Roman Church* obtained the cause, and *Saturday* became a *fast*, almost through all the parts of the Westerne world. I say the *Westerne* world, and of that alone: The *Easterne* Churches being so farre from altering their ancient custome, that in the sixth Councell of *Constantinople, Anno* 692, they did admonish those of *Rome* to forbeare fasting on that day, upon pain of censures. Which I have noted here, in its proper place, that we might know the better how the matter stood betweene the *Lord's Day*, and the *Sabbath;* how hard a thing it was for one to get the mastery of the other."—"*History of the Sabbath*," part 2, chap. 2, *pp. 44, 45. London: 1636. (The original spelling is retained.)*

This shows how the popes tried to get rid of the Sabbath. They knew that the churches generally would not give it up willingly, and as yet the popes did not have the power to force them to do it. But if the Sabbath was made a day of fasting, the children would soon tire of it, and after a few generations the majority would gladly give up the gloomy fast day. This effort continued from about A. D. 391 to 692, and even then it was hard for the Sunday to get the mastery over the Sabbath, says Dr. Heylyn. Here we can readily see that it was not changed at the time of the apostles.

Rev. Joseph Bingham, M. A., says:

The Sabbath in History

"The ancient Christians were very careful in the observation of Saturday, or the seventh day, which was the ancient Jewish Sabbath. Some observed it as a fast, others as a festival; but all unanimously agreed in keeping it as a more solemn day of religious worship and adoration. In the Eastern church it was ever observed as a festival, one only Sabbath excepted, which was called the Great Sabbath, between Good Friday and Easterday. . . . From hence it is plain, that all the Oriental churches, and the greatest part of the world, observed the Sabbath as a festival. . . . Athanasius likewise tells us, that they held religious assemblies on the Sabbath, not because they were infected with Judaism, but to worship Jesus, the Lord of the Sabbath, Epiphanius says the same."—"*Antiquities of the Christian Church,*" Vol. II, Book XX, chap. 3, Sec. 1, pp. 1137, 1138. *London: 1852.*

The Primitive Christians

Bishop Jeremy Taylor says:

"The primitive Christians did keep the Sabbath of the Jews; . . . therefore the Christians, for a long time together, did keep their conventions upon the Sabbath, in which some portions of the law were read: and this continued till the time of the Laodicean council; which also took care that the reading of the Gospels should be mingled with their reading of the law."— "*The Whole Works*" *of Jeremy Taylor, Vol. IX, p. 416 (R. Heber's Edition, Vol. XII, p. 416). London: 1822.*

The edict here mentioned is "Canon XVI," which reads:

"*Canon XVI.*—The Gospels are to be read on the Sabbath Day, with the other Scriptures."—"*Index Canonum,*" *John Fulton, D. D., LL. D., p. 255. New York: 1883.*

Dr. T. H. Morer (a Church of England divine) says:

"The primitive Christians had a great veneration for the Sabbath, and spent the day in devotion and sermons. And it is not to be doubted but they derived this practice from the apostles themselves, as appears by several scriptures to that purpose "—"*Dialogues on the Lord's Day," p. 189. London: 1701.*

Dr. Theodore Zahn (Lutheran Professor in Theology at the University of Erlangen) says:

"The Apostles could not have conceded to any other than one man the right to 'change the customs Moses had given:' the Son of Man, who had called Himself Lord also of the Sabbath day; but of Him they knew that He had neither transgressed nor abolished the Jewish Sabbath, but truly sanctified it. And they knew also, how He had threatened any of His disciples who might dare to abolish even one of the least of the commands of Moses.

"But this has no one dared to do with the Sabbath commandment during the time of the Apostles. Certainly not within the territory of the Jewish Christendom; for they continued to keep the actual Sabbath. . . . Nor could any one have thought of such a thing within the Gentile Christian domain as far as Paul's influence reached."—"*Sondagens Historie*" (*History of Sunday*), pp. 33, 34. Christiania: P. T. Mallings, 1879.

The Example and Command of Jesus

Dr. Zahn further says in regard to the early Christians:

"They observed the Sabbath in the most conscientious manner: otherwise, they would have been stoned. Instead of this, we learn from the book of the Acts that at times they were highly respected even by that part of their own nation that remained in unbelief. . . . That the observance of Sunday commenced among them would be a supposition which would have no seeming ground for it, and all probability against it. . . . The Sabbath was a strong tie which united them with the life of the whole people, and in keeping the Sabbath holy, they followed not only the example, but also the command of Jesus."- "*Geschichte des Sonntags*," pp. 13, 14.

Bishop Grimelund of Norway (Lutheran) says:

"The early Christians were of Jewish descent, and the first Christian church in Jerusalem was a Jewish-Christian church. It conformed, as could be expected, to the Jewish law and Sabbath-custom; it had no express instruction from the Lord to do otherwise."—"*Sondagens Historie,*" *p. 13. Christiania, Norway: Den norske Lutherstiftelses Forlag, 1886.*

After citing the fact that Christ arose on the first day, he continues:

"But, one could reason, that for all this it does not follow that one should give up and forsake the 'Sabbath' which God Himself has commanded, . . . nor that we should transfer this to another day of the week, even if that is such a memorable day. To do this would require an equally definite command from God, whereby the former command is abolished, but where can we find such a command? It is true, such a command is not to be found."—*Id., p. 18.*

Dr. John C. L. Gieseler says:

"While the Jewish Christians of Palestine retained the entire Mosaic law, and consequently the Jewish festivals, the Gentile Christians observed also *the Sabbath* and *the passover* (1 Corinthians 5: 6-8), with reference to the last scenes of Jesus' life, but without Jewish superstition."—"*A Compendium of Ecclesiastical History,*" *Vol. I, chap. 2, sec. 30, p. 92. Edinburgh: 1846.*

A little later we shall trace Christ's true followers from the days of the apostles to our own time, and show how they retained the Bible Sabbath with the other parts of the apostolic faith. But we will here break off this narrative, and trace step by step how Sunday-keeping came into the popular church, and the influences which worked together to accomplish the change from the seventh to the first day of the week.

Sunday in the Early Church

HE word "Sunday" is not found in the Bible, but the "first day" of the week is mentioned just nine times. Let us examine these nine texts.

1. The first day of the week originated as a work day. This world was created on a Sunday, so that, wherever one goes, he is reminded of God's Sunday work. (Genesis 1: 1-5.)

2. "In the end of the Sabbath, as it began to dawn toward the first day of the week, came Mary Magdalene." Matthew 28: 1. Here we notice that Sunday is an ordinary "week" day, not a holy day, and that the New Testament says the Sabbath is over when the first day begins.

3. "When the Sabbath was past, Mary Magdalene, and Mary the mother of James, and Salome, had bought sweet spices, that they might come and anoint Him. And very early in the morning the first day of the week, they came unto the sepulcher at the rising of the sun. And they said among themselves, Who shall roll us away the stone." Mark 16: 1-3. Here again we see that Sunday is a working day on which work was resumed.

(The fourth text we will examine a little later.)

5. Christ was buried on Friday, "and that day was the preparation" for the Sabbath. After the burial, His followers returned home "and prepared spices and ointments; and rested the Sabbath day according to the commandment. Now upon the first day of the week, very early in the morning, they came unto the sepulcher, bringing the spices." Luke 23: 54-56; 24: 1. Here three consecutive days are mentioned: They prepared the spices on Friday, rested on the Sabbath, and early Sunday morning they went to finish the work left over from Friday. So we see that Sunday is a working day, which follows immediately after the Sabbath of the New Testament.

Sunday in the Early Church

6. "The first day of the week cometh Mary Magdalene early, when it was yet dark, unto the supulcher." John 20:1. This is simply a repetition of the other texts.

7. "Then the same day at evening, being the first day of the week, when the doors were shut, where the disciples were assembled for fear of the Jews," Jesus appeared. John 20:19. "Here," says some one, "you see the disciples were gathered to keep the new Sabbath in memory of the resurrection." But the text does not say that they were gathered in honor of the day, but "for fear of the Jews." Let us now examine the fourth text.

4. "Now when Jesus was risen early the first day of the week, He appeared first to Mary Magdalene. . . . She went and told them that had been with Him, as they mourned and wept. And they, when they had heard that He was alive, and had been seen of her, *believed not*. After that He appeared" to the two who went to Emmaus. They returned and told the rest: "*neither believed they them*. Afterward He appeared unto the eleven as they sat at meat, and *upbraided them with their unbelief* and hardness of heart, because *they believed not* them which had seen Him after He was risen." Mark 16:9-14. This is the same meeting which is recorded in John 20:19. We ask: How could they be gathered to celebrate Sunday in honor of Christ's resurrection, when *they did not believe He had risen?* No, the disciples were simply in their common living quarters, and were having their evening meal when Jesus came, and they gave Him some fish and honey that was left. (Mark 16:14; Luke 24:36-43.)

8. In Acts 20:7 we have the only place in the New Testament where a religious meeting is said to be held on the "first day of the week," and this was a farewell meeting, when, of course, it was natural to celebrate the Lord's supper in parting. (Vs. 7, 25.) Besides this, the believers gathered "daily," "breaking bread" (Acts 2:46), so there was nothing in the act to indicate that the day was holy. Then too, the meeting at Troas was held on Saturday night. In the Bible reckoning, every day begins and ends at sunset, because God began the work of

creation with the dark part and ended the day with the light part. "The evening and the morning were the first day." Genesis 1: 1-5. "From even unto even, shall ye celebrate your Sabbath." Leviticus 23: 32.

"And at even, when the sun did set, they brought unto Him all that were diseased." Mark 1: 32. They would not bring them until after the Sabbath; but "at even, when the sun did set," the first working day of the week began. Therefore the Sabbath began at sunset Friday, and ended at sunset Saturday, and the first day of the week began at sunset on our Saturday evening, and ended at sunset on our Sunday evening. The only dark part of the first day, was therefore the night that preceded it, as the night following it was part of the second day. The meeting at Troas was held at night, for "there were many *lights* in the upper chamber, where they were gathered together," and Paul "continued his speech until midnight." Being "the first day of the week," it must have been our Saturday night. (Acts 20: 7, 8.) Having spent the Sabbath together, they simply had a farewell meeting in the evening. Professor McGarvey says:

"I conclude that the brethren met on the night after the Jewish Sabbath which was still observed as a day of rest by all of them who were Jews or Jewish proselytes; and considering this the beginning of the first day of the week, spent it in the manner above described. On Sunday morning Paul and his companions resumed their journey."—*Commentary on Acts,* under *Acts 20: 7.*

Conybeare and Howson write:

"It was the evening which succeeded the Jewish Sabbath. . . . On the Sunday morning the vessel was about to sail. The Christians of Troas were gathered together at this solemn time. . . . The night was dark. . . . Many lamps were burning in the room where the congregation was assembled."—*"Life and Epistles of the Apostle Paul," pp. 520, 521. New York.*

If Sunday was their holy day, why then would Paul stay with the brethren at Troas seven days, and leave them on

Sunday morning to walk eighteen and one-half miles that day, "for so had he appointed." This was planning quite a work for Sunday! (Acts 20: 6, 13.)

9. "Upon the first day of the week let every one of you lay by him in store." 1 Corinthians 16: 2. This text says that every one should "lay *by him* in store." The new Swedish and new Norwegian Bibles read, at "home by himself." Weymouth's reads: "Let each of you put on one side and store up at his home." Ballantine's translation reads: "Let each of you lay up at home." And the Syriac has it: "Let every one of you lay aside and preserve at home." So the text proves the opposite of what is often claimed for it.

The apostle Paul was instructing the believers to take time on Sunday to lay aside at home from the wages received during the preceeding week, such an amount as they could afford to give for the relief of their poor brethren at Jerusalem. If we always remembered on Sunday to take something from our previous week's earnings and lay it up at home, we would find a larger ready offering at hand, when the call comes, than if we wait, and give what we happen to have on hand. The fact that they should sit down and figure up their accounts to see how "God hath prospered" them, and give accordingly, would indicate that the day was not considered a holy day. Then, too, Sunday is never given a sacred title in the New Testament.

THE LORD'S DAY

Some claim that "the Lord's day" of Revelation 1: 10, refers to Sunday, but this text does not say which day is meant, and Sunday is not called the Lord's day in any other place in the New Testament. There is therefore no evidence that Sunday is meant here. It is generally agreed that John wrote his Gospel two years after he wrote Revelation. If the term "Lord's day" had become the designation for Sunday, when John wrote Revelation, then he would have used that name for it two years later when he wrote the Gospel, but he simply calls it "the first day of the week." John 20: 1. The only day which the Lord has designated as His day, is the seventh. (Exodus 20: 10; Isaiah 58: 13; Mark 2: 28.)

Dr. Summerbell says:

"Many suppose that they must denominate the first day of the week the '*Lord's day*'; but we have no certain Scripture for this. The phrase 'Lord's day,' occurs but once in the Bible: 'I was in the spirit on the *Lord's day*,' and there probably refers to the day of which Christ said: 'The Son of man is Lord even of the Sabbath day,' as the whole book of Revelation has a strong Jewish bearing."—"*History of the Christian Church,*" *p. 152. Cincinnati: 1873.*

W. B. Taylor says:

"If a current day was intended, the only day bearing this definition, in either the Old or New Testaments, is Saturday, the seventh day of the week."—"*Obligation of the Sabbath,*" *p. 296.*

Dr. Peter Heylyn remarks:

"Take which you will, either of the Fathers, or the Modernes, and we shall find no *Lord's day* instituted by any *Apostolic Mandate*, no *Sabbath* set on foot by them upon the *first day of the weeke*, as some would have it: much lesse than any such *Ordinance* should be hence collected, out of the words of the apostle." —"*History of the Sabbath,*" (*original spelling*), *Part 2, p. 27. London: 1636.*

The Conclusion

Dr. William Smith, LL. D., after carefully examining all the texts in the New Testament usually adduced in favor of the first day, comes to this conclusion:

"Taken separately, perhaps, and even all together, these passages seem scarcely adequate to prove that the dedication of the first day of the week to the purposes above mentioned was a matter of apostolic institution, or even of apostolic practice." —*A Dictionary of the Bible, art. "Lord's Day," p. 356. Hartford: Burr and Hyde, 1871.*

Sunday in the Early Church 93

The learned Dr. John Kitto sums up those texts in the following words:

"Thus far, then, we cannot say that the evidence for *any particular observance* of this day amounts to much; still less does it appear what *purpose* or object was referred to. We find no mention of any *commemoration,* whether of the resurrection or any other event *in the Apostolic records."—Cyclopædia of Biblical Literature (2-vol. ed.), Vol. II, art. "Lord's Day," p. 269. New York.*

"'But,' say some, 'it was *changed* from the seventh to the first day.' Where? when? and by whom? No man can tell. No, it never was changed, nor could it be, unless creation was to be gone through again: for the reason assigned must be changed before the observance, or respect to the reason, can be changed!! It is all old wives' fables to talk of the change of the Sabbath from the seventh to the first day. If it be changed, it was that august personage changed it who changes times and laws *ex officio*—I think his name is DOCTOR ANTICHRIST."—*Alexander Campbell, in " The Christian Baptist," revised by D. S. Burnet, from the Second Edition, with Mr. Campbell's last corrections, page 44. Cincinnati: D. S. Burnet, 1835.*

A tract widely circulated against those who keep the seventh day as the Sabbath has this to say in its fourteenth proposition:

"If Christians are to keep the Sabbath day, how do you account for the fact that the apostles preached the gospel in Jerusalem, Samaria, to Cornelius the Gentile, and to many others, without commanding a single individual to keep it? Did they under the inspiration of the Holy Spirit fail to properly instruct their converts?"

We answer: The Christians everywhere were keeping the seventh-day Sabbath, and there was an acknowledged law enforcing its observance. There was therefore no occasion for giving any commandment on this point. (Luke 23: 52-56: 16: 17; Matthew 5: 17-19; Romans 3: 31.) And the apostles by their example and teaching had educated both Jewish and Gentile believers to keep the seventh-day Sabbath. (Acts 13:

42-44; 18: 1-4; 17: 2; 16: 12, 13; 1 Corinthians 7: 19; Romans 7: 12; 3: 31.) What more could they have done in this direction?

But if a new day (Sunday) was to be instituted among God's people, how can we account for the fact that the apostles preached the gospel in Jerusalem, Samaria, to Cornelius the Gentile, and to many others, without ever mentioning the institution of Sunday in place of the Sabbath, or ever commanding any one to keep Sunday, the first day of the week? If the day of rest was changed from the seventh to the first day of the week, how can we account for the fact that the New Testament is entirely silent about any such change, and that the apostles wrote four Gospels, and twenty-one letters to instruct the churches, besides the Acts and the Revelation, and never instructed the Christians to keep Sunday, or even mentioned it with any sacred title, but always as a "week" day; that is, a work day? Did the apostles, under the inspiration of the Holy Spirit, fail to instruct their converts properly? (See Acts 20: 26, 27.)

The new Christian institutions of baptism and the Lord's supper are clearly taught in the New Testament. We can point to the chapter and verse where they are commanded. Then why should not so important an institution as a new Christian rest day be mentioned? To this there can be but one answer: The silence of the New Testament as to any change of the weekly rest day is an indisputable evidence that no such change was made till after the New Testament canon was closed.

Sunday a Working Day

Dr. Francis White, Lord Bishop of Ely, says:

"In S. Hieromes days [420 A. D.], and in the very place where he was residing, the devoutest Christians did ordinary worke upon the *Lord's day**, when the service of the Church was ended."—"*Treatise of the Sabbath-Day*," *p. 219. London: 1636.*

"The Catholic Church for more than six hundred yeares

---

* Sunday was called "Lord's Day" in England in the seventeenth century when Bishop White wrote this; he therefore uses this designation of the day. Jerome is here spelled Hierome.

after Christ, permitted labour, and gave license to many Christian people, to worke upon the Lord's-day [Sunday], at such houres, as they were not commanded to bee present at the publike service, by the precept of the church."—*Id., pp. 217, 218.*

Bishop Jeremy Taylor says:

"St. Ignatius expressly affirms: . . . 'The Christian is bound to labor, even upon that day.' . . . And the primitive Christians did all manner of works upon the Lord's day, even in the times of persecution, when they are the strictest observers of all the divine commandments: but in this they knew there was none."—*"Whole Works" of Jeremy Taylor, D. D. (R. Heber, ed.), Vol. XII, Book 2, chap. 2, rule 6, par. 59, p. 426. London: 1822.*

Dr. John Kitto, D. D., F. S. A., says:

"Chrysostom (A. D. 360) concludes one of his Homilies by dismissing his audience to their respective ordinary occupations."—*Cyclopædia of Biblical Literature, Vol. 2, art. "Lord's Day," p. 270.*

Dr. Peter Heylyn quotes St. Jerome as telling us that, when the services were ended on Sunday morning, the holy women, "after their returne from thence, . . . set themselves unto their tasks which was the making garments for themselves or others: a thing which questionlesse so good a woman had not done, and much lesse ordered it to be done by others; had it beene then accounted an unlawful Act. And finally S. Chrysostome . . . confesseth, . . . that after the dismission of the Congregation, every man might apply himselfe to his lawfull businesse. . . . As for the time appointed to these publicke exercises, it seemes not to be very long . . . an houre, or two at the most."—*"History of the Sabbath" (original spelling) Part 2, chap. 3, par. 7, 8, pp. 79, 80. London: 1636.*

Dr. Heylyn says further that the people in the country worked freely on Sunday, and that those "in populous cities" "might lawfully apply themselves to their *severall businesses,* the exercises being ended" in the church. (Id., pp. 80, 81.) And of the Christians of the East he says:

"It was neere 900 yeares from our Saviour's birth, if not quite so much, before restraint of husbandry on this day, had beene first thought of in the *East:* and probably being thus restrained, did finde no more obedience there, then it had done before in the *Westerne* parts."—*Id., chap. 5, par. 6, p. 140.*

"The *Sunday* in the *Easterne* Churches had no great prerogative above other dayes, especially above the *Wednesday* and the *Friday*."—*Id., chap. 3, par. 4, p. 73.*

Some may wonder why these early morning meetings were held on Sunday, when the Christians considered it only a working day. We shall see that there was a natural cause for it, when we learn that the heathen living around them were sun worshipers, who met at their temples Sunday morning, and prostrated themselves before the rising sun. Christians are a missionary people, and to win their neighbors they held a meeting at the time when their neighbors were used to worshiping their sungod. And, as it takes a crowd to draw a crowd, the church leaders requested their members to gather at this early morning hour, after which all went to their respective places of business. But this custom became a steppingstone toward eventually adopting the heathen Sunday, as we soon shall see. Other influences also led in the same direction.

Influences Toward Apostasy

MITHRAISM, an outwardly refined sun worship, invaded the Roman Empire in B.C. 67, and made way for itself by gathering under its wing all the gods of Rome, so that "in the middle of the third century [A. D.] Mithraism seemed on the verge of becoming the universal religion."— *Encyclopedia Britannica, Vol. XVIII, art. "Mithras," p. 624, 11th edition, 1911.*

That which made Mithraism so popular was the fact that the Roman Cæsars adopted it, and the soldiers planted its banner wherever they went. The higher schools of Greek learning also accepted it, as did also the nobility, or the better classes of society, which gave it great prestige. Its "Mysteries" had a bewitching and fascinating influence on the people. And Sunday, "the venerable day of the sun," was the popular holiday of Mithraism.

On the other hand, the primitive Christian religion appeared to the learned Greek scholastics and their followers of eminent nobility only as "foolishness" (see 1 Corinthians 1: 18-23), and the Romans looked down upon the Christians with disdain and utter contempt. After the Jews had rebelled against the Roman government (Jerusalem and its temple were destroyed by Titus, A. D. 70, and multitudes of the Jews were sold as slaves), hatred and contempt for them had become quite general among the Romans, and everything Jewish was despised. Thus Sunday, in the Roman world, stood for what was eminent and popular, while the Sabbath, kept by the Jews, stood for what was despised and looked down upon. The temptations placed before an aspiring man, therefore, lay all in one direction. Dr. J. L. Mosheim says:

"The profound respect that was paid to the Greek and Roman mysteries, and the extraordinary sanctity that was attributed to them, were additional circumstances that induced the Christians to give their religion a mystic air, in order to put it upon an equal footing, in point of dignity, with that of the Pagans. For this purpose, they gave the name of *mysteries* to the institutions of the Gospel, and decorated particularly the holy sacrament with that solemn title. They used in that sacred institution, as also in that of baptism, several of the terms employed in the Heathen mysteries, and proceeded so far, at length, as even to adopt some of the ceremonies of which those renowned mysteries consisted. . . . A great part, therefore, of the service of the Church, in this century, had a certain air of the Heathen mysteries, and resembled them considerably in many particulars."—"*History of the Church*" (*2-vol. ed.*) *Vol. I, Cent. 2, part 2, chap. 4, par. 5, p. 67. New York: 1871.*

Gradually, as the church lowered its standards, many of the Greek scholars accepted Christianity (while they retained their heathen philosophy), and they carried with them into the church more or less of their former viewpoint and teaching. Then, as heathenism assailed the church, and the Roman government persecuted it, these men, such as Origen, Tertullian, Justin Martyr, *et al.*, wrote "apologies" and "treatises" to vindicate Christianity. They, however, sadly mixed heathen sentiments with Christian doctrines, and the church gradually became permeated with the teachings of these men, who now had become the new leaders. Dr. Cummings says:

"The Fathers who were really most fitted to be the luminaries of the age in which they lived were too busy in preparing their flocks for martyrdom to commit anything to writing. . . . The most devoted and pious of the Fathers were busy teaching their flocks; the more vain and ambitious occupied their time in preparing treatises. If all the Fathers who signalized the age had committed their sentiments to writing, we might have had a fair representation of the theology of the church."—"*Lectures on Romarism,*" *p. 203; quoted in "History of the Sabbath," J. N. Andrews, pp. 199, 200.*

In a very short time, the customs of Mithraism became incorporated into Christianity. John Dowling, D. D., says: "There is scarcely anything which strikes the mind of the careful student of ancient ecclesiastical history with greater surprise, than the comparatively early period at which many of the corruptions of Christianity, which are embodied in the Romish system, took their rise."—*"History of Romanism,"* Book II, chap. 1, par. 1, p. 65.

Christianity soon became so much like Mithraism that there was only a step between them. Frantz Cumont (who is probably the best informed man of our age on the subject of Mithraism) says of Christianity and Mithraism:

"The two opposed creeds moved in the same intellectual and moral sphere, and one could actually pass from one to the other without shock or interruption. . . . The religious and mystical spirit of the Orient had slowly overcome the whole social organism and prepared all nations to unite in the bosom of a universal church."—*"Oriental Religions in Roman Paganism,"* pp. 210, 211. Chicago, Ill.: Open Court Pub. Co., 1911.

The Introductory Essay by Grant Showerman says:

"Nor did Christianity stop here. It took from its opponents their own weapons and used them; the better elements of paganism were transferred to the new religion."—*Id.*, pp xi, xii.

It would be too long a story to trace the doctrines of Mithraism that were brought into the church. We must confine ourselves to our subject, Sunday-keeping. Mr. Cumont says further:

"The ecclesiastical authorities purified in some degree the customs which they could not abolish."

"The pre-eminence assigned to the *dies Solis* [Sunday] by Mithraism also certainly contributed to the general recognition of Sunday as a holiday [among Christians]."—*"Astrology and Religion Among the Greeks and Romans,"* pp. 171, 162, 163. New York: 1912.

"Sunday, over which the Sun presided, was especially holy. . . .

"[The worshipers of Mithra] held Sunday sacred, and celebrated the birth of the Sun on the twenty-fifth of December."—

"*The Mysteries of Mithra*," pp. 167, 191. Chicago: Open Court Pub. Co., 1911.

Professor Gilbert Murray, M.A., D.Litt., LL.D., F.B.A., Professor of Greek in Oxford University, says:

"Now, since Mithras was 'The Sun, the Unconquered,' and the Sun was 'The royal Star,' the religion looked for a King whom it could serve as the representative of Mithras upon earth: . . . The Roman Emperor seemed to be clearly indicated as the true King. In sharp contrast to Christianity, Mithraism recognized Cæsar as the bearer of the divine Grace, and its votaries filled the legions and the civil service. . . .

"It had so much acceptance that it was able to impose on the Christian world its own Sun-Day in place of the Sabbath, its Sun's birthday, twenty-fifth December, as the birthday of Jesus."—"*History of Christianity in the Light of Modern Knowledge,*" Chap. III; cited in "*Religion and Philosophy,*" pp. 73, 74. New York: 1929.

Rev. William Frederick likewise states the same historic fact:

"The Gentiles were an idolatrous people who worshiped the sun, and Sunday was their most sacred day. Now, in order to reach the people in this new field, it seems but natural, as well as necessary, to make Sunday the rest day of the church. At this time it was necessary for the church to either adopt the Gentiles' day or else have the Gentiles change their day. To change the Gentiles' day would have been an offence and stumbling block to them. *The church could naturally reach them better by keeping their day.* There was no need in causing an unnecessary offence by dishonoring their day."—"*Sunday and the Christian Sabbath,*" pp. 169, 170; quoted in *Signs of the Times*, Sept. 6, 1927.

Thomas H. Morer makes a similar acknowledgement. He says:

"Sunday being the day on which the Gentiles solemnly adored that planet, and called it Sunday, . . . the Christians thought fit to keep the same day and the same name of it, that

they might not appear causelessly peevish, and by that means hinder the conversion of the Gentiles, and bring a greater prejudice than might be otherwise taken against the gospel."
—*"Dialogues on the Lord's Day," p. 23. London: 1701.*

The North British Review gives the following reasons for the Christians' adopting the heathen Sun-day:

"That very day was the Sunday of their heathen neighbors and respective countrymen, and patriotism gladly united with expediency in making it at once their Lord's day and their Sabbath. . . . That primitive church, in fact, was shut up to the adoption of the Sunday,—until it became established and supreme, when it was too late to make another alteration."—*Vol. XVIII, p. 409. Edinburgh: Feb., 1853.*

Thomas Chafie, a clergyman of the English Church, gives the following reasons why the early Christians could not continue to keep the Bible Sabbath among the heathen, nor change the heathen custom from Sunday to Saturday:

"Christians should not have done well in changing, or in endeavouring to have changed their [the heathen's] standing service-day, from Sunday to any other day of the week; and that for these reasons:

"1. Because of the contempt, scorn and derision they thereby should be had in among all the Gentiles with whom they lived; and toward whom they ought by St. Paul's rule to live inoffensively, 1 Cor. 10: 32, in things indifferent. If the Gentiles thought hardly, and spoke evil of them, for that they ran not into the same excess of riot with them: 1 Pet. 4: 4, what would they have said of Christians for such an innovation as would have been made by their change of their standing service-day? If long before this, the Jews were had in such disdain among the Gentiles for their Saturday-Sabbath, . . . how grievous would be their taunts and reproaches against the poor Christians living with them, and under their power, for their new set Sacred day, had the Christians chosen any other than the Sunday?

"2. Most Christians then were either Servants or of the

poorer sort of People: and the Gentiles (most probably) would not give their servants liberty to cease from working on any other set day constantly, except on their Sunday. . . .

"5. It would have been but labour in vain for them to have assayed the same, they could never have brought it to pass."
—*"A Brief Tract on the Fourth Commandment . . . About the Sabbath-Day," pp. 61, 62. London: St. Paul's Church Yard, 1692.*

Richard Verstegen, after much research, writes of the heathen nations:

"And it is also respectable, that the most ancient Germans being Pagans, and having appropriated their first Day of the Week to the peculiar adoration of the Sun, whereof that Day doth yet in our English Tongue retain the name of Sunday."— *"Restitution of Decayed Intelligence in Antiquities," p. 11. London: 1673.*

Speaking of the Saxons, he says:

"First then unto the day dedicated unto the especial adoration of the Idol of the Sun, they gave the name of Sunday, as much as to say the Sun's-day, or the day of the Sun. This Idol was placed in a Temple, and there adored and sacrificed unto, for that they believed that the Sun in the Firmament did with or in this Idol correspond and co-operate. The manner and form whereof was according to this ensuing Picture."— *Id., p. 74.* (*Capitalization as given in this ancient book.*)

It is hardly fair to accuse the Roman Catholic Church of exchanging God's holy Sabbath for a heathen festival without giving her the opportunity to deny or acknowledge this accusation; so we will now let her state the fact in her own words, frankly. She says:

"The Church took the pagan philosophy and made it the buckler of faith against the heathen. . . . She took the pagan Sunday and made it the Christian Sunday. . . . There is, in truth, something royal, kingly about the sun, making it a fit emblem of Jesus, the Sun of Justice. Hence the Church in these countries would seem to have said, 'Keep that old, pagan name. It shall remain consecrated, sanctified.' And thus the pagan

Sunday, dedicated to Balder, became the Christian Sunday, sacred to Jesus."—"*Catholic World,*" *March, 1894, p. 809.*

So willing were church leaders to adopt the popular heathen festivals, that even heathen authors reproached them for it. Faustus accused St. Augustine as follows:

"You celebrate the solemn festivals of the Gentiles, their calends and their solstices; and as to their manners, those you have retained without any alteration. Nothing distinguishes you from the pagans except that you hold your assemblies apart from them."—*Cited in "History of the Intellectual Development of Europe," Dr. J. W. Draper, Vol. I, p. 310. New York: 1876.*

Similar reproaches had been made earlier, for Tertullian answers them, making the following admission:

"Others, with greater regard to good manners, it must be confessed, suppose that the sun is the god of the Christians, because it is a well-known fact that we pray toward the east, or because we make Sunday a day of festivity. What then? Do you do less than this? . . . It is you, at all events, who have even admitted the sun into the calendar of the week; and you have selected its day, in preference to the preceding day. . . . You who reproach us with the sun and Sunday should consider your proximity to us."—"*Ad Nationes," Book I, chap. 13; in "Ante-Nicene Fathers," Vol. III, p. 123, ed. by Drs. Roberts and Donaldson. New York: 1896.*

Tertullian had no other excuse for their Sunday-keeping than that they did not do worse than the heathen. Not only did the Church adopt heathen festivals, but Gregory Thaumaturgus allowed their celebration in the degrading manner of the heathen:

"When Gregory perceived that the ignorant multitude persisted in their idolatry, on account of the pleasures and sensual gratifications which they enjoyed at the pagan festivals, he granted them a permission to indulge themselves in the like pleasures, in celebrating the memory of the holy martyrs, hoping that, in process of time, they would return of their own accord, to a more virtuous and regular course of life."—"*Ecclesiastical History," J. L. Mosheim, D.D., Vol. I, Second Century,*

Part II, chap. 4, par. 2, footnote (Dr. A. Maclaine's 2-vol. ed., p. 66). New York: 1871.

Cardinal Newman says:

"Confiding then in the power of Christianity to resist the infection of evil, and to transmute the very instruments and appendages of demon-worship to an evangelical use, . . . the rulers of the Church from early times were prepared, should the occasion arise, to adopt, or imitate, or sanction the existing rites and customs of the populace, as well as the philosophy of the educated class. . . .

"The same reason, the need of holy days for the multitude, is assigned by Origen, St. Gregory's master, to explain the establishment of the Lord's Day. . . .

"We are told in various ways by Eusebius, that Constantine, in order to recommend the new religion to the heathen, transferred into it the outward ornaments to which they had been accustomed in their own. . . . Incense, lamps, and candles; . . . holy water; asylums; holy days and seasons, . . . the ring in marriage, turning to the east, images . . . are all of pagan origin, and sanctified by their adoption into the Church."—*"Development of Christian Doctrine," pp. 371-373. London: 1878.*

"Real superstitions have sometimes obtained in parts of Christendom from its intercourse with the heathen. . . . As philosophy has at times corrupted her divines, so has paganism corrupted her worshipers."—*Id., pp. 377, 378.*

"The church . . . can convert heathen appointments into spiritual rites and usages. . . . Hence there has been from the first much variety and change, in the Sacramental acts and instruments which she has used."—*Id., p. 379.*

Speaking of the immoral pagan feast he says:

"It certainly is possible that the consciousness of the sanctifying power in Christianity may have acted as a temptation to sins, whether of deceit or of violence; as if the habit or state of grace destroyed the sinfulness of certain acts, or as if the end justified the means."—*Id., p. 379.*

The terrible nature of these sensual gratifications of the

pagan festivals, in which the leaders of the Church now allowed its members to indulge, a person can hardly imagine till the sickening facts are spread before one's eyes by Livy. (Hist., lib. xxxix, chap. 9-17.) The learned Englishman, George Smith, F.A.S., in his "Sacred Annals," Vol. III, on the "Gentile Nations," pp. 487-489, says that this "most revolting and abandoned villiany" was so general, that when the Roman Senate had to proceed against its worst features, "Rome was almost deserted, so many persons, feeling themselves implicated in the proceedings, sought safety in flight."

A church that will take in such members, without conversion, and then allow them to continue in the most putrid corruption, must have lost all respect for morality (not to say true Christianity), and cannot be in possession of the divine power of the gospel; which changes the hearts and lives of people. (Romans 1: 16; 2 Corinthians 5: 17.) The Apostle Paul had foretold this "falling away" of the church. (Acts 20: 28-30; 2 Thessalonians 2: 1-7.) And it was during this fallen condition that the Church changed its weekly rest day from the Sabbath to the Sunday. Dr. N. Summerbell says:

"The Roman church had totally apostatized. . . . It reversed the Fourth Commandment by doing away with the Sabbath of God's word, and instituting Sunday as a holiday."— *"The Christian Church," p. 415. Cincinnati: 1873.*

Now, long after the Sabbath has been changed, Protestants are at a loss to find authority in the Bible for this change. They have rejected the authority of the Roman church to legislate on Christian faith, and cannot accept tradition, therefore they know not where to turn. Professor George Sverdrup, a leading man in the Lutheran Church, gives expression to this predicament in the following words:

"For, when there could not be produced one solitary place in the Holy Scriptures which testified that either the Lord Himself or the apostles had ordered such a transfer of the Sabbath to Sunday, then it was not easy to answer the question: Who has transferred the Sabbath, and who has had the right to do it?"

—"*Samlede Skrifter i Udvalg,*" *Andreas Helland, Vol. I, pp. 342, 343. Minneapolis, Minn.: 1909.*

Walter Farquhar Hook, D.D., Vicar of Leeds, expresses the same thought:

"The question is, whether God has ordered us to keep holy the first day of the week. Baptism and the Lord's Supper are undoubted ordinances of God; we can quote the chapter and verse in which we read of their being ordained by God. But as to the Lord's Day [Sunday], we are not able to refer to a single passage in all the Scriptures of the New Testament in which the observance of it is enjoined by God. If we refer to tradition, tradition would not be of value to us on the point immediately under consideration. The Romanist regards the tradition of the Church as of authority equal to that of Scripture. But we are not Romanists. . . . But on this point there is not even tradition to support us. . . . There is no tradition that God ordained the first day of the week to be a Sabbath. . . . The change of the Sabbath from Saturday to Sunday was never mentioned, or, as far as I can discover, thought of by the early Christians. The Sabbath, that is to say, the observance of Saturday as a day to be devoted to God's service, to rest of body and repose of mind, was an ordinance of God. This ordinance relating to Saturday could be changed by God and by God only. We, as Protestants, must appeal to the Bible, and the Bible only, to ascertain the fact that God has changed the day—that God has Himself substituted Sunday for Saturday. . . . It is no answer to this to say that the apostles seem to have sanctioned the assembly of Christians for public worship on the Lord's Day, or that St. John in the Apocalypse speaks of the Lord's Day and may possibly allude to the Sunday festival. For this is one of those arguments which prove too much. We ourselves keep Easter Day; this is no proof that we do not keep Christmas Day, or that Easter has been substituted for Christmas. And if we have instances of the first day of the week being kept holy by the apostles, we have more instances of their observing the Jewish Sabbath."—"*Lord's Day,*" *p. 94. London: 1856; quoted in* "*The*

Influences Toward Apostasy

Literature of the Sabbath Question," Robert Cox, Vol. II, pp. 369, 370.

Dr. Edward T. Hiscox, author of the "Baptist Manual," says: "There was and is a commandment to keep holy the Sabbath day, but that Sabbath day was not Sunday. It will be said, however, and with some show of triumph, that the Sabbath was transferred from the seventh to the first day of the week, with all its duties, privileges, and sanctions. Earnestly desiring information on this subject, which I have studied for many years, I ask, where can the record of such a transaction be found? Not in the New Testament, absolutely not. There is no Scriptural evidence of the change of the Sabbath institution from the seventh to the first day of the week.

"I wish to say that this Sabbath question, in this aspect of it, is the gravest and most perplexing question connected with Christian institutions which at present claims attention from Christian people; and the only reason that it is not a more disturbing element in Christian thought and in religious discussions, is because the Christian world has settled down content on the conviction that somehow a transference has taken place at the beginning of Christian history. . . .

"To me it seems unaccountable that Jesus during three years' intercourse with His disciples, often conversing with them upon the Sabbath question, discussing it in some of its various aspects, freeing it from its false glosses, never alluded to any transference of the day; also that during forty days of His resurrection life, no such thing was intimated. Nor, so far as we know, did the Spirit, which was given to bring to their remembrance all things whatsoever that He had said unto them, deal with this question. Nor yet did the inspired apostles, in preaching the gospel, founding churches, counseling and instructing those founded, discuss or approach this subject.

"Of course, I quite well know that Sunday did come into use in early Christian history as a religious day, as we learn from the Christian Fathers and other sources. But what a pity that it comes branded with the mark of paganism, and christened with the name of the sun-god, when adopted and sanctioned by the papal apostasy, and bequeathed as a sacred legacy to Protestantism!"—*A paper read before a New York Ministers' Conference, held Nov. 13, 1893. From a copy furnished by Dr. Hiscox for the "Source Book," pp. 513, 514. Wash., D. C.: Review and Herald, 1922.*

Bishop Skat Rordam, of Denmark, says:

"As to when and how it became customary to keep the first day of the week the New Testament gives us no information....

"The first law about it was given by Constantine the Great, who in the year 321 ordained that all civil and shop work should cease in the cities, but agricultural labor in the country was permitted. . . . Still no one thought of basing this command to rest from labor on the 3rd [4th] commandment before the latter half of the sixth century. From that time on, little by little, it became the established doctrine of the church during its 'Dark Ages,' that the holy church and its teachers, or the bishops with the Roman Pope at their head, as the Vicar of Christ and His apostles on earth, had transferred the Old Testament Sabbath with its glory and sanctity over onto the first day of the week." —"*Report of the Second Ecclesiastical Meeting in Copenhagen, Sept. 13-15, 1887," P. Taaning, pp. 40, 41. Copenhagen: 1887.*

Bishop A. Grimelund, of Norway, says:

"Now, summing up what history teaches regarding the origin of Sunday and the development of the doctrine about Sunday, then this is the sum: *It is not the apostles, not the early Christians, not the councils of the ancient church which have imprinted the name and stamp of the Sabbath upon the Sunday, but it is the Church of the Middle Ages and its scholastic teachers.*"—"*Sondagens Historie" (The History of Sunday), p.37. Christiania:1886.*

"What do we learn from this historical review? . . . That it is a doctrine which originated in the papal church that the sanctification of the Sunday is enjoined in the 3rd [4th] commandment, and that the essential and permanent in this commandment is a command from God to keep holy one day in each week."—*Id., pp. 47, 48.*

Constantine

Constantine had been watching, he said, those Cæsars who had persecuted the Christians, and found that they usually had a bad end, while his father, who was favorable toward them, had prospered. So, when he and Licinius met at Milan in 313 A. D., they jointly prepared an edict, usually called "The Edict of Milano," which gave equal liberty to Christians and pagans. Had Constantine stopped here, he might have been honored as the originator of religious liberty in the Roman Empire, but he had different aims in view. The Roman Empire had been ruled at times by two, four, or even six Cæsars jointly, and in his ambition to become the sole Emperor, Constantine, as a shrewd statesman, soon saw that the Christian church had the vitality to become the strongest factor in the empire. The other Cæsars were persecuting the Christians. If he could win them without losing the good will of the pagans, he would win the game. He therefore set himself to the task of blending the two religions into one. As H. G. Heggtveit (Lutheran) says:

"Constantine labored at this time untiringly to unite the worshipers of the old and the new faith in one religion. All his laws and contrivances are aimed at promoting this amalgamation of religions. He would by all lawful and peaceable means melt together a purified heathenism and a moderated Christianity. . . . His injunction that the 'Day of the Sun' should be a general rest day was characteristic of his standpoint. . . . Of all his blending and melting together of Christianity and heathenism none is more easy to see through than this making of his Sunday law. 'The Christians worshiped their Christ, the heathen their sun-god; according to the opinion of the Emperor, the objects for worship in both religions were essentially the same.'"—*"Kirkehistorie"* (*Church History*), *pp. 233, 234. Chicago: 1898.*

Constantine's Sunday law of 321 A. D. reads as follows:

"On the venerable Day of the Sun let the magistrates and people residing in cities rest, and let all workshops be closed. In the country, however, persons engaged in agriculture may freely and lawfully continue their pursuits; because it often happens that another day is not so suitable for grain-sowing or for vine-planting; lest by neglecting the proper moment for such operations the bounty of heaven should be lost. (Given the 7th day of March, Crispus and Constantine being consuls each of them for the second time."—"*Codex Justinianus, lib. 3, tit. 12, 3*"; translated in "*History of the Christian Church,*" Philip Schaff, D. D., (7-vol. ed.) Vol. III, p. 380. New York: 1884.

Dr. A. Chr. Bang (Lutheran bishop, Norway), says:

"This Sunday law constituted no real favoritism towards Christianity. . . . It is evident from all his statutory provisions, that the Emperor during the time 313-323 with full consciousness has sought the realization of his religious aim: *the amalgamation of heathenism and Christianity.*"—"*Kirken og Romerstaten*" ("*The Church and the Roman State*"), *p. 256. Christiania: 1879.*

That Constantine by his Sunday law intended only to enforce the popular heathen festival is acknowledged by Professor Hutton Webster, Ph.D. (University of Nebraska), who says:

"This legislation by Constantine probably bore no relation to Christianity; it appears, on the contrary, that the emperor, in his capacity as Pontifex Maximus, was only adding the day of the sun, the worship of which was then firmly established in the Roman Empire, to the other ferial days of the sacred calendar."—"*Rest Days,*" p. 122. New York: 1916.

A. H. Lewis, D. D., who spent years of study and research on this subject, declares, that "the pagan religion of Rome had many holidays, on which partial or complete cessation of business and labor were demanded," and that Constantine by his Sunday law was "merely adding one more festival to the *festi* of the empire."—"*A Critical History of Sunday Legislation from 321 to 1888 A. D.,*" pp. 8, 12. New York: D. Appleton and Co., 1888.

This is clearly seen when we carefully examine all the circumstances presented by Dr. Lewis:

1. Constantine's Sunday edict was given March 7, 321. The

very next day he issued an edict commanding purely heathen superstition. We quote:

"The August Emperor Constantine to Maximus:

"If any part of the palace or other public works shall be struck by lightning, let the soothsayers, following old usages, inquire into the meaning of the portent, and let their written words, very carefully collected, be reported to our knowledge." —*Id., p. 19.*

2. The Cæsars for over a century had been worshipers of the sun-god, whose weekly holiday was Sunday. Dr. Lewis says: "The sun-worship cult had grown steadily in the Roman Empire for a long time."—*Id., p. 20.* He then quotes the following from Schaff in regard to Elagabalus, a Roman Cæsar of a century before Constantine's time:

"The abandoned youth, El-Gabal or Heliogabalus (218-222), who polluted the throne by the blackest vices and follies, tolerated all religions in the hope of at last merging them in his favorite Syrian worship of the sun with its abominable excesses. He himself was a priest of the god of the sun, and thence took his name."—*Id., pp. 20, 21.*

Dean H. H. Milman says:

"It was openly asserted that the worship of the sun, under the name of Elagabalus, was to supersede all other worship. If we may believe the biographies in the Augustan history, a more ambitious scheme of a universal religion had dawned upon the mind of the emperor. The Jewish, the Samaritan, even the Christian, were to be fused and recast into one great system, of which the Sun was to be the central object of adoration."— "*History of Christianity," Vol. II, Book 2, chap. 8, par. 22, p. 178, 179. New York: 1881.*

Dr. Lewis further says that Aurelian, who reigned from 270-276 A. D., embellished the temple of the Sun with "above fifteen thousand pounds of gold."—"*History of Sunday Legislation," p. 23.* Diocletian, who reigned from 284 to 305, "appealed in the face of the army to the all-seeing deity of the sun." —*Id., p. 24.*

"Such were the influences which preceded Constantine and surrounded him when he came into power. The following extract shows still plainer the character of Constantine and his attitude toward the sun-worship cults, when the first 'Sunday edict' was issued:

"'But the devotion of Constantine was more peculiarly directed to the genius of the Sun, the Apollo of Greek and Roman mythology. . . . The sun was universally celebrated as the invincible guide and protector of Constantine.'"—*Id., pp. 26, 27.*

"These facts combine to show that Sunday legislation was purely pagan in its origin."—*Id., p. 31.*

"In this law he only sought to give additional honor to the 'venerable day' of his patron deity, the sun-god."—*Id., p. 32.*

"His attitude toward Christianity was that of a shrewd politician rather than a devout adherent."—*Id., p. 6.*

Dr. Lewis quotes from Dr. Schaff a very fitting conclusion to his remarks regarding Constantine:

"'And down to the end of his life he retained the title and dignity of *pontifex maximus*, or high-priest of the heathen hierarchy. His coins bore on the one side the letters of the name of Christ, on the other the figure of the sun-god, and the inscription 'Sol invictus.'"—*Id., p. 10.*

That the Christians at this time were still keeping the Sabbath can be seen from the following statement of Hugo Grotius, quoted by Robert Cox, F. S. A. Scot.:

"He refers to Eusebius for proof that Constantine, besides issuing his well-known edict that labor should be suspended on Sunday, enacted that the people should not be brought before the law courts on the seventh day of the week, which also, he adds, was long observed by the primitive Christians as a day for religious meetings. . . . And this, says he, 'refutes those who think that the Lord's day was substituted for the Sabbath—a thing nowhere mentioned either by Christ or His apostles.'"

—"*Opera Omnia Theologica*," *Hugo Grotius (died 1645), (London: 1679); quoted in "Literature of the Sabbath Question," Cox, Vol. I, p. 223. Edinburgh: Maclachlan and Stewart, 1865.*

Pope Sylvester co-operated with Constantine to bring paganism into the Christian church (especially Sunday-keeping). This caused the true Christians to have repugnance for him. The Waldenses believed he was the Antichrist. Dr. Peter Allix quotes the following from a prominent Roman Catholic author regarding the Waldenses:

"'They say that the blessed Pope Sylvester was the Antichrist, of whom mention is made in the Epistles of St. Paul, as being the son of perdition, who extols himself above every thing that is called God; for, from that time, they say, the Church perished. . . .'

"He lays it down also as one of their opinions, 'That the Law of Moses is to be kept according to the letter, and that the keeping of the Sabbath . . . and other legal observances, ought to take place.'"—"*Ecclesiastical History of the Ancient Churches of Piedmont,*" *p. 169. Oxford: 1821. Page 154 in the edition of 1690.*

Having obtained a glimpse of the opposition of God's people to this falling away, let us now return to our subject, to get a view of the novel means Constantine employed to make converts in accordance with his amalgamation scheme. Edward Gibbon says:

"The hopes of wealth and honors, the example of an emperor, his exhortations, his irresistible smiles, diffused conviction among the venal and obsequious crowds which usually fill the apartments of a palace. . . . As the lower ranks of society are governed by imitation, the conversion of those who possessed any eminence of birth, of power, or of riches, was soon followed by dependent multitudes. The salvation of the common people was purchased at an easy rate, if it be true that, in one year, twelve thousand men were baptized at Rome . . . and that a white garment, with twenty pieces of gold, had been promised by the emperor to every convert."—"*Decline and Fall,*" *chap. 20, par. 18.*

Constantine gave the following instruction to the bishops

at the Council of Nicæa, which shows his constant policy: "'In all ways unbelievers must be saved. It was not every one who would be converted by learning and reasoning. Some join us from desire of maintenance; some for preferment; some for presents: nothing is so rare as a real lover of truth. We must be like physicians, and accommodate our medicines to the diseases, our teaching to the different minds of all.'"—"*Lectures on the History of the Eastern Church,*" Arthur Penrhyn Stanley, D. D., Lecture 5, p. 271. New York: 1875.

The bishops were only too willing to follow the emperor's instruction, and the result was disastrous to the church. J. A. W. Neander in the following paragraph gives us some of the results of this policy:

"Such were those who, without any real interest whatever in the concerns of religion, living half in Paganism and half in an outward show of Christianity, composed the crowds that thronged the churches on the festivals of the Christians, and the theaters on the festivals of the pagans."—"*History of the Christian Religion and Church,*" Vol. II, Sec. 3, Part 1, Div. 1, par. 1, p. 223. Boston: 1855.

No wonder Rev. H. H. Milman exclaims:

"Is this Paganism approximating to Christianity, or Christianity degenerating into Paganism?"—"*History of Christianity,*" pp. 341, 342. He answers this question later by saying: "With a large portion of mankind, it must be admitted that the religion itself was Paganism under another form."—*Id., p. 412.*

Eusebius, bishop of Cæsarea, and an admirer of Constantine, co-operated with him in bringing "the venerable day of the sun" into the Christian church. Speaking of Pope Sylvester, Constantine, and himself, he says:

"All things whatsoever that it was duty to do on the Sabbath. *these we have transferred to the Lord's day*, as more appropriately belonging to it, because it has a precedence and is first in rank, and more honorable than the Jewish Sabbath. For on that day, in making the world, God said, 'Let there be light, and there was light.'"—"*Commentary on the Psalms*"; quoted in

"*Literature on the Sabbath Question,*" *Robert Cox, Vol. I, p. 361.*

Eusebius evidently used the strongest argument he knew as proof for Sunday-keeping; but advocates of this new holiday had probably not yet conceived the idea that Christ's resurrection would be an argument in favor of Sunday-keeping, so he used creation instead.

OLD AND NEW CHURCH MEMBERS

The church at this time consisted of two widely different kinds of church members: 1. The *old* class, with their devoted leaders, had accepted Christianity in the primitive way, by genuine conversion and separation from the world, suffering for Christ and His unpopular truth. This class lived mostly in the country and in out-of-the-way places. 2. The *new* converts lived mainly in the large cities, and had come in through a mass movement, following the crowd in what was most popular, attracted by the hopes of temporal gain or honor, or they had been forced in by the secular arm. These were devoid of any personal Christian experience, but constituting the majority, they elected bishops of their own kind.

The elections of bishops were attended with secret corruption and bloody violence, which was only too natural for that kind of "Christians." Edward Gibbon says of these elections:

"While one of the candidates boasted the honors of his family, a second allured his judges by the delicacies of a plentiful table, and a third, more guilty than his rivals, offered to share the plunder of the church among the accomplices of his sacrilegious hopes."—*"Decline and Fall," chap. XX, par. 22.*

Rev. H. H. Milman says:

"Even within the Church itself, the distribution of the superior dignities became an object of fatal ambition and strife. The streets of Alexandria and of Constantinople were deluged with blood by the partisans of rival bishops."— *"History of Christianity," Book 3, chap. 5, par. 2, p. 410. New York: 1881.*

Schaff declares that "many are elected on account of their

badness, to prevent the mischief they would otherwise do."—
"*History of the Christian Church*," *Vol. III, Sec. 49, par. 2, note 5, p. 240*. Even the sanctity of the church was not respected by the fighting parties. Milman, speaking of the installation of a bishop at Constantinople, says:

"In the morning, Philip [the prefect of the East] appeared in his car, with Macedonius by his side in the pontifical attire; he drove directly to the church, but the soldiers were obliged to hew their way through the dense and resisting crowd to the altar. Macedonius passed over the murdered bodies (three thousand are said to have fallen) to the throne of Christian prelate."—"*History of Christianity*," *Vol. XI, p. 426. New York: 1870*. Socrates ("Ecclesiastical History," Bk. II, chap. 17, p. 96) gives the number slain as 3150.

Can we wonder at the lack of spiritual insight and sound judgment of such bishops when they met at their councils to formulate the creed of Christendom? They decreed in favor of image worship, purgatory, prayers for the dead, veneration of relics, and many other heathen customs, persecuting all who would not fall in line with their mongrel customs. At the Council of Laodicea, A. D. 364, they anathematized Sabbath-keepers in the following way:

"Christians must not judaize by resting on the Sabbath, but must work on that day, rather honoring the Lord's Day; and, if they can, resting then as Christians. But if any shall be found to be judaizers, let them be Anathema from Christ."—*Canon XXIX, "Index Canonum," John Fulton, D. D., LL. D., p. 259.*

That the Christians were then keeping the Sabbath we see from Canon XVI of the same council, in which they decreed:

"The Gospels are to be read on the Sabbath Day, with the other Scriptures."—*Id., p. 255.*

Dr. Heylyn also declares that the Christians were keeping the Sabbath at that time:

"Nor was this onely the particular will of those two and thirty Prelates, there assembled; it was the practice generally of the Easterne Churches; and of some churches of the west. . . .

Influences Toward Apostasy

For in the Church of Millaine [Milan]; . . . it seemes the Saturday was held in a farre esteeme. . . . Not that the Easterne Churches, or any of the rest which observed that day, were inclined to Iudaisme [Judaism]; but that they came together on the Sabbath day, to worship Iesus [Jesus] Christ the Lord of the Sabbath."—"*History of the Sabbath*" (*original spelling retained*), *Part 2, par. 5, pp. 73, 74. London: 1636.*

The true Christians paid very little attention to the anathema of the bishops, for they continued to keep the true Sabbath, as the following quotations show:

"From the apostles' time until the council of Laodicea, which was about the year 364, the holy observation of the Jews' Sabbath continued, as may be proved out of many authors; yea, notwithstanding the decree of the council against it."—"*Sunday a Sabbath,*" *John Ley, p. 163. London: 1640.*

That the Sabbath was kept, "notwithstanding the decree of the council against it," is also seen from the fact that Pope Gregory I (A. D. 590-604) wrote against "Roman citizens [who] forbid any work being done on the Sabbath day."—"*Nicene and Post-Nicene Fathers,*" *Second Series, Vol. XIII, p. 13, epist. 1.*

As late as 791 A. D. Christians kept the Sabbath in Italy. Canon 13 of the council at Friaul states:

"Further, when speaking of that Sabbath which the Jews observe, the last day of the week, *and which also our peasants observe,* He said only Sabbath, and never added unto it, 'delight,' or 'my.'"—*Mansi, 13, 851; Quoted in "History of the Sabbath," J. N. Andrews, p. 539. 1912.*

Bishop Hefele summarizes the canon in the following words:
"The celebration of Sunday begins with Saturday evening. It is enjoined to keep Sunday and other church festivals. The peasants kept Saturday in many cases."—"*Conciliengesch.,*" *3, 720, sec. 404; Quoted in "History of the Sabbath," Andrews, pp. 539, 540. 1912.*

The Waldenses

WHILE Constantine's purchased converts, and the superficial-minded multitude followed the popular church, there were many honest, God-fearing Christians, who resented this sinful compromise with paganism; and, when they saw that all their protests were useless, they withdrew to places where they could more freely follow their conscience and bring up their children away from the contamination of the fallen church, which they looked upon as the "Babylon" of Revelation 17. Several hundred Sabbath-keeping Christian churches were established in southern India, and some were found even in China. Likewise the original Celtic Church in England, Scotland, and Ireland kept the seventh-day Sabbath, as will be shown in the next chapter.

The majority of these original Christians settled, however, in the Alps, a place naturally suited for their protection, being situated where Switzerland, France, and Italy join. They could, therefore, more easily get protection in one or another of these countries, as it would be harder for the Papacy to get joint action of all these countries in case of persecution. Then, too, these mountains were so steep and high, the valleys so narrow, and the passes into them so difficult, that it would seem as though God had prepared this hiding place for His true church and truth during the Dark Ages. William Jones says:

"Angrogna, Pramol, and S. Martino are strongly fortified by nature on account of their many difficult passes and bulwarks of rocks and mountains; as if the all-wise Creator, says Sir Samuel Morland, had, from the beginning, designed that place as a cabinet, wherein to put some inestimable jewel, or in which to reserve many thousand souls, which should not bow the knee before Baal."—"*History of the Christian Church,*" *Vol. I, p. 356, third ed. London: 1818.*

Sophia V. Bompiani, in "A Short History of the Italian Waldenses" (New York: 1897), quotes from several unquestionable authorities to show that the Waldenses, after having withdrawn to the Alps because of persecution, fully separated from the Roman church under the work of Vigilantius Leo, the Leonist of Lyons, who vigorously protested against the many false doctrines and practices that had been adopted by the Church. Jerome (A. D. 403-406) wrote a very cutting book against him in which he says:

"'That monster called Vigilantius . . . has escaped to the region where King Cottius reigned, between the Alps and the waves of the Adriatic. From thence he has cried out against me, and, ah, wickedness! there he has found bishops who share his crime.'" Sophia V. Bompiani then remarks: "This region, where King Cottius reigned, once a part of Cisalpine Gaul, is the precise country of the Waldenses. Here Leo, or Vigilantius, retired for safety from persecution, among a people already established there of his own way of thinking, who received him as a brother, and who thenceforth for several centuries were sometimes called by his name [Leonists]. Here, shut up in the Alpine valleys, they handed down through the generations the doctrines and practices of the primitive church, while the inhabitants of the plains of Italy were daily sinking more and more into the apostasy foretold by the Apostles."—"*A Short History of the Italian Waldenses,*" *pp. 8, 9.*

"The ancient emblem of the Waldensian church is a candlestick with the motto, *Lux lucet in tenebris* ['The light shineth in darkness']. A candlestick in the oriental imagery of the Bible is a church, and this church had power from God to prophesy in sackcloth and ashes twelve hundred and sixty days or symbolic years."—*Id., p. 17.*

Dr. W. S. Gilly, an English clergyman, after much research, wrote a book entitled: "Vigilantius and His Times," giving the same information.

Roman Catholic writers try to evade the apostolic origin of the Waldenses, so as to make it appear that the Roman is the only apostolic church, and that all others are later novelties. And for this reason they try to make out that the Waldenses originated with Peter Waldo of the twelfth century. Dr. Peter Allix says:

"Some Protestants, on this occasion, have fallen into the snare that was set for them. . . . It is absolutely false, that these churches were ever founded by Peter Waldo. . . . It is a pure forgery."—"*Ancient Church of Piedmont*," *pp. 192. Oxford: 1821.*

"It is not true, that Waldo gave this name to the inhabitants of the valleys: they were called Waldenses, or Vaudes, before his time, from the valleys in which they dwelt."—*Id., p. 182.*

On the other hand, he "was called Valdus, or Waldo, because he received his religious notions from the inhabitants of the valleys."—"*History of the Christian Church*," *William Jones, Vol. II, p. 2.* See also Sir Samuel Morland's "History of the Evangelical Churches of the Valleys of Piedmont," pp. 29, 30.

Henri Arnaud, a leading pastor among the Waldenses, says:

"Their proper name, Vallenses, is derived from the Latin word *vallis*, and not, as has been insinuated, from Valdo, a merchant of Lyons."—"*The Glorious Recovery by the Vaudois*," *Henri Arnaud, p. xiii. London: 1827.*

The Roman Inquisitor, Reinerus Sacho, writing about 1230 A. D., says:

"The heresy of the Vaudois, or poor people of Lyons, is of great antiquity. Among all sects that either are, or have been, there is none more dangerous to the Church, than that of the Leonists, and that for three reasons: the first is, because it is the sect of the longest standing of any; for some say that it has been continued down ever since the time of Pope Sylvester; and others, ever since that of the apostles. The second is, because it is the most general of all sects; for scarcely is there any country to be found where this sect hath not spread itself. And the third, because it has the greatest appearance of piety; because, in the sight of all, these men are just and honest in their transactions, believe of God what ought to be believed, receive all the articles of the Apostles' Creed, and only profess to hate the Church of Rome."—*Quoted on page 22 of William Stephen Gilly's "Excursion," fourth edition. London: 1827.*

Now it must be clear as the noonday sun, that Reinerus would not have written as he did, if the Waldenses had originated with Peter Waldo, only seventy-five years before; nor could Waldo's followers have multiplied and spread over the whole world in so short a time, under great persecution, and with so slow means of travel.

Henri Arnaud, a Waldensian pastor, says of their origin: "Neither has their church been ever reformed, whence arises its title of *Evangelic*. The Vaudois are, in fact, descended from those refugees from Italy who, after St. Paul had there preached the gospel, abandoned their beautiful country and fled, like the woman mentioned in the Apocalypse, to these wild mountains, where they have to this day handed down the gospel from father to son in the same purity and simplicity as it was preached by St. Paul."—"*The Glorious Recovery by the Vaudois," p. xiv of preface by the Author, translated by Acland. London: 1827.*

THE WALDENSIAN FAITH

The Waldenses took the Bible as their only rule of faith, abhorred the idolatry of the papacy, and the main body rejected its traditions and holidays, but kept the seventh-day Sabbath, and used the apostolic mode of baptism. (See "Ancient Churches of Piedmont," by P. Allix, pp. 152-260.) Their old catechism shows that they believed in justification by faith in the grace of Christ alone, and that obedience to the Ten Commandments was the sure *fruit* of living faith:

"*Q.*—By what means do we hope for grace? *A.*—By the Mediator Jesus Christ. . . .

"*Q.*—What is a living faith? *A.*—That which worketh by charity. *Q.*—What is a dead faith? *A.*—According to St. James, that faith which is without works, is dead. . . .

"*Q.*—By what means canst thou know that thou believest in God? *A.*—By this: because I know that I have given myself to the observation of the commandments of God. Q.—How many commandments of God are there? A.—Ten, as it appeareth in Exodus and Deuteronomy. . . . Q.—Upon what do all these commandments depend? A.—Upon the two great commandments, that is to say: Thou shalt love God above all things, and thy neighbor as thyself."—"*Waldenses,*" *Perrin, Part III, Book I, pp. 1-10. (1624 A. D.)* "*The Glorious Recovery by the Vaudois,*" *Henri Arnaud, pp. xcvi, xcvii, cv. London: 1827.*

Dr. Peter Allix quotes the following from a Roman Catholic author: "'They say that blessed Pope Sylvester was the Antichrist, of whom mention is made in the Epistles of St. Paul, as being the son of perdition, who extols himself above everything that is called God; for, from that time, they say, the Church perished.' . . .

"He lays it down also as one of their opinions; 'That the Law of Moses is to be kept according to the letter, and that the keeping of the Sabbath, circumcision, and other legal observances, ought to take place.'"—"*Ancient Churches of Piedmont,*" *p. 169 (page 154, edition of 1690). Oxford: 1821.*

In regard to the accusation that the Waldenses practiced circumcision, Mr. Benedict truthfully says:

"The account of their practicing circumcision is undoubtedly a slanderous story, forged by their enemies, and probably arose in this way: because they observed the seventh day they were called, by way of derision, Jews, as the Sabbatarians are frequently at this day, and if they were Jews, it followed, of course, that they either did, or ought to, circumcise their followers."—"*General History of the Baptist Denomination,*" *Vol. II, p. 414, edition of 1813.*

That this was exactly the way this slander was fastened on Sabbath-keepers, we can see from the "Epistle" written against them by Pope Gregory I (A. D. 590-604), in which he says:

"It has come to my ears that certain men of perverse spirit have sown among you some things that are wrong and opposed to the holy faith, so as to forbid any work being done on the Sabbath day. . . .

"For, if any one says that this about the Sabbath is to be kept, he must needs say that carnal sacrifices are to be offered: he must say, too, that the commandment about the circumcision of the body is still to be retained."—*"Nicene and Post-Nicene Fathers" (Second Series), Vol. XIII, Book 13, epist. 1, p. 92. New York: 1898.*

Going back to Judaism was considered by the Roman Catholic Church as one of the most serious heresies, punishable with death. And any one at all familiar with the tactics of Romanists knows that it has been a practice, only too common among them, to blacken the character of those whom they would destroy, so as to justify their destruction. Dr. Peter Allix says:

"It is no great sin with the Church of Rome to spread lies concerning those that are enemies of the faith. . . . There is nothing more common with the Romish party, than to make use of the most horrid calumnies to blacken and expose those who have renounced her communion. . . . Calumny is a trade the Romish party is perfectly well versed in."—*"Ancient Church of Piedmont," pp. 224, 225. (Pages 205, 206 in edition of 1690.)*

William Jones says:

"Louis XII, King of France, being informed by the enemies of the Waldenses, inhabiting a part of the province of Province, that several heinous crimes were laid to their account, sent the Master of Requests, and a certain doctor of the Sorbonne, who was confessor to his majesty, to make inquiry into this matter. On their return, they reported that they had visited all the parishes where they dwelt, had inspected their places of worship, but that they had found there no images, nor signs of the ornaments belonging to the mass, nor any of the ceremonies of the Romish church; much less could they discover any traces of those crimes with which they were charged. On the contrary, they kept the Sabbath day, observed the ordinance of baptism, according to the primitive church, instructed their children in the articles of the Christian faith, and the commandments of

God. The King having heard the report of his commissioners, said with an oath that they were better men than himself or his people."—"*History of the Christian Church,*" *Vol. 2, pp. 71, 72, third edition. London: 1818.*

NAMES OF THE WALDENSES

John P. Perrin of Lyons writes of how the Waldenses went under different names, either from the territory in which they lived, or from the name of the missionary they had sent to that country. He says:

"First therefore they called them . . . Waldenses; of the countries of Albi, Albigeois [Albigenses]. . . .

"And from one of the disciples of Valdo, called Ioseph [Joseph], who preached in Dauphiney in the diocesse of Dye, they were called Iosephists [Josephites]. . . .

"Of one of their pastors who preached in Albegeois, named Arnold Hot, they were called Arnoldists. . . .

"And because they observed no other day of rest but the Sabbath dayes, they called them Insabathas, as much as to say, as they observed no Sabbath.

"And because they were alwayes exposed to continuall sufferings, from the Latin word Pati, which signifieth to suffer, they called them Patareniens.

"And for as much as like poore passengers, they wandered from one place to another, they were called Passagenes,"— "*Luther's Fore-Runners,*" (*original spelling*) *pp. 7, 8. London: 1624.*

This author quotes the following from the Waldensian faith:

"That we are to worship one only God, who is able to help us, and not the Saints departed; that we ought to keep holy the Sabbath day, but that there was no necessity of observing other feasts."—*Id., p. 38.*

Goldastus, a learned German historian (A. D. 1576-1635) says of them:

They were called "Insabbatati, not because they were

circumcised, but because they kept the Jewish Sabbath." "*Circumcisi forsan illi fuerint, qui aliis Insabbatati, non quod circumciderentur, inquit Calvinista* [Goldastus] *sed quod in Sabbato judaizarent.*"—*Robert Robinson, in "Ecclesiastical Researches," chap, 10, p. 303. (Quoted in "History of the Sabbath," J. N. Andrews, p. 412, ed. 1887.)*

David Benedict, M. A., says:

"Robinson gives an account of some of the Waldenses of the Alps, who were called *Sabbati, Sabbatati, Insabbatati*, but more frequently *Inzabbatati*. 'One says they were so named from the Hebrew word Sabbath, because they kept the Saturday for the Lord's day. Another says they were so called because they rejected all the festivals."—"*General History of the Baptist Denomination," Vol. II, p. 413. Boston: 1813.*

Dr. J. L. Mosheim says:

"Pasaginians . . . had the utmost aversion to the dominion and discipline of the church of Rome; . . . and celebrated the Jewish Sabbath."—"*Ecclesiastical History*" (*two-volume edition*), *Cent. 12, Part 2, Chap. 5, Sec. 14, Vol. I, p. 333. New York: Harper and Brothers, 1871.*

The papal author, Bonacursus, wrote the following against the "Pasagini":

"Not a few, but many know what are the errors of those who are called Pasagini. . . . First, they teach that we should obey the law of Moses according to the letter—the Sabbath, and circumcision, and the legal precepts still being in force. . . . Furthermore, to increase their error, they condemn and reject all the church Fathers, and the whole Roman Church."— "*D'Achery, Spicilegium I, f. 211-214; Muratory, Antiq. med. aevi. 5, f. 152, Hahn, 3, 209. Quoted in "History of the Sabbath," J. N. Andrews, pp. 547, 548. 1912.*

The Roman Catholic Church has always had a special enmity toward the Bible Sabbath and Sabbath-keepers. Mr. Benedict says:

"It was the settled policy of Rome to obliterate every vestige of opposition to her doctrines and decrees, everything heretical, whether persons or writings, by which the faithful would be liable to be contaminated and led astray. In conformity to this, their fixed determination, all books and records of their opposers were hunted up, and committed to the flames."—"*History of the Baptist Denomination,*" *p. 50. 1849.*

Dr. De Sanctis, who for years was a Catholic official at Rome, and at one time Censor of the Inquisition, but who later became a Protestant, reports in his book a conversation of a Waldensian scholar as he pointed to the ruins of the Palatine Hill at Rome:

"'See,' said the Waldensian, 'a beautiful monument of ecclesiastical antiquity. These rough materials are the ruins of the two great Palatine libraries, one Greek and the other Latin, where the precious manuscripts of our ancestors were collected, and which Pope Gregory I, called the Great, caused to be burned.'"—"*Popery, Puseyism, Jesuitism,*" *De Sanctis, p. 53.*

Eternity alone will reveal how many precious manuscripts have been destroyed by Rome in its effort to blot out all traces of apostolic Christianity.

We have now seen that the ancient apostolic church, scattered by persecution, and often in hiding, went under various names. Being peaceful, virtuous, and industrious citizens, they were tolerated, or even shielded, by princes who understood their value to the country, while the Catholic Church hunted them down like wild beasts. After the Waldenses and Albigenses had lived quietly in France for many years, Pope Innocent III wrote the following instruction to his bishops:

"Therefore by this present apostolical writing we give you a strict command that, by whatever means you can, you destroy all these heresies and expel from your diocese all who are polluted with them. You shall exercise the rigor of the ecclesiastical power against them and all those who have made themselves suspected by associating with them. They may not appeal from your judgments, and if necessary, you may cause the princes and people to suppress them with the sword."—"*A Source Book for Mediæval History,*" *Oliver J. Thatcher and E. H. McNeal, p. 210. New York: Charles Scribner's Sons, 1905.*

Philippus van Limborch, Professor of Divinity at Amsterdam, speaking of the way the liberty of the people was suppressed after 1050, says:

"In the following ages the affairs of the church were so managed under the government of the Popes, and all persons so strictly curbed by the severity of the laws, that they durst not even so much as whisper against the received opinions of the church. Besides this, so deep was the ignorance that had spread itself over the world, that men, without the least regard to knowledge and learning, received with a blind obedience every thing that the ecclesiastics ordered them, however stupid and superstitious, without any examination; and if any one dared in the least to contradict them, he was sure immediately to be punished; whereby the most absurd opinions came to be established by the violence of the Popes."—"*History of the Inquisition*," p. 79. London: 1816.

Ignorance and superstition generated vice of the basest sort, and brought the Christian world into the darkest of the Dark Ages, which made the Reformation of the sixteenth century an absolute necessity. And, as "the darkest hour of the night is just before dawn," so the twelfth to the fifteenth centuries were the darkest in the Christian Era. For a time, however, there were still a few lights shining on the religious horizon, shedding their mild gospel light into the dense darkness. But when these were extinguished, the darkness became well-nigh complete. 1. The Celtic church of Scotland and Ireland had sent their missionaries with an open Bible into almost every country of Europe. The gospel lamp of Scotland was extinguished in 1069; that of Ireland in 1172; that of the ancient Albigenses in 1229; the Assyrian lamp of the East was extinguished at Malabar, India, by the Inquisition in 1560; and the Waldensian lamp, that had been shining the longest, and had sent its mild rays over Europe for centuries, was extinguished in 1686. The history of these evangelical churches during this dark period is very interesting and has many valuable lessons for our day.

The Waldenses and Albigenses were quiet and industrious

people, and followed the Bible standard of morality, which actually caused their persecution.

"But their crowning offence was their love and reverence for Scripture, and their burning zeal in making converts. The Inquisitor of Passau informs us that they had translations of the whole Bible in the vulgar tongue, which the Church vainly sought to suppress, and which they studied with incredible assiduity. . . . Many of them had the whole of the New Testament by heart. . . . Surely if ever there was a God-fearing people it was these unfortunates under the ban of Church and State. . . . The inquisitors . . . [declare] that the sign of a Vaudois, deemed worthy of death, was that he followed Christ and sought to obey the commandments of God."—"*History of the Inquisition of the Middle Ages,*" *H. C. Lea, Vol. I, pp. 86, 87. New York: Harper and Brothers, 1888.*

"In fact, amid the license of the Middle Ages ascetic virtue was apt to be regarded as a sign of heresy."—*Id., p. 87.*

On the other hand, the licentious lives of the Catholic clergy placed insurmountable barriers for a Waldensian ever to become a Catholic. When in 1204 Pope Innocent III sent his commissioners to crush the peaceful Waldenses and Albigenses in Southern France "with fire and sword," these monks returned to the pope asking for help to reform the lives of the Catholic priests. Lea says:

"The legates . . . appealed to him for aid against prelates whom they had failed to coerce, and whose infamy of life gave scandal to the faithful and an irresistible argument to the heretic. Innocent curtly bade them attend to the object of their mission and not allow themselves to be diverted by less important matters."—*Id., p. 129.*

Professor Philippus van Limborch writes:

"It was the entire study and endeavour of the popes, to crush, in its infancy, every doctrine that any way opposed their exorbitant power. In the year 1163, at the synod of Tours, all the bishops and priests in the country of Tholouse, were commanded 'to take care, and to forbid, under the pain of excom-

The Waldenses

munication, every person from presuming to give reception, or the least assistance to the followers of this heresy, *which first began in the country of Tholouse*, whenever they shall be discovered. Neither were they to have any dealings with them in buying or selling; that by being thus deprived of the common assistances of life, they might be compelled to repent of the evil of their way. Whosoever shall dare to contravene this order, let them be excommunicated, as a partner with them in their guilt. As many of them as can be found, let them be imprisoned by the Catholic princes, and punished with the forfeiture of all their substance.'

"Some of the Waldenses, coming into the neighbouring kingdom of Arragon, king Ildefonsus, in the year 1194, put forth, against them, a very severe and bloody edict, by which 'he banished them from his kingdom, and all his dominions, as enemies of the cross of Christ, prophaners of the Christian religion, and public enemies to himself and kingdom.' He adds: 'If any, from this day forwards, shall presume to receive into their houses, the aforesaid Waldenses and Inzabbatati, or other heretics, of whatsoever profession they be, or to hear, in any place, their abominable preachings, or to give them food, or to do them any kind office whatsoever; let him know, that he shall incur the indignation of Almighty God and ours; that he shall forfeit all his goods, without the benefit of appeal, and be punished as though guilty of high treason.'"—*"History of the Inquisition," pp. 88, 89. London: 1816.*

To destroy completely these heretics Pope Innocent III sent Dominican inquisitors into France, and also crusaders, promising "a plenary remission of all sins, to those who took on them the crusade . . . against the Albigenses." When Raymond VI, Earl of Tholouse, shielded these innocent people, who were such an asset to his country, he was "deposed by the pope." * Being frightened by the savage crusaders Raymond submitted, and

---

* Catholic Encyclopedia, Vol. XII, art. "Raymond VI," p. 670.

the papal legate had him publicly whipped twice till "he was so grievously torn by the stripes" that he had to leave the church by a back door. (Id., pp. 98, 100.) He later appealed to Innocent III. "The pope, however, ceded the estates of Raymond to Simon de Montfort," (1215)*. Thousands of God's people were tortured to death by the Inquisition, buried alive, burned to death, or hacked to pieces by the crusaders. While devastating the city of Biterre the soldiers asked the Catholic leaders how they should know who were heretics; Arnold, Abbot of Cisteaux, answered: "Slay them all, for the Lord knows who is His."—*Id., pp. 98, 101.*

In 1216 to 1221 Raymond reconquered his land, and after his death (1221) his son became Earl, and "the Inquisition was banished from the country of Tholouse." But Pope Honorius III "proclaimed an holy war, to be called the 'Penance war,' against the heretics," and "to subdue the Earl of Tholouse, he sent letters to King Louis" of France to make war on Raymond, which he did. But treachery, which has always been one of the most successful weapons of the Papacy against God's people, had to be resorted to here: When the Pope's legate saw that he could not take the city of Avignon by force, he "scrupled not to adopt the vilest treachery and to practice the basest hypocrisy.—He offered to suspend hostilities, and to pave the way for peace, if the besieged would admit a few priests, only to inquire concerning the faith of the inhabitants: and those terms being agreed upon and sealed by mutual oaths; the priests entered, but in direct violation of their solemn engagement, brought the French army with them, who thus fraudulently triumphed over the unsuspecting citizens; they plundered the city, killed or bound in chains the inhabitants."—*Id., pp. 104-106.*

(This is in perfect harmony with the Catholic teaching and practice, that they need not keep faith with a heretic, as carried out in the case of John Huss. In spite of the safe-conduct from the Emperor Sigismund, he was imprisoned, November 28, 1414, and burned July 6, 1415.)

---

* Catholic Encyclopedia, Vol. XII, art. "Raymond VI," p. 670.

The Waldenses

HUNTED LIKE WILD BEASTS

The Earl of Tholouse was finally forced to bow to Rome, and God's people were hunted as wild beasts everywhere. Here are some of the laws of Louis IX, King of France, A. D. 1229: "*Canon 3.*—The lords of the different districts shall have the villas, houses, and woods diligently searched, and the hiding-places of the heretics destroyed. *Canon 4.*—If any one allows a heretic to remain in his territory, he loses his possession forever, and his body is in the hands of the magistrates to receive due punishment. *Canon 5.*—But also such are liable to the law, whose territory has been made the frequent hiding-place of heretics, not by his knowledge, but by his negligence. *Canon 6.*—The house in which a heretic is found, shall be torn down, and the place or land be confiscated. *Canon 14.*—Lay members are not allowed to possess the books of either the Old or the New Testament."—"*Hefele's Councils,*" *Vol. V, pp. 981, 982.* ("*History of the Sabbath,*" *New, p. 558*).

These laws were only echoes of the "Bulls" of the popes. But while the Waldenses on the French side of the Alps were being exterminated, the pope had a more difficult task to destroy them in the Piedmont Alps. From Pope Lucius III (A. D. 1181-1185) to the Reformation in the sixteenth century the persecution of the Waldenses was the subject of many papal "anathemas." Army after army was sent against them, and all manner of trickery was resorted to in order to destroy these honest, plain, Christian people. In 1488 Albert Cataneo, the papal legate came with an army into the midst of Val Louise. The inhabitants fled into a cavern for shelter, and the soldiers started a fire at the mouth of the cavern and smothered the entire population of 3,000, including 400 children. Then Cataneo entered the Piedmont side. Here the Waldenses retreated to Pra del Tor, their "Shiloh of the Valleys." Cataneo ordered his soldiers into the dark, narrow chasm that formed the only path to this citadel. The poor Waldenses were now bottled up, and their enemies were proceeding towards them, sure of their prey, but God heard earnest prayers:

"A white cloud, no bigger than a man's hand, unobserved by the Piedmontese, but keenly watched by the Vaudois, was seen to gather on the mountain's summit.. . . . That cloud grew rapidly bigger and blacker. It began to descend. . . . It fell right into the chasm in which was the Papal army. . . . In a moment the host were in night; they . . . could neither advance nor retreat. [The Waldenses] tore up huge stones and rocks, and sent them thundering down into the ravine. The papal soldiers were crushed where they stood. . . . Panic impelled them to flee, . . . they threw each other down in the struggle; some were trodden to death; others were rolled over the precipice, and crushed on the rocks below, or drowned in the torrent, and so perished miserably."—"*History of the Waldenses*," *J. A. Wylie, pp. 48, 49.*

In 1544 the treacherous and heartless Catholic leader, D'Oppede caused the terrible butchery of thousands of Waldenses. At Cabrieres he wrote a note to the people, saying that if they would open the gates of their city he would do them no harm. They, in good faith, opened the gates, and D'Oppede cried out: "Kill them all." Men, women, and children were massacred or burned alive. In 1655 there was another massacre of Waldenses. After the Catholic leaders had made several vain attempts to break into the fastnesses of the mountains where the Waldenses lived, and were defeated, the Marquis of Pianesse wrote the various Waldensian towns to entertain certain regiments of soldiers to show their good faith. These Christian people, who always had such sacred regard for their own word, never seemed to learn that it is a fundamental Catholic doctrine, that Catholics need not, and should not, keep faith with heretics, when the interest of the "Church" is at stake. After they had sheltered the soldiers, and fed them of their scanty store, a signal was given at 4 A. M., April 24, 1655, and the butchery began.

"Little children, Leger says, were torn from the arms of their mothers, dashed against the rocks, and cast carelessly away. The sick or the aged, both men and women, were either burned in their houses, or hacked in pieces; or mutilated, half murdered,

The Waldenses

and flayed alive, they were exposed in a dying state to the heat of the sun, or to flames, or to ferocious beasts."—*"Israel of the Alps," Dr. Alexis Muston, Vol. I, pp. 349, 350.*

These people suffered tortures too terrible to mention, which only devils in human form could have invented. The towns in the beautiful valleys were left smoldering ruins. A few people saved themselves by flight to the mountains.

Further Destruction

In 1686 another terrible edict was issued against them, and an army raised to exterminate them. And again it was the same story of treachery. Gabriel of Savoy himself wrote them:

"'Do not hesitate to lay down your arms; and be assured that if you cast yourselves upon the clemency of his royal highness, he will pardon you, and that neither your persons nor those of your wives or children shall be touched.'"—*"Israel of the Alps," Alexis Muston, Vol. I, p. 445.*

The Waldenses accepted the official document in good faith and opened their entrenchments. But the Catholic officials, true to the nature of their church doctrines, rushed in and butchered men, women, and children in cold blood. Unspeakable tortures were inflicted on the innocent people, while a few escaped to the mountains. All the towns of the valleys were smoldering and charred ruins. Rome had at last quenched the ancient lamp. "The school of the prophets in the Pra del Tor is razed. No smoke is seen rising from cottage, and no psalm is heard ascending from dwelling or sanctuary, . . . and no troop of worshipers, obedient to the summons of the Sabbath bell, climbs the mountain paths."—*"History of the Waldenses," Wylie, p. 173.*

As these exiled Waldenses fled from country to country, they were persecuted and harassed, but they sowed the seeds of truth as they went. Let us now consider the experiences of other branches of the apostolic church, that were scattered by persecution and by early missionary endeavors to the outskirts of civilization. (See the chapter "Wycliffe, Huss," etc.)

Celtic Sabbath-Keepers

WE KNOW from several sources that Christianity entered the British Isles in apostolic times. (Colossians 1:23.) Rev. Richard Hart, B. A., Vicar of Catton, says: "That the light of Christianity dawned upon these islands in the course of the first century, is a matter of historical certainty."—"*Ecclesiastical Records,*" *p. vii. Cambridge: 1846.* Tertullian, about 200 A. D., included the Britons among the many nations which believed in Christ, and he speaks of places among "the Britons—inaccessible to the Romans, but subjugated to Christ."—"*Answer to the Jews,*" *chap. vii.* Dr. Ephraim Pagit, in his "Christianography," printed in London, 1640, gives an interesting account of the early Christians in these islands.

Before the church in the British Isles was forced under the papal yoke, it was noted for its institutions of learning. The Rev. Mr. Hart says:

"That learning and piety flourished in these islands during the period of their independence is capable of the most satisfactory proof, and Ireland in particular was so universally celebrated, that students flocked thither from all parts of the world." —"*Ecclesiastical Records,*" *p. viii.*

He says, some came to "Ireland for the sake of studying the Scriptures."—*Id., p. xi.*

The Coming of Patrick

Patrick, a son of a Christian family in southern Scotland, was carried off to Ireland by pirates about 376 A. D. Here, in slavery, he gave his heart to God and, after six years of servitude, escaped, returning to his home in Scotland. But he could not forget the spiritual need of these poor heathen, and after ten years he returned to Ireland as a missionary of the Celtic

Celtic Sabbath-Keepers 135

church. "He had now reached his thirtieth year [390 A. D.]."—
"*The Ancient British and Irish Churches*," William Cathcart,
D. D., p. 70.

Dr. E. Pagit says that "Saint Patricke had in his day founded there 365 churches."—"*Christianography*," Part 2, p.10.

Dr. August Neander says of Patrick:

"The place of his birth was Bonnaven, which lay between the Scottish towns Dumbarton and Glasgow, and was then reckoned to the province of Britain. This village, in memory of Patricius, received the name of Kil-Patrick or Kirk-Patrick. His father, a deacon in the village church, gave him a careful education."—"*General History of the Christian Religion and Church*," Vol. II, p. 122. Boston: 1855.

Patrick himself writes in his "Confession":

"I, Patrick, . . . had Calpornius for my father, a deacon, a son of the late Potitus, the presbyter. . . . I was captured. I was almost sixteen years of age . . . and taken to Ireland in captivity with many thousand men."—"*The Ancient British and Irish Churches*," William Cathcart, D. D., p. 127.

Patrick Not a Catholic

To those who have heard of Patrick only as a Catholic saint, it may be a surprise to learn that he was not a Roman Catholic at all, but that he was a member of the original Celtic church. There is no more historic evidence for Patrick's being a Roman Catholic saint, than for Peter's being the first pope. Catholics claim that Pope Celestine commissioned Patrick as a Roman Catholic missionary to Ireland; but William Cathcart, D. D., says:

"There is strong evidence that Patrick had no Roman commission in Ireland."

"As Patrick's churches in Ireland, like their brethren in Britain, repudiated the supremacy of the popes, all knowledge of the conversion of Ireland through his ministry must be suppressed [by Rome, at all cost.]"—*Id.*, p. 85.

The popes who lived contemporary with Patrick never mentioned him. "There is not a written word from one of them rejoicing over Patrick's additions to their church, showing clearly that he was not a Roman missionary. . . . So completely buried was Patrick and his work by popes and other Roman Catholics, that in their epistles and larger publications, his name does not once occur in one of them until A. D. 634."—*Id., p. 83.*

"Prosper does not notice Patrick. . . . He says nothing of the greatest success ever given to a missionary of Christ, apparently because he was not a Romanist."—*Id., p. 84.*

"Bede never speaks of St. Patrick in his celebrated 'Ecclesiastical History.'"—*Id., p. 85.*

But, writing of the year 431, Bede says of a Catholic missionary: "Palladius was sent by Celestinus, the Roman pontiff, to the Scots [Irish] that believed in Christ."—"*Ecclesiastical History,*" *p. 22. London: 1894.*

But this papal emissary was not received any more favorably by the church in Ireland, than was Augustine later received by the Celtic church of Scotland, for "he left because he did not receive respect in Ireland."—"*The Ancient British and Irish Churches,*" *William Cathcart, D. D., p. 72.*

No Roman Catholic church would have dared to ignore a bishop sent them by the pope. This proves that the churches in the British Isles did not recognize the pope.

Dr. Todd says:

"The 'Confession' of St. Patrick contains not a word of a mission from Pope Celestine. One object of the writer was to defend himself from the charge of presumption in having undertaken such a work as the conversion of the Irish, rude and unlearned as he was. Had he received a regular commission from the see of Rome, that fact alone would be an unanswerable reply. But he makes no mention of Pope Celestine, and rests his defense altogether on the *divine call* which he believed himself to have received for his work."—*Id., pp. 81, 82.*

"Muirchu wrote more than two hundred years after Patrick's death. His declaration is positive that he *did not go to Rome*."—*Id., p. 88.*

There are three reasons why Patrick could not have been a Roman Catholic missionary: 1. Early Catholic historians and popes avoided mentioning Patrick or his work; until later legendary histories represented him as a Catholic Saint.* 2. When papal missionaries arrived in Britain, 596 A. D., the leaders of the original Celtic church refused to accept their doctrines, or to acknowledge the papal authority, and would not dine with them. (Compare 1 Corinthians 5: 11; 2 John 8-11.) They "acted towards the Roman party exactly 'as if they had been pagans.' "—*"Ecclesiastical Records," by Richard Hart, pp. viii, xiv.* 3. The doctrines of the Celtic church of Patrick's day differed so widely from those of the Roman church, that the latter could not have accepted it as "Catholic." Patrick must have been a Sabbath-keeper, because the churches he established in Ireland, as well as the mother church in Scotland and England, followed the apostolic practice of keeping the seventh-day Sabbath, and of working on Sunday, as we soon shall see. But this was considered deadly heresy by the Papacy.

COLUMBA

Another leader in the Celtic church deserves to be mentioned: Columba, who was born in Ireland, A. D. 521. Animated by the zeal and missionary spirit he found in the schools established by Patrick, Columba continued the work of his predecessor, and selecting twelve fellow workers, he established a missionary center on the island of Iona. This early Celtic church sent its missionaries not only among the heathen Picts of their own country, but also into the Netherlands, France, Switzerland, Germany, and Italy. This Sabbath-keeping church (as did their Waldensian brethren) kept the torch of truth burning during the long, dark night of papal supremacy, till finally they

---

* These legendary histories of St. Patrick, written during the Dark Ages, are so full of childish superstition and fabricated miracles, that they have to be rejected as actual history.

were conquered by Rome in the twelfth century. Professor Andrew Lang says of them:

"They worked on Sunday, but kept Saturday in a Sabbatical manner."—"*A History of Scotland from the Roman Occupation,*" *Vol. I, p. 96. New York: Dodd, Mead, and Co., 1900.*

Dr. A. Butler says of Columba:

"Having continued his labors in Scotland thirty-four years, he clearly and openly foretold his death, and on Saturday, the ninth of June, said to his disciple Diermit: 'This day is called the Sabbath, that is, the rest day, and such will it truly be to me; for it will put an end to my labors.'"—"*Butler's Lives of the Saints,*" *Vol. I, A. D. 597, art " St. Columba," p. 762. New York: P. F. Collier.*

In a footnote to Blair's translation of the Catholic historian, Bellesheim, we read:

"We seem to see here an allusion to the custom, observed in the early monastic Church of Ireland, of keeping the day of rest on Saturday, or the Sabbath."—"*History of the Catholic Church in Scotland,*" *Vol. I, p. 86.*

Professor James C. Moffatt, D. D., Professor of Church History at Princeton, says:

"It seems to have been customary in the Celtic churches of early times, in Ireland as well as Scotland, to keep Saturday, the Jewish Sabbath, as a day of rest from labor. They obeyed the fourth commandment literally upon the seventh day of the week."—"*The Church in Scotland,*" *p. 140. Philadelphia: 1882.*

But the church of Rome could never allow the light of pure apostolic Christianity to shine anywhere, for that would reveal her own religion to be apostasy. Pope Gregory I, in 596, sent the imperious monk Augustine, with forty other monks, to Britain. Dr. A. Ebrard says of this "mission":

"Gregory well knew that there existed in the British Isles, yea, in a part of the Roman dominion, a Christian church, and that his Roman messengers would come in contact with them. By sending these messengers, he was not only intent upon the conversion of the heathen, but from the very beginning he was

Celtic Sabbath-Keepers 139

also bent upon bringing this Irish-Scotch church, which had hitherto been free from Rome, in subjection to the papal chair." —"*Bonifacius*," *p. 16. Guetersloh, 1882. (Quoted in Andrews' "History of the Sabbath," fourth edition, revised and enlarged, p. 532).*

Through political influence, and with magnificent display, the Saxon king, Ethelbert of Kent, consented to receive the pope's missionaries, and "Augustine baptized ten thousand pagans in one day" by driving them in mass into the water. Then, relying on the support of the pope and the sword of the Saxons, Augustine summoned the leaders of the ancient Celtic church, and demanded of them: "'Acknowledge the authority of the Bishop of Rome.' These are the first words of the Papacy to the ancient Christians of Britain." They meekly replied: "'The only submission we can render him is that which we owe to every Christian.'"—"*History of the Reformation*," *D'Aubigne, Book XVII, chap. 2.* "'But as for further obedience, we know of none that he, whom you term the Pope, or Bishop of Bishops, can claim or demand.'"—"*Early British History*," *G. H. Whalley, Esq., M. P., p. 17 (London: 1860): and "Variation of Popery," Rev. Samuel Edger, D. D., pp. 180-183. New York: 1849.* Then in 601, when the British bishops finally refused to have any more to do with the haughty messenger of the pope, Augustine proudly threatened them with secular punishment. He said:

"'If you will not have peace from your brethren, you shall have war from your enemies; if you will not preach life to the Saxons, you shall receive death at their hands.' Edelfred, King of Northumbria, at the instigation of Augustin, forthwith poured 50,000 men into the Vale Royal of Chester, the territory of Prince of Powys, under whose auspices the conference had been held. Twelve hundred British priests of the University of Bangor having come out to view the battle, Edelfred directed his forces against them as they stood clothed in their white vestments and totally unarmed, watching the progress of the battle—they were massacred to a man. Advancing to the university itself, he put to death every priest and student therein, and destroyed by fire the halls, colleges, and churches of the university itself; thereby fulfilling, according to the words of the great Saxon authority called the Pious Bede, the prediction, as he terms it, of the blessed Augustine. The ashes of this noble monastery were smoking; its libraries, the collection of ages, having been wholly consumed."—"*Early British History,*" *G. H. Whalley, Esq., M. P., p. 18. London: 1860.* See also "*Six Old English Chronicles,*" *pp. 275, 276; edited by J. A. Giles, D. C. L. London: 1906.*

D'Aubigne says of Augustine: "A national tradition among the Welsh for many ages pointed to him as the instigator of this cowardly butchery. Thus did Rome loose the savage Pagan against the primitive church of Britain."—"*History of the Reformation,*" *D'Aubigne, book 17, chap. 2.*

This was a master stroke of Rome, and a great blow to the native Christians. With their university, their colleges, their teaching priests, and their ancient manuscripts gone, the Britons were greatly handicapped in their struggle against the ceaseless aggression of Rome. Still they continued the struggle for more than five hundred years longer, till finally, in the year 1069, Malcolm, the King of Scotland, married the Saxon princess, Margaret, who, being an ardent Catholic, began at once to Romanize the primitive church, holding long conferences with its leaders. She was assisted by her husband, and by prominent Catholic officials. Prof. Andrew Lang says:

"The Scottish Church, then, when Malcolm wedded the sainted English Margaret, was Celtic, and presented peculiarities odious to the English lady, strongly attached to the establishment as she knew it at home. . . . The Celtic priests must have disliked the interference of an Englishwoman.

"First there was a difference in keeping Lent. The Kelts did not begin it on Ash Wednesday. . . . They worked on Sunday, but kept Saturday in a sabbatical manner."—"*History of Scotland,*" *Vol. I, p. 96.*

William F. Skene says:

"Her next point was that they did not duly reverence the

Lord's day, but in this latter instance they seem to have followed a custom of which we find traces in the early Monastic Church of Ireland, by which they held Saturday to be the Sabbath on which they rested from all their labours."—"*Celtic Scotland,*" *Vol. II, p. 349. Edinburgh: David Douglas, printer, 1877.*

"They held that Saturday was properly the Sabbath on which they abstained from work."—*Id., p. 350.*

"They were wont also to neglect the due observance of the Lord's day, prosecuting their worldly labours on that as on other days, which she likewise showed, by both argument and authority, was unlawful."—*Id., p. 348.*

SCOTLAND UNDER QUEEN MARGARET

Professor Andrew Lang relates the same fact thus:

"The Scottish Church, then, when Malcolm wedded the saintly English Margaret, was Celtic, and presented peculiarities odious to an English lady, strongly attached to the Establishment as she knew it at home. . . .

"They worked on Sunday, but kept Saturday in a sabbatical manner. . . . These things Margaret abolished."—"*A History of Scotland from the Roman Occupation,*" *Vol. I, p. 96. New York: Dodd, Mead, and Co., 1900.*

The Catholic historian, Bellesheim, says of Margaret:

"The queen further protested against the prevailing abuse of Sunday desecration. 'Let us,' she said, 'venerate the Lord's day, inasmuch as upon it our Saviour rose from the dead: let us do no servile work on that day.' The Scots in this matter had no doubt kept up the traditional practice of the ancient monastic Church of Ireland which observed Saturday, rather than Sunday, as a day of rest."—"*History of the Catholic Church in Scotland,*" *Vol. I, pp. 249, 250.*

Finally the queen, the king, and three Roman Catholic dignitaries held a three-day council with the leaders of the Celtic church. Turgot, the queen's confessor, says:

"It was another custom of theirs to neglect the reverence

due to the Lord's day, by devoting themselves to every kind of worldly business upon it, just as they did upon other days. That this was contrary to the law, she proved to them as well by reason as by authority. 'Let us venerate the Lord's day,' said she, 'because of the resurrection of our Lord, which happened upon that day, and let us no longer do servile works upon it; bearing in mind that upon this day we were redeemed from the slavery of the devil. The blessed Pope Gregory affirms the same, saying: "We must cease from earthly labour upon the Lord's day."' . . . From that time forward . . . no one dared on these days either to carry any burdens himself or to compel another to do so."—"*Life of Queen Margaret,*" *Turgot, Section 20; cited in "Source Book," p. 506, ed. 1922.*

Thus Rome triumphed at last in Scotland. In Ireland also the Sabbath-keeping church established by Patrick was not long left in peace:

"Giraldus Cambrensis informs us that in the year 1155 [Henry II, King of England, was entrusted by Pope Adrian IV with the mission of] invading Ireland [with devastating war] *to extend the boundaries of the church,* [so that even the Irish would become] faithful to the Church of Rome." The pope wrote Henry:

"'You, our beloved son in Christ, have signified to us your desire of invading Ireland, . . . and that you are also willing to pay to St. Peter the annual sum of one penny for every house. We therefore grant a willing assent to your petition, and *that the boundaries of the Church may be extended,* . . . permit you to enter the island.'"—"*Ecclesiastical Records of England, Ireland, and Scotland,*" *Rev. Richard Hart, B. A., pp. xv, xvi.*

Thus we see, that in Scotland an English queen "introduced changes which, in Ireland, came in the wake of conquest and the sword. For example, the ecclesiastical novelties which St. Margaret's influence gently thrust upon Scotland, were accepted in Ireland by the Synod of Cashel (1172) under Henry II. Yet there remained, in the Irish Church, a Celtic and an Anglo-Norman party, 'which hated one another with as perfect a hatred as if they rejoiced in the designation of Protestant and Papist.'"—"*History of Scotland,*" *Andrew Lang, Vol. I, p. 97.*

But whether this triumph of Catholicism over the native Celtic faith was accomplished by the devastating wars of Henry II, or by Queen Margaret's appeal to Pope Gregory, and her threat of the civil law, in either case it lacked an appeal to plain Bible facts, accompanied by the convicting power of the Holy Spirit. And, while the *leaders* of the Celtic church might reluctantly yield to the civil authorities, the *people*, who had kept the Bible Sabbath for centuries, requested divine authority for Sunday-keeping. For some time the papal missionaries, who preached this strange gospel to the Britons, fabricated all kinds of stories about miraculous punishments that had befallen those who worked on Sunday: Bread baked on Sunday, when it was cut, sent forth a flow of blood; a man plowing on Sunday, when cleaning his plow with an iron, had it grow fast to his hand, so that he had to carry it around to his shame for two years.

Forged Letter From Christ

When the Abbot Eustace, 1200 A. D., was continually confronted with requests for a divine command for Sunday-keeping, he finally retired to Europe, and returned the next year with a spurious letter from Jesus Christ, claimed to have fallen down from heaven upon St. Simon's altar at Golgotha. This letter declared:

"I am the Lord. . . . It is my will, that no one, from the ninth hour on Saturday [3 P. M.] until sunrise on Monday, shall do any work. . . . And if you do not pay obedience to this command, . . . I swear to you . . . I will rain upon you stones, and wood, and hot water, in the night. . . . Now, know ye, that you are saved by the prayers of my most holy Mother, Mary."
—"*Roger de Hoveden's Annals,*" *Vol. II, pp. 526, 527, Bohn's edition. London: 1853.*

In that superstitious age such childish fabrications might, to some extent, satisfy some people, but four hundred years later the trouble flared up again.

"Upon the publication of the 'Book of Sports' in 1618, a violent controversy arose among English divines on two points: first, whether the Sabbath of the fourth commandment was in force among Christians; and, secondly, whether, and on what ground, the first day of the week was entitled to be distinguished and observed as 'the Sabbath.' In 1628 Theophilus Brabourne, a clergyman, published the first work in favor of the seventh day, or Saturday, as the true Christian Sabbath. He and several others suffered great persecution."—*Haydn's Dictionary of Dates*, art. "*Sabbatarians*," p. 602. New York: Harper and Brothers, 1883.

Several ministers arose in England about this time who defended the Bible Sabbath, and who were bitterly persecuted by the state church. John Trask was put in prison; his wife, a schoolteacher of a devout Christian character, remained in prison for fifteen years. On November 26, 1661, John James, a godly Sabbath-keeping preacher, was hanged for advocating the Sabbath truth, "and his head was set upon a pole opposite the meeting house in which he had preached the gospel."— "*History of the Baptists*," Dr. J. M. Cramp, p. 351. London: Elliot Stock, 1868. Dr. Thomas Bampfield,* who had been speaker in one of Cromwell's parliaments, wrote two books defending the seventh-day Sabbath (1692, 1693), but he also was imprisoned. In 1664, Edward Stennet, an English minister, wrote a book entitled: "The Seventh Day Is the Sabbath of the Lord." But like the rest, he had to spend a long time in prison. In 1668 he wrote the following letter to his Sabbath-keeping brethren in America:

"Abington, Berkshire, England,
"February 2nd, 1668.

"Edward Stennet, a poor unworthy servant of Jesus Christ, to the remnant in Rhode Island, who keep the commandments of God, and the testimonies of Jesus, sendeth greeting:

"Dearly Beloved:

---

* See Robert Cox's "Literature of the Sabbath Question," Vol. II, pp. 86-91.

"I rejoice in the Lord on your behalfs that He hath been graciously pleased to make known to you His holy Sabbath in such a day as this, when truth falleth in the streets, and equity cannot enter. And with us we can scarcely find a man that is really willing to know whether the Sabbath be a truth or not, and those who have the greatest parts, have the least anxiety to meddle with it.

"We have passed through great opposition for the truth's sake, repeatedly from our brethren, which makes the affliction heavier; I dare not say how heavy, lest it should seem incredible; but the Lord has been with us, affording us strength according to our day. And when lovers and friends seem to be moved far from us, the Lord was near us, comforting our souls, and quickening us, with such quick and eminent answers to our prayers, has encouraged and established us in the truth for which we suffer. But the opposers of truth seem much withered, and at present the opposition seems declining away; the truth is strong, and this spiritual fiery law will burn all those thorns which men set up before it. For was there ever any ceremonial law given us? But this law was given from the mouth of God, in the ears of so many thousands—written on tables of stone with His own finger—promised to be written on the tables of their hearts—and confirmed by a miracle for the space of forty years in the wilderness, the manna not keeping good any other day but the Sabbath. . . .

"It is our duty as Christians, to carry it with all meekness and tenderness to our brethren, who, through the darkness of their understanding in this point, differ from us. We have abundant reason to bless our dear Father, who hath opened our eyes to behold the wonders in His law, while many of His dear servants are in the dark; but the Lord has in this truth as in others, first revealed it unto babes, that no flesh shall glory in His presence. Our work is to be at the feet of the Lord in all humility, crying unto Him, that we may be furnished with all grace to fit us for His work; that we may be instruments in His hands, to convince our brethren (if the Lord will) who at present differ from us. . . .

"Truly, dear brethren, it is a time of slumbering and sleeping with us, though God's rod is upon our backs. Oh! pray for us to the Lord, to quicken us, and set us upon watch-towers. Here are, in England, about nine or ten churches that keep the Sabbath, besides many scattered disciples, who have been eminently preserved in this tottering day, when many once eminent churches have been shattered in pieces. The Lord alone be exalted, for the Lord has done this, not for our sakes, but for His own name's sake. My dear brethren, I write these lines at a venture, not knowing how they will come to your hand. I shall commit them and you to the blessing of our dear Lord, who hath loved us, and washed away our sins in His own blood. If these lines come to you safely, and I shall hear from you, hereafter I will write to you more largely. . . . The grace of our Lord Jesus Christ be with you all. Amen.

"Edward Stennet."

—"*An Original History of the Religious Denominations,*" *I. Daniel Rupp, p. 71. Philadelphia: 1844.*

Wycliffe, Huss, and Zinzendorf

THE Inqusition and the devastating wars which the popes and the Councils directed against the Albigenses and Waldenses during the twelfth and thirteenth centuries, had scattered some of them over Europe, where they settled mostly in Germany, Poland, and Bohemia. "Others turning to the west obtained refuge in Britain."* Everywhere these God-fearing people worked quietly for the salvation of souls, and thus prepared the way for the Reformation. But the books of heaven alone contain the true record of the work done by these humble Waldenses.

"John Wycliffe was the herald of reform, not for England alone, but for all Christendom. The great protest against Rome which it was permitted him to utter, was never to be silenced. That protest opened the struggle which was to result in the emancipation of individuals, of churches, and of nations." —"*The Great Controversy,*" *pp. 79, 80.*

In Bohemia, Huss and Jerome were, in their labor, animated by the writings of Wycliffe, so that the light of truth, which the Papacy had quenched in the "Vallies" was flaring up in England and Bohemia. Dr. Fr. Nielsen, of Denmark, says of the papal opposition:

"The struggle against the Waldenses . . . was as nothing compared to the trouble that broke out in the Bohemian church when Wycliffism had taken root in that country. . . . About the year 1400 Jerome, M.A., of Prague had been at Oxford, and from thence had brought with him to Prague Wycliffe's 'Dialogus' and 'Trialogus,' and in 1403 John Huss stepped out openly as one of Wycliffe's disciples."—"*Haandbog i Kirkens Historie*"

---

* See "Dissertation on the Prophecies," by Bishop Thomas Newton, p. 518, and "History of the Evangelical Churches of . . . Piedmont," by Samuel Morland, Esq., p 191. (London, 1658).

(*Handbook of Church History*), *Vol. II, p. 874, ed. of 1893. Copenhagen.*

After Huss was burned, July 6, 1415, and Jerome, May 30, 1416, their work of reform was carried on by their followers. But they were divided into two camps, the conservative of Prague, and the radical of Tabor. Dr. Nielson continues:

"All Hussites were agreed upon yielding obedience to the 'law of God.' . . . Those of Prague . . . rejected only that which conflicted with the law of God, [while the] Taborites . . . would acknowledge only what was expressly mentioned in the Scriptures. . . . The Taborites read the Scriptures with their own eyes. . . . The radical party rejected all holidays, even Sunday. . . . Some longed for the condition of the apostolic times. . . . The religious enlightenment among the Taborites was great, and their women had a better knowledge of the Scriptures than the Italian priests. . . . In Germany the Waldenses had, without doubt, as in Bohemia, several places prepared the way for the Hussitism. . . .

"If any one after the middle of the fifteenth century wanted to find genuine disciples of Wycliffe and Huss in Bohemia he had to go to the eastern border where the remnant of the Taborites, as 'the quiet in the land' in strict discipline endeavored to follow the law of God. At the close of the fifteenth century there were in Bohemia and Moravia about two hundred churches of the 'Brethren,' who rejected all connection with the Roman church and had their own ministers and bishops, who through a Waldensian Bishop from Austria believed they had preserved the apostolic succession. . . . Time and again they were subject to bloody persecutions."—*Id., pp. 886-888, 896, 897.*

We shall now show that these Waldensian and Hussite brethren were Sabbath-keepers. Dr. R. Cox says: "I find from a passage in Erasmus that at the early period of the Reformation when he wrote, there were Sabbatarians in Bohemia, who not only kept the seventh day, but were said to be . . . scrupulous in resting on it." Erasmus' statement follows: "Now we hear that among the Bohemians a new kind of Jews has arisen called

Sabbatarians, who observe the Sabbath."—"*Literature of the Sabbath Question,*" *Cox, Vol. II, pp. 201, 202.*

Bishop A. Grimelund of Norway speaks of them as "the anciently arisen, but later vanished sect of Sabbatarians in Bohemia, Moravia, and Hungary."—"*Sondagens Historie*" (*History of Sunday*), *pp. 46, 47. Christiania: 1886.*

About the year 1520 many of these Sabbath-keepers found shelter on the estate of Lord Leonhard, of Lichtenstein, "as the princes of Lichtenstein held to the observance of the true Sabbath."—"*History of the Sabbath,*" *J. N. Andrews, p. 649, ed. 1912.* Lord Leonhard asked the Sabbatarians to submit to him a statement of their belief, which was sent to Wolfgang Capito, a leading Strassburg Reformer, and to Caspar Schwenkfeld. This document is lost, but Schwenkfeld's answer to it (printed in 1599) contains several quotations from it, showing that their arguments for the seventh day were much the same as those used by Seventh-day Adventists today. In 1535 they were driven from their homes by persecution, but "once more they were granted respite." Finally in 1547 the king of Bohemia, yielding to the constant urging of the Roman church, expelled them. "The Jesuits contrived to publish this edict just before harvest and vintage. . . . They allowed them only three weeks and three days for their departure; it was death to be found even on the borders of the country beyond the expiration of the hour. . . . At the border they filed off, some to Hungary, some to Transylvania, some to Wallachia, others to Poland." See J. N. Andrews, "History of the Sabbath," pp. 641-649.

Count Zinzendorf

Scattered and torn by persecution, the old sect of Moravian Brethren wandered about till about the year 1720 Count Zinzendorf invited them to his estate, later called Herrnhut. He began to keep the Sabbath, and became the leader of these Brethren and the head of a great missionary movement. Bishop A. G. Spangenberg says of him:

"He loved to stick to the plain text of the Scriptures, believing that rather simplicity than art is required to understand it. When he found anything in the Bible stated in such plain language that a child could understand, he could not well bear to have one depart from it."—"*Leben des Grafen Zinzendorf*" (*Life of Count Zinzendorf*), *pp. 3, 546, 547, 1774.*

In 1738 Zinzendorf wrote of his keeping the Sabbath thus:

"That I have employed the Sabbath for rest many years already, and our Sunday for the proclamation of the gospel—that I have done without design, and in simplicity of heart." —"*Budingsche Sammlung," Sec. 8, p. 224. Leipzig: 1742.*

Spangenberg gives some of Zinzendorf's reasons for keeping the seventh day holy:

"On the one hand, he believed that the seventh day was sanctified and set apart as a rest day immediately after creation; but on the other hand, and principally, because his eyes were directed to the rest of our Saviour Jesus Christ in the grave on the seventh day."—"*Leben des Grafen Zinzendorf" pp. 5, 1422, note.*

In 1741 he journeyed to Bethlehem, Pa., where some Moravian Brethren had settled. Of his work there Spangenberg relates:

"As a special instance it deserves to be noticed that he is resolved with the church at Bethlehem to observe the seventh day as rest day. The matter had been previously considered by the church council in all its details, and all the reasons pro and con were carefully weighed, whereby they arrived at the unanimous agreement to keep the said day as Sabbath."—*Id., pp. 5, 1421, 1422.* (See also "*Varnhagen von Ense Biographische Denkmale," pp. 5, 301. Berlin: 1846.*

The church records of the Bethlehem Moravian Church (now in the Moravian Seminary archives, and dated June 13 O. S., or June 24 N. S., 1742) has this paragraph:

"The Sabbath is to be observed in quietness and in fervent communion with the Saviour. It is a day that was given to all nations according to the law for rest, for the Jews observed it not so much as Jews as human beings."

PERSECUTION IN THE UNITED STATES

But even in the United States, Sabbath-keepers had endured more or less persecution, and when, on the second of October, 1798, a member of their Ephrata society was haled into court for working on Sunday, the judge read a letter, which George Washington wrote to the Baptists of Virginia, dated August 4, 1798, in which he assured them of full religious liberty. It was not easy, however, for the people to grasp the truth that religious liberty is an inherent right, and that governments are instituted to protect the individual in his God-given rights, and that church and state are to be kept separate. (Luke 20: 25.) The champions of liberty had a long, hard fight to secure the adoption and ratification of the Federal Constitution and its First Amendment, and it will take the utmost watchfulness by the friends of freedom to retain the liberty there guaranteed.

When the Constitution was drafted and made its appearance, the friends of religious liberty, especially those who had been oppressed under the religious establishments of the colonies, felt that liberty of conscience was not sufficiently secured by the proposed Constitution. While Article 6 forbade religious tests as a qualification for office under the government, there was no guaranty against religious tests and religious intolerance to those *not* in office. So on May 8, 1789, the United Baptist churches of Virginia addressed a communication to George Washington, in which they gave expression to the prevailing fears in this matter. Washington replied as follows: "If I could have entertained the slightest apprehension that the Constitution framed by the convention where I had the honor to preside might possibly endanger the religious rights of any ecclesiastical society, certainly I would never have placed my signature to it; and if I could now conceive that the general government might ever be so administered as to render the liberty of conscience insecure, I beg you will be persuaded that no one would be more zealous than myself to establish effectual barriers against the horrors of spiritual tyranny and every species of religious persecution. For, you doubtless remember, I have often expressed my sentiments that any man, conducting himself as a good citizen and being accountable to God alone for his religious opinions, ought to be protected in worshiping the Deity according to the dictates of his own conscience."—"*History of the Baptists,*" *Thomas Armitage, D. D., pages 806, 807.*

About a month later, James Madison, with the approval of George Washington, introduced in the first Congress that met under the new Constitution, the first ten amendments, commonly known as the Bill of Rights, the first of which enjoins Congress from all religious legislation. It is as follows:

"Congress shall make no law respecting an establishment of religion, or prohibiting the free exercise thereof; or abridging the freedom of speech or of the press; or the right of the people peaceably to assemble, and to petition the government for a redress of grievances."

Thus the champions of liberty secured for the citizens of the new republic full liberty of conscience to worship, freedom of speech and of the press, and it will take eternal vigilance to retain these rights unimpaired. See "American State Papers," William Addison Blakely, pp. 152, 153, revised edition. Washington, D. C.: 1911.

Sabbath-Keepers In India

APOSTOLIC ORIGIN

WE SHALL now briefly trace the apostolic Christian Sabbath-keepers from Antioch in Syria to their farthest mission stations in old China. Thomas Yeates in his "Indian Church History" (London: 1818), has collected from several sources statements that all agree on the points he presents, that the apostle Thomas traveled through Persia into India, where he raised up many churches. "From thence he went to China, and preached the gospel in the city of Cambala, [which is] supposed to be the same with Pekin, and there he built a church."—"*Indian Church History,*" *p. 73.* "In the year 1625, there was found in a town near Si-ngan-fu, the metropolis of the province of Shin-si, a stone having the figure of a cross, and inscriptions in two languages, . . . Chinese and Syriac . . . as follows: '*This Stone was erected to the honor and eternal memory of the law of light and truth brought from Ta-Cin, and promulgated in China.*' [The inscription consists of 736 words, giving] a summary of the fundamental articles of the Christian faith."—*Id., pp. 86-88.*

That the missionaries who brought the gospel to China were Sabbath-keepers can be seen by the following extract from the inscription:

"On the *seventh day* we offer sacrifice, after having purified our hearts, and received absolution for our sins. This religion, so perfect and so excellent, is difficult to name, but it enlightens darkness by its brilliant precepts."—"*Christianity in China,*" *M. l'Abbe Huc, Vol. I, chap. 2, pp. 48, 49, seq. New York: 1873.*

Returning to India we shall find traces of the Sabbath among those churches also. And they had retained the Bible in the ancient language used by the church at Antioch, where the name "Christians" originated. (Acts 11:26.)

"It was in these sequestered regions that copies of the Syriac Scriptures found a safe asylum from the search and destruction of the Romish inquisitors, and were found with all the marks of ancient purity."—"*Indian Church History*," *T. Yeates, p. 167.*

"Whatever may be the future use and importance of those manuscripts, one thing is certain, and that is, they establish the fact that the Syrian Christians of India have the pure unadulterated Scriptures in the language of the ancient church of Antioch, derived from the very times of the Apostles."—*Id., p. 169.*

Thomas Yeates shows that they kept "Saturday, which amongst them is a festival day, agreeable to the ancient practice of the church."—*Id., pp. 133, 134.*

The Armenians of India and Persia had evidently received their faith from the same source as the other Christians of India. Rev. Claudius Buchanan, D. D., says of them:

"The Armenians in Hindostan are our own subjects. . . . They have preserved the Bible in its purity; and their doctrines are, as far as the Author knows, the doctrines of the Bible. Besides, they maintain the solemn observance of Christian worship, throughout our Empire, on the seventh day; and they have as many spires pointing to heaven among the Hindoos, as we ourselves."—"*Christian Researches in Asia*," *p. 143. Philadelphia: 1813.*

The Jacobites, another branch of the original Christians of India, can add one more link to this evidence. Samuel Purchas, the noted geographer and compiler, said of them:

"They keep Saturday holy, nor esteem the Saturday fast lawful, but on Easter even. They have solemn service on Saturdays, eat flesh, and feast it bravely, like the Jews."—"*Pilgrimmes*," *Part 2, Book 8, chap. 6, p. 1269. London: 1625.* (We must remember that the papal church demanded all to fast on the Sabbath, but these Christians refused to obey her.)

J. W. Massie says of these Indian Christians:

"Remote from the busy haunts of commerce, or the populous seats of manufacturing industry, they may be regarded as the

Sabbath-Keepers in India

Eastern Piedmontese, the Vaudois of Hindustan, the witnesses prophesying in sackcloth through revolving centuries, though indeed their bodies lay as dead in the streets of the city which they had once peopled."—"*Continental India,*" *Vol. 2, p. 120.*

PAPAL PERSECUTION

Mr. Massie further says of these Christians:

"Separated from the Western world for a thousand years, they were naturally ignorant of many novelties introduced by the councils and decrees of the Lateran; and *their conformity with the faith and practice of the first ages* laid them open to the unpardonable guilt of heresy and schism, as estimated by the church of Rome. 'We are Christians, and not idolaters,' was their expressive reply when required to do homage to the image of the Virgin Mary. . . . LaCroze states them at fifteen hundred churches and as many towns and villages. They refused to recognize the pope, and declared they had never heard of him; they asserted the purity and primitive truth of their faith since they came, and their bishops had for thirteen hundred years been sent, from the place where the followers of Jesus were first called Christians."—*Id., Vol. II, pp. 116, 117.*

When the Portuguese (Roman Catholics) came to Malabar, India, in 1503, "they were agreeably surprised to find upwards of a hundred Christian churches on the coast of Malabar. But when they became acquainted with the purity and simplicity of their worship, they were offended. 'These churches,' said the Portuguese, 'belong to the Pope.' 'Who is the Pope?' said the natives, 'we never heard of him.' The European priests were yet more alarmed, when they found that these Hindoo Christians maintained the order and discipline of a regular church under Episcopal jurisdiction: and that, for 1300 years past, they had enjoyed a succession of Bishops appointed by the Patriarch of Antioch. 'We,' said they, 'are of the true faith, whatever you from the West may be; for we came from the place where the followers of Christ were first called Christians.'"—"*Christian*

Researches in Asia," Claudius Buchanan, D. D., p. 60. Philadelphia: 1813.

"These Christians met the Portuguese as natural friends and allies, and rejoiced at their coming:—but the Portuguese were much disappointed at finding the St. Thome Christians firmly fixed in the tenets of a primitive church; and soon adopted plans for drawing away from their pure faith this innocent, ingenuous, and respectable people."—"*Indian Church History,*" *Thomas Yeates, p. 163. London: 1818.*

When the Jesuit, Francis Xavier, and his colaborers, were sent to India, they displayed the true spirit of Romanism. "The Inquisition was set up at Goa, in the Indies, at the instance of Francis Xaverius, who signified by letter to Pope [King] John III, Nov. 10, 1545, 'that the Jewish wickedness spread every day more and more in the parts of the East Indies, subject to the kingdom of Portugal, and therefore he earnestly besought the said king, that to cure so great an evil, he would take care to send the office of the Inquisition into those countries. [Accordingly the Inquisition was erected there.] The first Inquisitor was Alexius Diaz Falcano, sent by Cardinal Henry, March 15, A. D. 1560. . . . The language of F. Xavier, used on this occasion, is truly suspicious, and that under the mask of correcting 'the Jewish wickedness,' is rather to be construed an avowed design against the liberties, the independence, and the firmness of the native Christians of Malabar, who refused to acknowledge the Pope's supremacy, and with a true Protestant zeal bravely resisted the Catholic tyranny."—*Id., pp. 139, 140.*

"The Jewish wickedness" of which Xavier complained was evidently the Sabbath-keeping among those native Christians, as we shall see in our next quotation. When one of these Sabbath-keeping Christians was taken by the Inquisition, he was accused "of having *Judaized;* which means, having conformed to the ceremonies of the Mosaic law; such as not eating pork, hare, fish without scales, &c., of having attended the solemnization of the Sabbath."—"*Account of the Inquisition at Goa,*" *Dellon, p. 56. London: 1815.*

"The Inquisitors, by degrees, begin to urge him in this way—'If thou hast observed the law of Moses, and assembled on the Sabbath day as thou sayest, and thy accusers have seen thee there, as appears to have been the case; to convince us of the sincerity of thy repentance, tell us who are thine accusers, and those who have been with thee at these assemblies.'" Dellon then suggests that in the mind of the Inquisitors "the witnesses of the Sabbath are considered as accomplices." —*Id., p. 58.*

Some have thought that these Sabbath-keepers were relapsed Jews, but Dellon declares:

"Of an hundred persons condemned to be burnt as Jews, there are scarcely four who profess that faith at their death; the rest exclaiming and protesting to their last gasp that they are Christians, and have been so during their whole lives."—*Id., p. 64.*

"The prisoner, who was entirely innocent, would be given over to the civil arm to be burned, unless he confessed the very crimes of which he was accused, and signed his confession, and also named six or seven of his accusers. But, not being told who they were, he might have to name many before striking the right ones, and, as his accusers were supposed to have been eyewitnesses to his Sabbath-keeping, they might be Sabbath-keepers, who, like himself, were in the clutches of the Inquisition. His only hope, therefore, was to name some of his brethren, who would then be taken by the inquisitors, and forced to repeat the same experience to free themselves. Thus the prison would be filled with people who were tortured for guilt of which they were innocent, or to remain in solitary confinement and terrible suspence and agony of mind until the Auto da Fe, or public burning, which took place every two or three years."—*Id., pp. 53-60, 67.* And whether they were released or executed, their property was confiscated to the Inquisition. Dr. C. Buchanan says:

"When the power of the Portuguese became sufficient for their purpose, they invaded these tranquil Churches, seized some of the Clergy, and devoted them to the death of heretics. . . .

They seized the Syrian Bishop Mar Joseph, and sent him prisoner to Lisbon: and then convened a Synod at one of the Syrian Churches called Diamper, near Cochin, at which the Romish Archbishop Menezes presided. At this compulsory Synod 150 of the Syrian Clergy appeared. They were accused of the following practices and opinions: 'That they had married wives; that they owned but two Sacraments, Baptism and the Lord's Supper; that they neither invoked Saints, nor worshipped Images, nor believed in Purgatory; and that they had no other orders of names of dignity in the church, than Bishop, Priest, and Deacon.' These tenets they were called on to abjure, or to suffer suspension from all Church benefices. It was also decreed that all Syrian books on ecclesiastical subjects that could be found, should be burned; 'in order,' said the Inquisitors, 'that no pretended apostolical monuments may remain.'"—"*Christian Researches in Asia,*" *p. 60.*

The papacy had adopted the policy that all remains of the pure, apostolic church, whether persons or books, should be carefully eradicated, so that no trace of them might betray the sad fact that the Roman church had fallen away from the apostolic purity. And she has also tried to destroy all accounts of her persecution during the Dark Ages, so that her tracks would be covered up.

The Reformation

Necessary Because the Church Had Fallen

THE Roman church was sadly in need of a reformation, but she refused to surrender the elements that corrupted her, and slew those who tried to save her. There were two papal ordinances which especially contributed toward the terrible and widespread depravity of her priesthood: (1) enforced celibacy (forbidding priests to marry), and (2) exemption of the clergy from the domain of civil law, so that government officials could not punish them for any crime. H. C. Lea says of the Roman Catholic clergyman:

"No matter what crimes he might commit, secular justice could not take cognizance of them, and secular officials could not arrest him. He was amenable only to the tribunals of his own order, which were debarred from inflicting punishments involving the effusion of blood, and from whose decisions an appeal to the supreme jurisdiction of distant Rome conferred too often virtual immunity."—"*History of the Inquisition of the Middle Ages*," *Vol. I, p. 2. New York: 1888.*

This author makes a further statement concerning a "complaint laid before the pope by the imperial Diet held at Nurnberg early in 1522. . . . The Diet, in recounting the evils arising from the ecclesiastical jurisdiction which allowed clerical offenders to enjoy virtual immunity, adduced, among other grievances, the license afforded to those who, debarred by the canons from marriage, abandoned themselves night and day to attempts upon the virtue of the wives and daughters of the laity, sometimes gaining their ends by flattery and presents, and sometimes taking advantage of the opportunities offered by the confessional. It was not uncommon, indeed, for women to be openly carried off by their priests, while their husbands and fathers were threatened with vengeance if they should attempt to recover them. As regards the sale to ecclesiastics of licenses to indulge in habitual lust, the Diet declared it to be a regular and settled matter, reduced to the form of an annual tax, which in most dioceses was exacted of all the clergy without exception, so that when those who perchance lived chastely demurred at the payment, they were told that the bishop must have the money, and that after it was handed over they might take their choice whether to keep concubines or not."—*"An Historical Sketch of Sacerdotal Celibacy in the Christian Church," pp. 431, 432, and Note 1. Boston: Houghton Mifflin and Co., Riverside Press, 1884.*

Let the reader remember that those "complaints were made by the highest authority in the empire."—*Ibid.*

Professor Philip Limborch records the same fact, and adds:

"Erasmus says: 'There is a certain German bishop, who declared publicly at a feast, that in one year he had brought to him 11,000 priests that openly kept women': for they pay annually a certain sum to the bishop. This was one of the hundred grievances that the German nation proposed to the Pope's nuncio at the convention at Nuremberg, in the years 1522 and 1523. Grievance 91."—*"History of the Inquisition," p. 84.*

H. C. Lea says:

"The extent to which the evil sometimes grew may be guessed from a case mentioned by Erasmus, in which a theologian of Louvian refused absolution to a pastor who confessed to having maintained illicit relations with no less than two hundred nuns confided to his spiritual charge."—*"An Historical Sketch of Sacerdotal Celibacy," pp. 567, 568.*

While the pope had ample machinery in the Inquisition for correcting his sinning priests, yet he was very lenient with them, except for "heresy." In fact, heinous depravity seemed to have been worse where the Inquisition reigned supreme. H. C. Lea continues:

"It is rather curious that in Spain, the only kingdom where heresy was not allowed to get a foothold, the trouble seems to have been greatest and to have first called for special remedial measures."—*Id., p. 568.*

The Reformation

Of the "remedial" laws enacted in 1255, 1274, and 1302, Lea says:

"However well meant these efforts were, they proved as useless as all previous ones, for in 1322 the council of Valladolid, under the presidency of the papal legate, [enacted still more laws]. The acts of this council, moreover, are interesting as presenting the first authentic evidence of a custom which subsequently prevailed to some extent elsewhere, by which parishioners were wont to compel their priests to take a female consort for the purpose of protecting the virtue of their families from his assaults."—*Id., p. 310.* "The same state of affairs continued until the sixteenth century was well advanced."—*Id., p. 312.*

"We have already seen ecclesiastical authority for the assertion that in the Spanish Peninsula the children sprung from such illicit connections rivaled in numbers the offspring of the laity." —*Id., p. 336.*

Such conditions seem almost unbelievable. But, when in 1900 W. H. Taft was sent to the Philippines to establish civil government with a public school system there, he reported finding in those islands conditions similar to those described above. See Senate Document No. 190, 56th Congress, 2nd Session: "Message from the President of the United States, 1901 A. D."

If some Protestants of today had known the conditions existing at the time of the Reformation they would not have judged Dr. Martin Luther so critically for his harsh statements. That the Reformation was the inevitable result of the fallen condition of the Catholic Church, was acknowledged by the speakers at the Council of Trent. H. C. Lea says:

"Even in the Council of Trent itself, the Bishop of St. Mark, in opening its proceedings with a speech, January 6th, 1546, drew a fearful picture of the corruption of the world, which had reached a degree that posterity might possibly equal but not exceed. This he assured the assemblied fathers was attributable solely to the wickedness of the pastors, who drew their flocks with them into the abyss of sin. The Lutheran heresy had been provoked by their own guilt, and its suppression was only to be hoped for by their own reformation. At a later session, the Bavarian orator, August Baumgartner, told the assembled fathers that the progress of the Reformation was attributable to the scandalous lives of the clergy, whose excesses he could not describe without offending the chaste ears of his auditory. He even asserted that out of a hundred priests there were not more than three or four who were not either married or concubinarians —a statement repeated in a consultation on the subject of ecclesiastical reform drawn up in 1562 by order of the Emperor Ferdinand, with the addition that the clergy would rather see the whole structure of the church destroyed than submit to even the most moderate measure of reform."—"*An Historical Sketch of Sacerdotal Celibacy," pp. 518, 519.*

"Sale of Indulgences" Aroused Protest

The subject of indulgences is of great importance at this time, for the strenuous protest of Romanists against any discussion of this subject has changed both our schoolbooks and our encyclopedias. We therefore invite the reader to a careful investigation of this subject. The grossest doctrines that ever disgraced the church of Rome, usually began as apparently innocent injunctions, which developed for centuries into the final monstrosity. This was the case with "indulgence." It began simply as a release from some ecclesiastical punishment.

Catholic authorities today teach that there are *two* kinds of punishments for sin, *one eternal* and *the other temporal*. Dr. M. J. Scott, S. J., says:

"The forgiveness of sin is . . . the remission of the eternal chastisement. . . .

"After the guilt and eternal punishment have been remitted there remains the temporal chastisement, . . . which must be suffered either here or . . . hereafter . . . by the suffering of Purgatory."—"*Things Catholics Are Asked About," p. 145. New York: P. J. Kenedy and Sons. 1927.*

The debt in purgatory may be settled in this life by penances, masses, or by indulgences. On the cost of having masses celebrated see "Fifty Years in the Church of Rome" by Charles Chiniquy, chap. XXV. Catholic authors admonish a Catholic to settle his account with the church in this life, for when he dies "his family might have hundreds of Masses offered up for his soul," before it affects him in purgatory.—"*Things Catholics Are Asked About*," *p. 147.* As some Catholics may be unwilling to pay such sums for their deceased relatives, Dr. J. T. Roche warns them:

"The last will and testament of a Catholic in which there is no provision made for Masses gives evidence of an oversight which is truly deplorable. Children and heirs-at-law are the same the world over. In many instances they are dissatisfied with the bequests made to them individually. Their disappointment precludes the possibility of having Masses said for the dead testator. Some of them too are so selfish and grasping that they cannot think of parting with even a small portion of their inheritance to comply with what is clearly a duty."—"*Masses for the Dead*," *pp. 23, 24.* (*This booklet bears the sanction of the Catholic Church and its censor*).

THE POPE'S SPIRITUAL BANK

The Roman Catholic Church teaches that a person can by his good works and penances, pay off his own debt, and have some to spare. These extra good works form a Spiritual Bank from which the pope can draw for the benefit of those who lack, as the following quotations show. Dr. M. J. Scott says:

"A sinner has it in his own power to merit forgiveness and mercy while he lives."—"*Things Catholics Are Asked About*," *p. 148.*

Rev. J. Procter writes:

"Some holy ones of God more than satisfy the debt of temporal punishment which they owe to the Eternal Father. . . . All these 'satisfactions,' these merits, these uncalled-for penances, are not lost, nor are they useless and in vain. They form a spiritual treasure-house, a 'bank' we have called it, upon which the Church can draw for the benefit of her needy children."—*"Indulgences"* (*Roman Catholic*), *p. 9. London: Catholic Truth Society.*

Canon Law says: "To the Roman Pontiff is committed by Christ the entire spiritual treasury of the Church, wherefore only the Pope and those to whom he has given participation in the power by law, have the ordinary power to grant indulgences." (Canon 912)."—*"The New Canon Law," Rev. S. Woywod, O. F. M., pp. 143, 144. New York: 1918.*

The Catholic Encyclopedia testifies:

"According to Catholic doctrine, therefore, the source of indulgences is constituted by the merits of Christ and the saints. This treasury is left to the keeping, not of the individual Christian, but of the Church.

"This treasure He . . . entrusted to Blessed Peter, the keybearer, and his successors."—*Vol. VII, pp. 785, 784.*

"By a plenary indulgence is meant the remission of the entire temporal punishment due to sin so that no further expiation is required in purgatory. A partial indulgence commutes only a certain portion of the penalty.

"An indulgence is valid both in the tribunal of the Church and in the tribunal of God."—*Id., p. 783.*

"When the church, therefore, by an indulgence, remits this penalty, her action, according to the declaration of Christ, is ratified in heaven."—*Id., p. 785.*

"Here, as in many other matters, the love of money was the chief root of the evil; indulgences were employed by mercenary ecclesiastics as a means of pecuniary gain."—*Id., p. 787.*

We shall now enter into a careful examination of the two questions: (1) whether Catholic authorities, before the Protestant Reformation, had begun to represent indulgences as actual remissions of sin; and (2) if these indulgences could be purchased for money. Professor William E. Lunt says of the period following 1095 A. D.:

"The commercialization of indulgences began with those issued in connection with the Crusades."—*"Papal Revenues in*

The Reformation

the Middle Ages," Vol. I, p. 115. Columbia University Press, 1934.

"Boniface IX (1389-1404) issued several bulls of plenary indulgence to aid the building of the dome of the cathedral at Milan. In the course of the fifteenth century plenary indulgences for similar purposes became common. . . . One third or one half was the share most commonly taken by the pope, occasionally it amounted to two thirds."—*Id.*, p. 114.

"The general Summons of Pope Innocent III to a Crusade A. D. 1215 [requested all civil rulers] for the remission of their sins [to furnish soldiers. To all who joined in the Crusade, and also to those who could not go themselves, but who paid the expense of sending a substitute, the pope declared:] 'We grant full pardon of their sins.' [To those who went at their own expense, he promised not only] full pardon of their sins, [but he says:] 'We promise them an increase of eternal salvation.'"— "*Bullarium Romanum, editio Taurinensis,*" *Vol. III, p. 300; copied in "Select Historical Documents of the Middle Ages," E. F. Henderson, pp. 337, 339, 343. London: 1892.*

This papal permission to secure an indulgence by paying for a substitute in one's place, to fight in the Crusades, soon developed into a system of paying for indulgences. Another means of enormous income to the Holy See was started by Pope Boniface VIII, by inaugurating the "Jubilees" with their indulgences. We read of these:

"*Jubilees.*—On the 22nd of February of the present Year 1300, he issued a Bull, granting a full Remission of all Sins to such as should in the present Year, beginning and ending at *Christmas,* or in every other Hundreth Year, visit the Basilica of the two Apostles *St. Peter* and *St. Paul* [on fifteen different days.]—*Bower's* "*History of the Popes," Vol. VI, year 1300, p. 474.*

Herbert Thurston, S. J., in his book: "The Roman Jubilee," bearing the sanction of the Catholic Church, and of its "censor," says:

"And the same year, since a solemn remission of all sins, to wit, both of guilt and of penalty (*solemnis remissio omnium peccatorum, videlicet culparum et pœnarum*), was granted by Pope Boniface to all who visited Rome, many—both Christians and Tartars—came to Rome for the aforesaid indulgence."—*Id., p. 12. London and Edinburgh: 1925, abridged edition.*

Of the Jubilee of 1450 we read:

"Large sums of money were brought as offerings by the pilgrims, and we learn that money was scarce at this time, because 'it all flowed into Rome for the Jubilee.' . . . Early in the following year the Pope . . . despatched legates to certain foreign countries, to extend the Jubilee indulgence to the faithful who were unable to visit Rome. The conditions usually enjoined were a visit, or series of visits, to the cathedral of the Diocese, and an alms to be offered there for a special intention."—*Id., p. 27.*

During one of these Jubilees, we are told, there were millions in Rome, and the plague that had broken out carried off innumerable victims. Graves were to be seen all along the roads. H. C. Lea declares: "The pilgrim who went to Rome to secure pardon came back much worse than he started." And any one who joined the "crusades" against the Turks or the "heretics" to gain a "plenary indulgence," if he came back alive, "was tolerably sure to return a lawless bandit."—"*The Inquisition of the Middle Ages," Vol. I, pp. 42, 43.*

Pope Alexander VI ordered a Jubilee in 1500, but great as the crowds were who sought the papal indulgence at Rome, there remained a still greater number in the British Isles, "who were prevented from seeking Rome"; and so the pope issued another "Bull dated 9 December 1500," proclaiming a Jubliee in 1501 for Britain. Professor William E. Lunt quotes the following from Polydore Vergil's "Historiæ Anglicæ":

"*A Chronicler's Account of the Sale of Jubilee Indulgences in England.*—It was not gratuitous liberality, for Alexander . . . had decreed what was the price of his grace for providing for the salvation of men."—"*Records of Civilization Sources and Studies," No. XIX, "Papal Revenues In the Middle Ages," Vol. II, p. 477.*

The Reformation

Professor Lunt informs us that this Papal Bull is found in the "British Museum, Cottonian MS, Cleop. E. III, fol. 157V," "as entitled by Gairdner, *Letters and Papers Illustrative of the Reigns of Richard III and Henry VII*, II, 93-100," from which we quote the following:

"The Article of the Bull of the holy Jubilee of full remission and great joy granted to the realm of England, Wales, Ireland, and Garnesey, . . . by granting of great indulgence and remission of sins and trespasses."

Those who "at any time after the publication hereof to the last evensong of the Octaves of Easter next coming, truly confessed and contrite, visit such churches as shall be assigned . . . and there put into the chest for the intent ordained such sum or gratuity of money, gold or silver, as is limited and taxed here following in the last end of this paper, to be spent for the defense of our faith, shall have the same indulgence, pardon, and grace, with remission of all their sins, which they should have had if they had gone personally to Rome in the year of grace." —*Id., pp. 478, 479.*

Then follows the "Tax List":

"Tax that every man shall put into the chest that will receive this great grace of their jubilee.

"First, every man and woman, . . . having lands, tenements, or rents, amounting to the yearly value of £2,000 or above, must pay, or cause to be paid, . . . and effectually, without fraud or deceit, put into the chest . . . lawful money current in that country where they be, £3, 6s. and 8d.*

"Also, every man and woman having tenements and rents to the yearly value of £1,000 or above, to the sum of £2,000 exclusive, must pay for themselves and their wives and children 40s."—*Id., pp. 481, 482.*

This sliding scale goes down to the payment of 12d.

"The Pope . . . granted full authority and power to the venerable father in God, Jasper Powe, his orator and commissary, to absolve [any one who] hath committed simony, . . .

---
* £1 is $4.80, 1s. 24 cents, and 1d. is 2 cents.

with all those that occupy evil gotten goods, all usurers, and all such that wrongfully and unlawfully occupyeth or witholdeth other men's goods, . . . that they may lawfully keep and occupy the same goods, first making composition for the same with said commissary of some certain sum of money to be spent in the foresaid holy use."—*Id., pp. 482, 483.*

Hon. Thomas E. Watson, U. S. Senator from Georgia, writes:

"Claude d'Espence was Rector of the University of Paris in the sixteenth century. He published a 'Commentary on the Epistle to Titus.' He was [a] devoted Roman Catholic and his standing was high in his church. . . . Here is what he wrote and published about the 'Tariff on Sins':

"'Provided money can be extorted, everything prohibited is permitted. There is almost nothing forbidden that is not dispensed with for money. . . . They give permission to priests to have concubines. . . . There is a printed book which has been publicly sold for a considerable time, entitled, 'The Taxes of the Apostolical Chancery,' from which one may learn more enormities and crimes than from all the books of the Summists. And of these crimes, there are some which persons may have liberty to commit for money, while absolution from all of them, after they have been committed, may be bought.'

"In the British Museum are two small volumes which contain the Pope's Chancery Taxes, and his Penitential Taxes. These books—in manuscript bound in vellum—were taken from the archives of Rome, upon the death of Innocent XII. The Prothonotary, Amyon, was the abstractor. One of the booklets bears date, '6 February, 1514': the other '10 March, 1520.' The inscription is '*Mandatum Leonis, Papæ X.,*'—which, freely rendered, means that the compilation of these Taxes was ordered by Pope Leo X."*—"*The Watsonian,*" *October, 1928, Vol. II, No. IX, pp. 275, 276.*

---

* Of these "Tax Tables" forty-seven editions were issued, eighteen at Rome itself. They itemize all classes of sins: "simony," "perjury," "murder," "rape," etc., stating the exact amount of "tax" for "absolution" of each class of crime. See "Spiritual Venality of Rome," Rev. Joseph Mendham, M. A.,."Traffic in Pardons," George Hodson, and "Philosophical Dictionary," Voltaire, Vol. II, pp. 474-478. See also "The Pope and the Council," Dollinger, pp. 351-353.

"POPE COULD EMPTY PURGATORY"

Henry Charles Lea says:

"An enthusiastic Franciscan taught at Tournay, in 1482, that the pope at will could empty purgatory. . . . The same year . . . the church of Saintes, having procured a bull of indulgence from Sixtus IV, announced publicly that, no matter how long a period of punishment had been assigned by divine justice to a soul, it would fly from purgatory to heaven as soon as three sols were paid in its behalf to be expended in repairing the church. . . . The doctrine . . . was pronounced to be unquestionable Catholic truth by the Dominican Silvestro Mozzolino, in his refutation of Luther's Theses, dedicated to Leo X. (F. Silvest. Prieriatis Dialogus, No. 27.) As Silvestro was made general of his order and master of the sacred palace, it is evident that no exceptions to his teaching were taken at Rome. Those who doubt that the abuses of the system were the proximate cause of the Reformation can consult Van Espen, Jur. Eccles. Universi P. II., tit. vii, cap. 3, No. 9-12."—"*History of the Inquisition in the Middle Ages,*" *Vol. I, p. 43, note.*

Some Roman Catholic writers claim that the "taxes" charged in those "Tax Tables" were simply registration fees for the absolutions or pardons granted. If this were true, why are they called "taxes," and why should the registration fee for one man be fifty times as much as for another that had committed the same sin? Or why should registration fees vary so greatly for the different sins?

William Coxe, F. R. S., F. A. S., speaking of the time of Luther, says:

"The sale of indulgences gave rise to the schism of a great part of Europe from the church of Rome.

"Indulgences, in the early ages, were merely a diminution of ecclesiastical penances, at the recommendation of confessors or persons of peculiar sanctity. This license soon degenerated into an abuse, and being made by the popes a pretext for obtaining money, was held forth as an exemption from the pains of purgatory, and afterwards as a plenary pardon for the commission of all sins whatsoever; and this unchristian doctrine* was justified on the principle no less absurd than impious and immoral.

"With a view to replenish the exhausted treasury of the church, Leo X had recourse to the sale of indulgences, an expedient which had been first invented by Urban II, and continued by his successors; Julius II had bestowed indulgences on all who contributed towards building the church of St. Peter, at Rome, and Leo founded his grant on the same pretence. But . . . this scandalous traffic had been warmly opposed in Germany. . . . These indulgences were held forth as pardons for the most enormous crimes; they were publicly put up for sale, and even forced upon the people, and Tetzel and his coadjutors indulged themselves in drunkenness, and every other species of licentiousness, in which they squandered their share of the profits, and not unfrequently produced indulgences as stakes at the gaming table."—"*History of the House of Austria,*" *Vol. I, pp. 384-386.*

Professor Coxe continues in a footnote:

"We subjoin the form of absolution used by Tetzel:

"'May our Lord Jesus Christ have mercy upon thee, and absolve thee by the merits of his most holy passion. And I, by his authority, by that of his blessed apostles, Peter and Paul, and of the most holy pope, granted and committed to me in these parts, do absolve thee, first, from all ecclesiastical censures, in whatever manner they have been incurred; and then from all thy sins, transgressions, and excesses, how enormous soever they may be, even from such as are reserved for the cognizance of the Holy See; and as far as the keys of the holy church extend, I remit to thee all punishment which thou deservest in purgatory on their account; and I restore thee to the holy sacraments of the church, to the unity of the faithful, and to that innocence and purity which thou possessest at baptism; so that when thou diest, the gates of punishment shall be shut, and the gates of the paradise of delight shall be opened; and if thou shalt not die at present, this grace shall remain in full force when thou art at the point of death. In the name of the Father, and of the Son,

---

* The doctrine of the "treasury" containing the surplus of good works.

and of the Holy Ghost,'—*Seckend. Comment Lib. I, p. 14.*"
—*Id., p. 385.*

The author has several photographic reproductions of these "Indulgences." The "Congregation of the Propaganda" at Rome, 1883, published a book called "Il Tesoro dele Sacre Indulgence," which attempts to justify the sale of indulgences by monks at the time of Martin Luther. (Chap. III.)

Dr. William Robertson gives the same facts in the "History of the Reign of the Emperor Charles the Fifth," Vol. I, pp. 460-463, as have been quoted from Dr. Coxe. In a footnote Dr. Robertson adds the following of Tetzel's arguments:

"'The souls confined in purgatory, for whose redemption indulgences are purchased, as soon as the money tinkles in the chest, instantly escape from that place of torment and ascend into heaven. . . . For twelve pence you may redeem the soul of your father out of purgatory; and are you so ungrateful that you will not rescue your parent from torment?'"—*Id., p. 462.*

Turning the Tables on Tetzel

John Dowling, D. D., relates:

"A gentleman of Saxony had heard Tetzel at Leipsic, and was much shocked by his impostures. He went to the monk, and inquired if he was authorized to pardon sins *in intention*, or such as the applicant intended to commit? 'Assuredly,' answered Tetzel; 'I have full power from the Pope to do so.' 'Well,' returned the gentleman, 'I want to take some slight revenge on one of my enemies, without attempting his life. I will pay you ten crowns, if you will give me a letter of indulgence that shall bear me harmless.' Tetzel made some scruples; they struck their bargain for thirty crowns. Shortly after, the monk set out from Leipsic. The gentleman, attended by his servants, laid wait for him in a wood between Juterboch and Treblin,—fell upon him, gave him a beating, and carried off the rich chest of indulgence-money the inquisitor had with him. Tetzel clamored against this act of violence, and brought an action before the judges. But the gentleman showed the letter signed by Tetzel himself, which exempted him beforehand from all responsibility. Duke George who had at first been much irritated at this action, upon seeing this writing, ordered that the accused should be acquitted."—"*History of Romanism,*" *p. 445. New York: 1870.*

Some people finally began to feel that, if the pope could empty purgatory at will, he must be very hard-hearted to leave so many millions in the flames just because the people did not buy sufficient indulgences to free them! Was not the pope more concerned about the souls of his spiritual children in purgatory, than about the building of a magnificent church at Rome? Should not the shepherd be more concerned about his sheep than about their wool? People had begun to break the shackles and think for themselves. A storm was brewing, only waiting for some one to take the lead.

When God's hour strikes, He always has His instruments ready for action. On the 31st of October, 1517, Dr. Martin Luther stepped up to the beautiful Castle Church at Wittenberg, and nailed on its door the ninety-five theses he had written against the sale of indulgences. In two weeks "these propositions were circulated over all Germany. . . . In a month they had made the tour of Europe."—"*History of Protestantism,*" *J. A. Wylie, Vol. I, chap. X, p. 267.* Thus the Reformation began, and it continued till a large part of Europe broke away from the Roman Church; and only by the work of Jesuits were some of these countries brought back to the Roman fold.

We shall now leave it with the reader to decide, whether or not sufficient proof has been given of the corrupt condition of the medieval church to justify a Reformation. When the Church refused to be reformed, turned against the Reformers, and bitterly opposed all attempts to place the Bible in the hands of the common people, then the time had come to separate from her communion, and establish churches where the people would be fed with the word of God, and where there was liberty to obey it.

Finishing the Reformation

THE Reformers of the sixteenth century had done much to bring people back to the primitive Christianity of apostolic times. While they did not live long enough to see their work fully carried through, they had laid a deep and broad foundation for their children to build upon; namely, faith in "the Bible, and the Bible only." They expected their followers to carry their work through to a triumphant conclusion. But after the death of the Reformers, the Jesuits nearly wrecked the work of the Reformation, and some of the Protestant countries formed state churches to protect themselves from utter annihilation.

The popes and the Jesuits worked incessantly in conjunction with the bishops and the heads of the larger Catholic states to force the smaller Protestant countries back under the papal rule. This compelled Protestant princes to make common cause and stand together to save the day, as was the case in the Thirty Years' War.

After the worst storm had blown over, the Protestant churches found themselves under the protection and control of the state. They were no longer free to accept more light, and to progress along the way they originally had started. The state now dictated what they should believe and teach, who should be taken into church fellowship, and who should be their leaders. Their growth was stunted, their spiritual life stifled. Instead of progressing along the line of reform, they retrograded and gave up several of the points of truth held by the Reformers. This was especially true during the period of Rationalism in Europe. But God's work must go on to completion. No human consideration can stop it, and the time has now come for the work of the Reformation to be finished.

It is a remarkable and fascinating study to see how God

offered one religious denomination after another the privilege of carrying the Reformation to a finish, and how they, one by one, rejected God's plan.

The Church of England

God is no respecter of persons; He will use everyone who allows himself to be used by Him. In the seventeenth century He brought the Church of England face to face with the troublesome Sabbath question, but they declined the opportunity of becoming His chosen instrument to complete the Reformation on this and other important points, and many books were written in England to justify this refusal.

"Upon the publication of the 'Book of Sports' in 1618, a violent controversy arose among English divines on two points: first, whether the Sabbath of the fourth commandment was in force among Christians; and, secondly, whether, and on what ground, the first day of the week was entitled to be distinguished and observed as 'the Sabbath.'"—*Haydn's Dictionary of Dates, art. "Sabbatarians," p. 602. New York: Harper Brothers, 1883.*

Leaders of the church found themselves divided into three camps: One party claimed that Sunday is the "Christian Sabbath" and, from the fourth commandment, urged its observance in a Puritanical manner. Another party claimed that there is no Bible proof for the change of the Sabbath from the seventh day of the week to the first, but that Sunday is merely a church ordinance, the same as Christmas and Easter, and that we should obey the ordinances of the church, but without Puritanical rigor. A third, small minority, through this discussion, began to see that the only Sabbath in the New Testament is the one Christ and His apostles kept, and they began to teach and to write in favor of the seventh day (Saturday). Thus the Church of England had its call, and was forced to make its decision.

The Baptist

The English divines who began the observance of the seventh-day Sabbath in London during the seventeenth century, also practiced immersion as baptism, and they are now reckoned as a branch of the Baptists. After some of them had emigrated to the United States, they felt a special call from God during the first half of the nineteenth century to bring the Sabbath truth to their Christian brethren. It seemed as though the time had come for a Sabbath reform; for not only Baptists, but God-fearing men in different denominations, were simultaneously impressed with the importance of the Bible Sabbath, and that, seemingly, independent of one another. Dr. Edward T. Hiscox, author of the "Baptist Manual," says: "There was and is a commandment to keep holy the Sabbath day, but that Sabbath day was not Sunday. It will be said, however, and with some show of triumph, that the Sabbath was transferred from the seventh to the first day of the week, with all its duties, privileges, and sanctions. Earnestly desiring information on this subject, which I have studied for many years, I ask, Where can the record of such a transaction be found? Not in the New Testament, absolutely not. There is no Scriptural evidence of the change of the Sabbath institution from the seventh to the first day of the week."

A series of articles appeared in the organ of the Swedish Baptist church, *Evangelisten* (The Evangelist), Stockholm, May 30 to August 15, 1863. The articles, which appeared as editorials, took a bold stand against the abolition of the Sabbath commandment, and proved the binding claims of the Sabbath, from its institution, and from the teaching of Christ and His apostles. In regard to the abolition of the Sabbath the editor says:

"In opposition to this doctrine we will now endeavor to show that the sanctification of the Sabbath has its foundation and its origin in a law which God at creation itself established for the whole world, and as a consequence thereof is binding on all men in all ages."—*May 30, 1863, p. 169.*

"Thus we find that the Sabbath commandment is placed side by side with the other eternally binding commands, which God has given as a rule and guide for the whole human race.

Therefore, he who will maintain that the Sabbath commandment is only a ceremonial command, and so binding only for a certain time, can with equal right explain all the other of the ten commandments as ceremonial commands, with which we have nothing to do in the new covenant."—*Id., July 31, 1863, p. 235.*

This agitation was not without its effect. Pastor M. A. Sommer began observing the seventh day, and wrote in his church paper, *Indovet Kristendom*, No. 5, 1875, an impressive article about the true Sabbath. In a letter to Elder John G. Matteson, he says:

"Among the Baptists here in Denmark there is great agitation regarding the Sabbath commandment. . . . However, I am probably the only preacher in Denmark, who stands so near to the Adventists, and who for many years has proclaimed Christ's second coming."—"*Advent Tidende," May, 1875, p. 154.*

"The Confession of Faith," which the Danish Baptists received from Hamburg in 1852, contained the following:

"'*Art. 12. Concerning the Law.*—Here is emphasized the absolute and eternal validity of the Jewish law, especially *the ten commandments.* And by this is inculcated the sanctification of the Sabbath (Sunday).' What the brethren, who wrote the Confession of faith had in mind, was the violation of the Lord's day, and they did not realize that they shot over the mark. But when the Adventists came, they took advantage precisely of this article; it was namely an easy matter for them to point out, that 'the Sabbath day' was *Saturday*, and not Sunday. This brought the leading brethren to a real investigation of this matter, and when they met at the Conference in 1878 it had become clear to them . . . that we Christians have nothing to do with the Jewish law, and that we should keep Sunday as a day of rest, because the first Christians did so, and not because of the Sabbath commandment."—"*History of the Danish Baptists," S. Hansen and P. Olsen, pp. 162, 163. Copenhagen: 1896.*

In their new "Handbook" by W. J. Anderson (1903) there is no mention of the Ten Commandments, nor of the moral law. Thus they had made their decision.

Finishing the Reformation 177

On the other hand the American "Baptist Church Manual," by J. Newton Brown, 1853, and the "Star Book" by Dr. Edward Hiscox, both of whom wrote as representatives of Sunday-keeping denominations, have the following statement concerning the moral law, or the Ten Commandments:

"We believe the Scriptures teach that the Law of God is the eternal and unchangeable rule of His moral government; that it is holy, just, and good; and that the inability which the Scriptures ascribe to fallen men to fulfill its precepts, arises entirely from their sinful nature; to deliver them from which, and to restore them through a Mediator to unfeigned obedience to the holy law, is one great end of the gospel, and of the means of grace connected with the establishment of the visible church."
—"*Manual*," *p. 15, and "Star Book," p. 18. Philadelphia: American Baptist Pub. Soc., 1880.*

Thus we see that God, who is no respecter of persons, offered to the different denominations the honor and privilege of finishing the work so nobly begun by the great Protestant Reformers, that of digging up the precious truths of God's Word, which the Papacy had buried beneath it's traditions for so many centuries. Daniel 8:12; 7:25. This effort of God to bring His people back to the whole truth of His Word, will be seen more clearly in the next two chapters.

Sabbath Reform In Scandinavia

THERE were many Sabbath-keepers in Norway even in the days of Catholicism. The Sabbath seems to have been brought to the Scandinavian countries partly by the Waldenses, and partly as a direct work of the Spirit of God. But Rome was no more favorable towards the Sabbath there than in other parts of the world. When the Inquisition of the twelfth century scattered the Waldenses, they were forced to flee to more obscure places and to countries lying on the outskirts of civilization, and as the persecution continued, they gradually drifted into Scandinavia. Then, too, in the "Catechism" that was used during the fourteenth century, the Sabbath commandment read thus: "Thou shalt not forget to keep the seventh day."* We are told by Swedish historians that the Sabbath-keeping public claimed that angels had appeared to them, instructing them to keep the Sabbath on Saturday. Of the church council held at Bergen, Norway, August 22, 1435, we read:

"The first matter concerned a superstitious keeping holy of Saturday. It had come to the ear of the archbishop that people in different places of the kingdom, 'partly from the weakness of nature, partly by the deceptions and promptings of the devil,' had ventured to adopt and keep holydays, which neither God nor the holy Church had ordained or sanctioned, but on the contrary is against the commands of both, 'namely the keeping holy of Saturday, which Jews and heathen used to keep, but not Christians.' It is strictly forbidden—it is stated—in the Church-Law, for any one to keep or to adopt holydays, outside of those which the pope, archbishop, or bishops appoint."— *"The History of the Norwegian Church under Catholicism," R. Keyser, Vol. II, p. 488. Oslo: 1858.*

---
* This is quoted from "Documents and Studies Concerning the History of the Lutheran Catechism in the Nordish Churches," p. 89. Christiania: 1893.

At another church conference, held at Oslo, the next year, the same archbishop commanded:

"It is forbidden under the same penalty to keep Saturday holy by refraining from labor."—*Id., p. 491.*

In another old publication from nearly the same period we find this accusation against the priests:

"Also the priests have caused the people to keep Saturdays as Sundays."—"*Theological Periodicals for the Evangelical Lutheran Church in Norway,*" *Vol. I, p. 184. Oslo: P. T. Mallings, 1871.*

Sabbath-keepers continued to keep the Bible Sabbath in Norway, in spite of persecution, for we read of new laws made against them in 1544:

"I, Christoffer Whitefeldt, [governor] over Bergenhus, Stavanger, and Vaardoem, greet all you peasants kindly and with good wishes, who live in the district of Bergen. Dear friends: Mr. Gieble Pederson, superintendent of the district of Bergen, related to me that some of you have kept Saturday holy, especially at Arendal in Sogen, contrary to the ordinance given you last year by Peter Ottesen, my brother, and Niels Bernsen, who had charge of the palace by my authority, in my absence, in which you have done very wrong, and would receive great damage if I would punish you. But, however, because of the solicitation of Mr. Gieble, the superintendent, I will still forbear with you. But now it has been determined at the public Parliament for these two districts, Bergen and Stavanger, that whoever is found keeping Saturday holy shall be fined ten mark in money. So now ye know what ye have to go by.

"In the next place you are rebellious and disobedient in the Holydays you keep, and are not willing to be satisfied with those which the priest announces which are contained in the ordinance. We now command you in the name of His Majesty, the King, that you solemnly obey the ordinance of His Grace. And whoever disobeys, he shall by my sheriff be punished for his rebellion as a rebellious and disobedient citizen, and be fined ten mark."—"*History of King Christian the Third,*" *Niels Krag and*

S. Stephanius, Vol. II, *"Statutes and Ordinances,"* p. *379.* Copenhagen: 1778.

IN SWEDEN AND FINLAND

Sabbath-keepers were also scattered over Sweden and Finland. Bishop L. A. Anjou says that there was a peaceful but continued movement on foot in these two countries for the keeping of the seventh-day Sabbath, "one that required the sanctification of Saturday as Sabbath day. The first known origin of this goes back to the middle of the preceding century, when King Gustav I, in the year 1554, wrote a letter of warning to Finland against those who alleged that they through visions and dreams had come to the conviction that famine, etc., were God's punishments because people did not keep Saturday holy. In the beginning of the seventeenth century the same faith was found in Sweden, and even there it was founded on alleged revelations. It was zealously opposed in 1602 by Charles IX."— *"Swedish Church History from the Meeting at Upsala, Year 1593,"* p. *353.* Stockholm: 1866.

"Segregated from any movements opposed to the church, we must consider those who kept Saturday holy, and on this day abstained from labor, but otherwise did not separate themselves from the church. We do not find that those who held this view . . . observed any other Jewish habits or customs. . . . Had this movement been connected with anything that could be considered apostasy from Christianity, then without doubt the accusations against it would have been stronger and the laws more stringent.

"Independent of older influences, the inculcation of Sabbath-keeping could easily bring up the question of keeping Saturday holy, by questioning whether the Sabbath law had any validity if it was not applied to the Sabbath day previously appointed in the Old Testament. . . . The customary reading of the Bible, and the appeal to the law of God . . . could attract the attention to the commandment which required Saturday to be kept holy."—*Id.,* p. *355.*

"This keeping of Saturday holy did not stand alone, at least in most cases, but was part of the Pietism [pious worship] of that age, and was connected with sermons on repentance and warnings against prevailing sins and vices."—*Id., p. 355.*

Theodore Norlin, another important Swedish Church historian, says of these Sabbath-keepers:

"We can trace these opinions over almost the whole extent of Sweden of that day—from Finland and northern Sweden, Dalarne, Westmanland, Nerike, down to West-Gotland and Smaland.

"In the district of Upsala the farmers kept Saturday in place of Sunday. . . . At several places they pressed their requests so vehemently upon the priests, that they yielded to their wishes to the extent of beginning to hold services on Saturday. At the time of Gustaf Adolphus we see this peculiar faith arising at different places in the country.

"About the year 1625 . . . in West-Gotland, Smaland, and Nerike, revelations and visions of angels were related in which the necessity of keeping Saturday holy was strictly commanded, and in which warnings were given against the sins that were secretly practiced. This religious tendency became so pronounced in these countries, that not only large numbers of the common people began to keep Saturday as the rest day, but even many priests did the same, which gave occasion for no small schism."—"*History of the Swedish Church," Vol. I, part 2, chap. 3, p. 256.*

But the enemy of souls could not endure this revival of primitive Christianity, and Sabbath-keeping in Sweden and Finland was finally suppressed. But when the work of the Holy Spirit was suppressed in these Scandinavian churches, the same dire fruit of spiritual declension was seen, as formerly in the apostolic church. Whenever the warning voices are hushed up, spiritual darkness sets in. Dr. Scharling, Lutheran Professor of Theology, says:

"Luther's great work of Reformation was still far from having been accomplished, it was followed by a continual retrogression, a deeper sinking of the religious consciousness, until it at last reached its zero point in Ritualism. . . . Little by little the Evangelical church becomes chilled, . '. . and it takes on an unpleasant similarity to the Romish church."—"*Menneskehad og Kristendom,*" *Vol. 2, p. 248.*

A church in a lukewarm condition does not usually concern itself with spiritual reforms. But in the early part of the nineteenth century, when the great spiritual revival passed over almost every country, and affected nearly all denominations, Sabbath reform came to the front again, and deeply impressed the honest in heart. We find leading men in different denominations reaching out to find Bible proof for the change of the Sabbath, and when this could not be found, they either accepted the Bible Sabbath, or gave up their former faith in the immutability of the Ten Commandments.

THE LUTHERAN CHURCH IN AMERICA

Pastor A. C. Preus, in an article in *Kirkelig Maanedstidende* [Monthly Church Tidings], of August, 1855, endeavored to quiet an agitation on the Sabbath question that had arisen in Wisconsin, by claiming that the Sabbath commandment simply required the keeping of one day in seven. He wrote:

"It is a moral law, founded on a moral necessity, that a rest day must be appointed; . . . but it is ceremony, resting on outward occasion of circumstances, whether one day or another is established.

"We know that 'the law is a lamp and the commandment a light,' and woe be to us if we would 'abolish' even one of the least commandments and 'teach men so.' But the law, the unchangeable moral law, which proceeds from the nature of God, says nothing about which day. The third [fourth] commandment simply reads thus: 'Remember that thou keep holy the rest day,' it does not say the seventh day!"*—*Kirkelig Maanedstidende, August, 1855, pp. 94-97. Inmansville, Wis.*

---

* The Catholic Church dropped the second commandment out of their catechism, and the Lutherans followed the same numbering, making the Sabbath command the third. In the Lutheran catechism it reads as Pastor Preus here quotes it, and not as given in Exodus 20: 1-17.

A few Lutheran ministers saw in this article a direct blow against the sanctity of Sunday, others took exception to the claim that the Sabbath commandment is binding on us. The struggle that ensued is spoken of in their book on "The Jubilee of the Norwegian Synod, 1853-1903;" in the following statement: "The struggle which began against the sects outside of the Lutheran Church thus soon became a controversy with those who had false ideas within the Lutheran Church itself, a controversy which was kept up till well towards the eighties, when it gradually died away, because other points of dispute arrested the attention."—"*Festskrift,*" *p. 239. Decorah, Iowa: 1903.*

During this long controversy much was written in their official organ, *Kirkelig Maanedstidende* [Monthly Church Tidings], in *Emigranten,* and in their *Synodical Reports,* especially from 1863 to 1866, and discussions continued in their "Synods." The one side held to the "Explanation of Luther's Catechism" (Oslo, 1905), which says that the ceremonial law was abolished at the cross, but that "the moral law, which is contained in the Ten Commandments, . . . is still in force, . . . because, it is founded on God's holy and righteous nature, and hence is immutable as God Himself."—*Pp. 5, 6.*

The other party said:

"Either the words in the 3rd [4th] commandment regarding the seventh day on which God rested are binding on us, and then we must and shall keep Saturday, or, if these words are not in force for us, then we have nothing to do with any definite day, or any day whatever. . . . We notice that the 3rd [4th] commandment does not speak of one day in seven, or a seventh day, but only and solely of the seventh day, that is Saturday. As long as they will acknowledge this, which every honest Christian with common sound judgment certainly must, and they also acknowledge that the New Testament nowhere institutes or commands any other day, or says that one day in seven shall be taken in its place, then it also must be acknowledged that there is no word in Scripture to sustain the assertion that one day in seven is a moral command."—"*Record of the First Extraordinary*

Synod of the Norwegian-Evangelical-Lutheran Church in America," held at Holden, Minnesota, reported in Kirkelig Mannedstidende [Monthly Church Tidings], Aug. 1, 1862, p. 232.

"To say, that the commandment regarding outward rest (Exodus 20: 10, 11) [refers to one day in seven] is only arbitrary misrepresentation and falsification of God's word, for it does not say 'every seventh,' but 'the seventh day, on which God rested,' and that, every one knows, was Saturday. If therefore this commandment concerning outward rest for man and beast is in force as a moral command for us Christians, then we must rest on Saturday, as that is the only day on which such rest was commanded."—*Id., April 1, 1862, p. 99.*

Having called attention to the fact that the fourth commandment enjoins observance of the definite seventh day (Saturday) they then referred to Romans 14 and Colossians 2 as proof that the Sabbath was abolished. But those who held that the moral law is still in force, answered:

"In regard to the places, Romans 14 and Colossians 2, these refer . . . to the appointed days of the Old Testament, which the contents in the whole chapter show. . . . By 'Sabbaths' is not to be understood the weekly Sabbath, which, before Moses, yea already at Creation, was instituted [Genesis 2], but [they refer] to other feasts, which have been types of Christ, and ceased at Christ's coming."—*Id., September, 1863, pp. 271, 272.*

The other side answered:

"Sunday, no doubt, had sacred memories, but so had the day of Christ's death and the day of His ascension, without Friday and Thursday thereby becoming appointed days for weekly meetings, and even if Sunday had the most glorious memories, there would not be in that the least obligation to keep it. . . . After all, examples prove nothing, they only illustrate what has already been proved. And here it actually is incumbent on those who would make Sunday-keeping a divine ordinance to show us a definite command of God for it."—*Id., September, 1863, pp. 261, 262.*

The former, in their review, quoted Matthew 5: 17-19 and James 2:10, 11, and declared:

"If it is so dangerous to offend on one commandment, what must it be then to wholly throw away one commandment? . . . God has distinctly commanded that every tittle in His law is to be kept. And how it will fare with those who take away from, or add anything to, God's word we can read in Revelation. [The writer then referred to the fate of the priests of Baal in 1 Kings 18.]"—*Id., April, 1866, p. 103.*

We recognize that this was an argument in which two groups of Sunday-keepers were engaged, and in which each in his own way was trying to present reasons for the observance of the first day of the week. But in fact, the truths brought to light by this close study of the question prove that the fourth commandment enjoins the careful observance, not of one day in seven, but of the seventh day of the week in particular, that the Sabbath was instituted at creation, that while the ceremonial feasts, which were types of Christ, ceased at the cross, the seventh-day Sabbath did not pass away at that time, that there is no definite command in Scripture for Sunday observance, and that those who attempt to remove a jot or a tittle from the holy law of God by substituting the first day of the week for the seventh day fall under the curse of Revelation 22: 19.

IN NORWAY

The controversy in America had its counterpart in Norway and Denmark. At the "Ecclesiastical Association in Christiania [Oslo]," February 8-10, 1854, and at the "Theological Association of the Deans of Drammen," held August 15, 1854, the Sabbath question was the great subject for discussion. At first some seemed to think only of the proper observance of Sunday, but the question soon arose, how the sacredness of the Sabbath could be transferred from the seventh to the first day of the week. Pastor Kaurin thought it could, but Pastor W. A. Wexels declared that this could not be done, for "God Himself cannot transfer the reason for sanctifying the seventh day (God's rest at creation) to another day. Besides this we have no certainty of any transference of the day."—"*Theologisk Tidsskrift for den*

Norske Kirke," Vol. VI, pp. 629, 630. Oslo: P. T. Mallings, 1855.

Some of the speakers felt that the only way to get around this troublesome question was to teach that the Sabbath commandment was abolished, but "Dean Lange found it incomprehensible that any one who knew the sermon on the mount [Matthew 5] could urge the abolition of the Sabbath commandment."—*Id., p. 533.* And Wexels pointed out that the Sabbath commandment forms such an integral part of the moral law that what was said against one command affected the whole law. But he felt that as Christ had "finished" His work on the cross Friday evening, and rested on the Sabbath, "the Christians have [thus an appeal] on Saturday to live in . . . the memory *of the Lord's own rest* after His work on earth was finished, and of the Sabbath rest. . . . If these sacred Sabbath-memories, considered as the common property of the church, should seek an expression in a united outward service on Saturday, it would be entirely becoming."—*Id., pp. 608, 609.*

During these long debates one cannot but see a carefully worded attempt to return to the only Bible Sabbath, but who had the courage of a staunch reformer, daring to stand out alone on Bible truths?

Dean Fr. Schiorn, of Oslo, says:

"It has been claimed, that the relation of Jesus to the Sabbath commandment was one of protest against the continued validity of this command in the New Testament. On the whole it may be safely considered that the effort to remove the Decalogue as the unchangeable rule of divine authority can be traced principally to the fact that they want to blot out the Sabbath commandment. They can, of course, see, that it is impossible to take this one commandment out of the series of commandments as long as they acknowledge the other nine binding and obligatory. The Ten Commandments form such a definite circumscribed unity that they must stand or fall together. So they would sooner let all fall than to let the third [fourth] commandment remain standing."—"*Relation of the New Testament to the Old Testament Legislation," p. 11. Oslo: 1894.*

"It is clear also that this commandment belongs to the divine law for the church. It has always been a mystery to me, why many have such a living interest in getting this commandment blotted from the Decalogue. That the enemies of Christianity want the Sabbath day, or its divine validity, removed, that I can naturally understand. But why living Christians, zealous workers in the church, want it removed, that I cannot understand."—*Id., p. 12.*

"Has Jesus anywhere expressed Himself against the Sabbath commandment or the continuance of its validity? Has He ever violated it, or advised His disciples to violate it? Never! He has combated the misuse of the Sabbath commandment by the Pharisees in the same way that He combated their misuse of prayer, fasting, tithing, almsgiving, etc., that is, all self-righteous piety by works, all spiritless use of the Sabbath, but never the Sabbath commandment itself. . . . He says (Mark 2: 27): 'The Sabbath was made for man.' . . . God gave man —not only the Jews—the Sabbath . . . and He has protected this His gift by a definite command, which has its continued validity for the new covenant people as well as for the people of the old covenant, because their need and circumstances are essentially the same.

"When it is said that the third [fourth] commandment does not obligate the church, because Jesus has not imposed on us any Sabbath commandment, then this is to me very strange and incomprehensible talk. The commandment was already given in the law, which Jesus would not abolish, but fulfill. It was therefore a piece of superfluity for Jesus to give a Sabbath command. He, as Lord of the Sabbath, has caused His church to retain it, for which His church owes Him the very greatest thanks."— *Id., pp. 14, 15.*

On the other hand Pastor L. Dahle declared:

"The third [fourth] commandment is abolished for us Christians, and has no more as a command any binding claim.

"It is a false imagination, if any one thinks he obeys the third [fourth] commandment in the law of Moses by keeping holy the first day (Sunday) instead of the seventh; for the commandment does not at all speak of one day in seven, but of the seventh day of the week. If therefore the commandment continued to be in force, then without doubt, were the Jews and the Adventists right, when they say that if we will obey God's command, we must keep Saturday holy. There cannot be the least doubt about this. Every attempt to explain away this fact will and must fail.

"It is therefore only an imagination that we keep holy our Sunday according to the requirements of the third [fourth] commandment.

"Consequently it is an established fact, that if the third [fourth] commandment is still in force, then we must acknowledge the Adventists to be right, and begin to keep Saturday holy. If we are unwilling to do this, we must prove from the word of God that the Sabbath commandment is abolished in the New Testament and is no more binding on us Christians."—*"The Adventists, Sabbath, and Sunday," pp. 23, 24. Stavanger: 1903.*

Pastor K. A. Dachsel says, significantly:

"For this reason many godly Christians have solemnly upbraided the Christian church for keeping Sunday instead of Saturday: it [the church] can have no right to change God's commandment, and if in the catechism the whole commandment had been embodied verbatim from Exodus 20: 8-11, as has been done in the Heidelberg Catechism, then we should still keep Saturday holy, and not Sunday."—*"Edifying Instruction in the Catechism," p. 24. Bergen: 1887.*

Thus we see how the truth was forced upon the minds of leading churchmen by this prolonged discussion, and all were given the opportunity to make their choice. But, as is always the case, no one wishes to step out alone, they wait for all to step out in a body, a thing which has never occurred during the whole history of the world. God's work is an individual matter, not a mass movement.

In the discussion carried on in Denmark, Bishop Skat Rordam and Dr. Fr. Nielson took the same stand as Pastor L.

Dahle in Norway, and "The Norwegian Synod" in America, that the Sabbath commandment was abolished, but that the church keeps Sunday as a proper church regulation. (See Bishop Rordam's remarks on p. 108.)

On the other side stood Dean C. O. C. E. Krogh; Pastors John Clausen, Wilh. Beck, I. Vahl, P. Krag, A. G. Fich, and I. S. D. Branth, who declared that we have not nine, but ten commandments. "And the Ten Commandments are God's commandments for all men in all ages. It is that law which Christ would not destroy, but fulfill, and the Sabbath commandment is a part of it," declared Dean I. Vahl. Pastor P. Krag said:

"When Paul in the letter to the Colossians speaks about the law being abolished by Christ, he refers to the middle wall that separated Jews and Gentiles, the law of Moses. The Ten Commandments, in which Moses had no part, were given by God's own voice, and this God wrote with His own hand as an evidence that they should be in force for all times."—"*Report of the Second Church Meeting in Copenhagen," Sept. 13-15, 1887, P. Taaning, pp. 68, 69. Copenhagen: 1887.*

The reports of these discussions are very interesting and illuminating, but our limited space does not permit us to quote further. This, however, is sufficient to show how God led one by one of the leading denominations to investigate the Sabbath truth, and offered them the grand privilege of carrying the Reformation to completion. If they had accepted the Sabbath truth, He would have led them on step by step till they had reached the divine standard of the apostolic faith. Many of the truths of God's word, which the Roman church, during the Dark Ages, had buried beneath the rubbish of human tradition, still lay untouched, as costly jewels beneath the sand of centuries. These must be dug up, so that the "remnant" church could stand forth in its apostolic purity, possessing the complete "faith which was once delivered to the saints"; for those who shall meet the Lord in peace, when He comes in glory, must "keep the commandments of God, and the faith of Jesus." Jude 3; Revelation 12: 17; 14: 12.

The Taiping Revolution

WHILE the advent message was just beginning in America, there was a most remarkable movement going on in the heart of China. A heathen Chinese, without any acquaintance with Christianity, had, in 1837, a series of remarkable visions, in which he was shown the principal points in the Christian religion. In his visions Hung-sui-tshuen was first taken to a river, where the celestial visitors said to him: "Why hast thou kept company with yonder people and defiled thyself?" He was then washed clean, his heart was taken out, and a new heart was given him. (How could a heathen be given a better idea of conversion and baptism?) He was then brought in before "a man, venerable in years," "sitting in an imposing attitude upon the highest place," whom he called "Our Heavenly Father." He also "met with a man of middle age," whom he called "our Celestial Elder Brother."

"Sui-tshuen's whole person became gradually changed, both in character and appearance. He was careful in his conduct, friendly and open in his demeanor."

When Sui-tshuen, in his visions, was brought in before "Our Heavenly Father" he was shown the sinfulness of idolatry. God "began to shed tears, and said, 'All human beings in the whole world are produced and sustained by Me; they eat My food and wear My clothing,'" but they have no "'heart to remember and venerate Me'"; "'they take of My gifts and therewith worship demons.'" "And thereupon he led Sui-tshuen out, told him to look down from above, and said, 'Behold the people upon the earth! Hundredfold is the perverseness of their souls.' Sui-tshuen looked, and saw such a degree of depravity and vice that his eyes could not endure the sight, nor his mouth express their deeds." He was then told to go and rescue his brethren and sisters from the demons, and was given "a seal, by which he would overcome the evil spirits," and our "Elder Brother" "instructed him how to act," and "accompanied him upon his wanderings." When "he woke from his trance" he started on his God-given work.

Before this Hung had received from a stranger on the street nine small books, which he had not read. Now he started to read them, and was joined by his cousin Le. The books contained some chapters from the Bible which presented the same picture of God and Christianity that he had seen in his visions. "Sui-tshuen felt as if awakening from a long dream. He rejoiced in reality to have found a way to heaven, and a sure hope of everlasting life." He and Le then baptized each other. They prayed to God, and decided to obey His commands, and then felt their hearts overflowing with joy. "They thereupon cast away their idols and removed the table of Confucius." Through their earnestness and joy in the new-found salvation, many were soon won, and in answer to prayer the power of God was manifested among them in healing the sick. They had also the "gift of prophecy" among them.

"At this time, Hung prohibited the use of opium, and even tobacco, and all intoxicating drinks, and the Sabbath was religiously observed."—*"The Ti-Ping Revolution," by Lin-Le, an officer among them, Vol. I, pp. 36-48, 84. London: 1866.*

"The seventh day is most religiously and strictly observed. The Taiping Sabbath is kept upon our Saturday." The Sabbath is ushered in with prayer, and "two other services are held. . . . Each service opens with the Doxology:

"We praise thee, O God, our Heavenly Father;
　We praise thee, Jesus, the Saviour of the world;
　We praise the Holy Spirit."

—*Id., p. 319.*

When the Manchu government made war on the followers of Hung, they organized their own government, and millions of Chinese gladly flocked to their standard, because of the kindness and strict justice of their government. During the wars, their soldiers were not allowed to drink the water nor eat the food of the conquered without paying for them, and no crime was committed by them, under death penalty. The Taipings printed the Bible and spread it among their people, and the Ten Commandments were strictly followed.

In 1862 there were 85,000 converted Sabbath-keeping Christians among them, besides more than 45,000,000 others who gladly yielded themselves under their government, but were not accepted as church members. Their territory covered 90,000 square miles in the heart of China, and liquor, tobacco, opium, and idols were totally banished from its whole extent. Had the Christian nations kept out of the struggle, China today might have been a Sabbath-keeping Christian country. But two influences conspired against the Taipings, or God-worshipers, as they were called: 1. English opium-traders became alarmed about the probable destruction of opium and the loss of the millions they earned annually in the opium trade in China. 2. The Taipings did not understand the difference between the images of saints, used by the French Jesuits in their worship and the idols used by the heathen Manchus, so the Taipings opposed them indiscriminately, which aroused the ire of the Jesuits, and finally Christian countries assisted in completely destroying the Taipings. Lin-Le, heart-sickened at the thought of this "cruel sacrifice of the greatest Christian movement this world has ever witnessed," exclaims:

"What excuse can missionaries give for their surprising negligence of . . . the 70,000,000, and upwards, of those who might have become Christians under the Taiping authority during 1861-1862."—*Id., pp. 310, 312.*

The terrible massacre of the Taipings was so heart-rending that we must not describe it here, but will refer the reader to the description of it given by H. L. Hastings, in his book: "Signs of the Times," pages 149-151. We can see in this another evidence of the vigilant spirit that eagerly watches and determinedly opposes every effort to wrest souls out of his grasp, or to bring the true knowledge of God to mankind. (Revelation 12: 17.)

The Two Mysteries

THE Bible speaks of two mysteries: "the mystery of godliness," and "the mystery of iniquity." 1 Timothy 3: 16; 2 Thessalonians 2: 7. Seeing that these two mysteries are fundamental principles of two opposing powers, each claiming the sole sovereignty over the souls of men, and requiring man's unconditional surrender and obedience, the study of these two mysteries becomes both important and interesting.

The Mystery of Godliness

Ever since the fall, man's nature has been inclined toward evil; and while he still has the power of choice, he cannot in his own strength break with sin, change his nature, or live a godly life. The Bible declares: "Can the Ethiopian change his skin, or the leopard his spots? Then may ye also do good, that are accustomed to do evil." Jeremiah 13: 23. Yea, "he shall be holden with the cords of his sins." Proverbs 5: 22. The Apostle Paul realized this when in his struggle against the evil of his nature he cried out: "The good that I would I do not: but the evil which I would not, that I do. . . . O wretched man that I am! Who shall deliver me from the body of this death?" Romans 7: 19, 24.

There is only one who can deliver man from sin, and He is abundantly able and always willing to do it. "Thou shalt call His name JESUS: for He shall save His people from their sins," and His gospel is "the power of God unto salvation to every one that believeth." Matthew 1: 21; Romans 1: 16. Here is abundant power available to all who will believe and accept it, so that there is no excuse for continuing in known sin. And sin brings us no happiness, for it always carries with it a trail of woe. God's Father-heart of infinite love has been wrung with anguish for the sufferings of man, and He has settled it that sin with its terrible consequences shall never be permitted to enter His eternal kingdom; therefore our only hope of entering heaven is to part company with evil.

But as man cannot in his own strength rid himself of sin, his only hope is to let Christ take charge of his life. When Christ dwells in our hearts by His Holy Spirit, He changes our aspirations, our likes, and our dislikes. Sinful habits, which we in vain have tried to break, fall off as the leaves of autumn, and we receive the power of His love to conquer sin and live a happy Christian life. (John 15: 5; Romans 8: 10-13.) And while Christ would gladly do this work for everyone, for He wants "all men to be saved," yet He will not use force to accomplish it, but is patiently standing at the door of every heart asking permission to come in and supply the needed power to conquer sin. (1 Timothy 2: 3, 4; Revelation 3: 20.) Sad to say, most people refuse Him admittance. "But as many as received Him, to them gave He power to become the sons of God, even to them that believe on His name." John 1: 12.

Here, then, is the secret of victory in Christian life: "the mystery of godliness," "which is Christ in you, the hope of glory." 1 Timothy 3: 16; Colossians 1: 27. Then we are not left alone in our struggles, for He works in us "mightily" (v. 29), but He always wants our co-operation: "Work out your own salvation with fear and trembling. For it is God which worketh in you both to will and to do of His good pleasure." Philippians 2: 12, 13. By this co-operation of the human and the divine such marvelous changes are wrought in human lives and such Christlike character is developed that angels marvel at it, and even worldlings are forced to recognize in the change from sin to godliness a mysterious power with which they are unacquainted.

The life of Jesus on earth was a living demonstration of this mystery. He combined in His own person both the human and the divine natures. "And without controversy great is the mystery of godliness: God was manifest in the flesh." 1 Timothy 3: 16.

The Two Mysteries

THE MYSTERY OF INIQUITY

It is evident that the "mystery of iniquity" is a counterfeit of the "mystery of godliness," or in other words, some human substitution for the divine plan of salvation, in which man would take the place of Christ, and human efforts would be substituted for the divine presence in the soul. And this is exactly what the Apostle Paul declared it to be, when he foretold that there would "come a falling away" of the apostolic church, and that in this fallen church there would arise "that man of sin, . . . who opposeth and exalteth *himself* above all that is called God, or that is worshiped; so that he as God sitteth in the temple of God, showing himself that he is God. . . . For the mystery of iniquity doth already work." 2 Thessalonians 2: 3-7. Speaking to the church he further says: "Ye are the temple of God." 1 Corinthians 3: 16, 17. This prophecy plainly shows that after the "falling away" of the early church some "man" would attempt to take Christ's place in the church, which is God's temple, or dwelling place.

The fulfillment of this prophecy is so clearly seen in the history of the Papacy that God's people have always recognized it whenever they have been spiritually awake. Every well-read person knows that the early Christian church fell away from its apostolic purity and corrupted its doctrines by adopting heathen customs, baptizing them with Christian names, so that the church entirely changed its face within four hundred years after the apostles' death. The "mysteries of Mithras" were substituted for the "mystery of godliness"; "the sacrifice of the mass" took the place of the sacrifice made on the cross; righteousness gained by self-torture and human efforts took the place of Christ's righteousness received by simple faith in Jesus as a personal Saviour; receiving a sacramental Christ by eating the wafer took the place of an indwelling Christ received by faith in God's promises; a multitude of human mediators were substituted for Christ, the "one mediator between God and man." 1 Timothy 2: 5. We shall enter more fully into the details of this in the following chapters.

The Antichrist

Defining the Name Antichrist

HE name "antichrist" is found in only three chapters of the Bible, and in every instance it was emphatically stated that he was already in the world. We read:
"Ye have heard that antichrist shall come, even now are there many antichrists. . . . Who is a liar but he that denieth that Jesus is the Christ? He is antichrist, that denieth the Father and the Son." 1 John 2: 18, 22. "This is that spirit of antichrist, whereof ye have heard that it should come; and even now already is it in the world." 1 John 4: 3. "For many deceivers are entered into the world, who confess not that Jesus Christ is come in the flesh. This is a deceiver and an antichrist." 2 John 7. How can anyone, in the light of these plain texts, say that the antichrist here spoken of is not yet come, when the very texts declare that he is here already?

These texts also reveal the fact that the apostle did not believe antichrist to be only one individual, but rather an antichristian tendency in the church: an organization dominated by "the spirit of antichrist," having a man at its head, so that when he died another would take his place, and the antichristian system would continue. Thus there would be "many antichrists," as the apostle says, but only *one* system; and this system had already made such progress before the apostle died, that it was about to capture the church. Its leader would not accept the Apostle John, one leader "forbiddeth them that would, and casteth them out of the church." 3 John 9, 10. This accounts for the warnings in John's epistles against these "many antichrists." 1 John 2: 18.

The Apostle Paul, during his last journey among the churches, gathered "the elders," or bishops, and warned them against the coming apostasy of the church, which was to be brought about

The Antichrist

by its leaders. He says: "For I know this, that after my departing shall grievous wolves enter in among you, not sparing the flock. Also *of your own selves* shall men arise, speaking perverse things, to draw away disciples *after them.*" Acts 20: 29, 30. Later the apostle reminded the believers, that the day of Christ's return was not then at hand: "For that day shall not come, except there come a *falling away* first, and that man of sin be revealed, the son of perdition; who opposeth and exalteth himself above all that is called God, or that is worshiped; so that he as God sitteth in the temple of God [the church, 1 Corinthians 3: 10, 16], showing himself that he is God. Remember ye not, that, when I was yet with you, I told you these things? . . . For the mystery of iniquity doth already work." 2 Thessalonians 2: 3-7.

These prophecies point out clearly that the "elders" (later called bishops) would "draw away" the people from the truth of the Bible, to follow men, and that this "falling away," which had "already" begun in Paul's day, would develop, until a "man" would exalt himself to take the place of Christ in the church. Every thoughtful student of prophecy can see that this points unmistakably to the Papacy, and it accords exactly with the significance of the name "antichrist."

Dr. James Strong says that "antichrist" comes from two Greek words, *antee* and *khristos*, and gives the following definition of *antee:* "Opposite, i.e. instead or because of, . . . for, in the room of. Often used in composition to denote . . . substitution."—*Exhaustive Concordance, Greek Dictionary, entries Nos. 500, 473.* Thomas Sheldon Green says: "*Anti*, prep, over against; hence, in correspondence to; in place of . . ."—*Greek-English Lexicon, p. 14. Boston: 1896.* The meaning, therefore, of "antichrist," as it is used in the New Testament, is a *rival* to Christ, or one who attempts to take the place of Christ as His "vicar." This significance of the prefix "anti" is also seen in the word "anti-pope." (For further information on this point see "The Papacy Is Antichrist," by J. A. Wylie, pp. 2-18. Edinburgh: George M'Gibbon.) We shall now see that this is exactly the position which Catholics claim for the pope, that he holds the place of Christ on earth. Rev. T. L. Kinkead says:

"Our Holy Father the Pope, the Bishop of Rome, is the vicar of Christ on earth and the visible head of the Church."

"'Vicar'—that is, one who holds another's place and acts in his name."—"*Explanation of the Baltimore Catechism,*" *p. 130. Benziger Brothers.* (*Sanctioned by Cardinal Gibbons, five archbishops, nineteen bishops, and other dignitaries.*)

Rev. William Humphrey, S. J., says:

"A vicar is put in the place of him whom he represents. He is invested with his power, he is furnished with his authority. . . . He personates his principal. . . . The master, by his appointment of a vicar, binds himself to ratify his vicar's acts, and to recognize them as his own."—"*The Vicar of Christ,*" *p. 4. New York: Benziger Brothers, 1892.*

Thomas Morell, D. D., and Prof. John Carey, LL.D., says:

"Vicarius, a, um. adj. That is in stead, or place of another; that supplies another's room; a deputy. . . . One who performs the office, or duty, of another; a deputy, a substitute."—*An Abridgement of Ainsworth's Latin Dictionary, Designed for the Use of Schools, p. 604. London: 1826.*

When the force of this similarity between the antichrist of prophecy and the pope of Rome dawned upon the mind of Cardinal Newman, he declared:

"The gibe, 'If the Pope is not Antichrist, he has had bad luck to be so like him,' is really another argument in favour of the claims of the Pope; since Antichrist simulates Christ, and the Pope is an image of Christ, Antichrist must have some similarity to the Pope, if the latter be the true Vicar of Christ."—*Catholic Encyclopedia, Vol. I, p. 561, art. "Antichrist."*

Thus it is claimed that the pope is the vicar of Christ on earth. But Christ left an altogether different Vicar, or Representative, in His place; namely, the Holy Spirit. (John 14: 15-18; 16: 7.) Of this Representative Christ says: "He shall teach you all things." "He will guide you into all truth." John 14: 26; 16: 13. (Compare 1 John 2: 20, 27.) The Holy Spirit,

being the author of the Bible (2 Peter 1: 21), certainly should be the proper interpreter of it. To this the Roman church answers:
"Nor can it be said that being a divinely inspired book, its prime Author, the Holy Spirit, will guide the reader to the right meaning.
"The Church which made the Bible, likewise interprets the Bible."—"*Things Catholics Are Asked About,*" *Martin J. Scott, S. J., Litt. D., pp. 119, 120. N. Y.: Kenedy, 1927.*

Pope Leo XIII says:
"But the supreme teacher in the Church is the Roman Pontiff. Union of minds, therefore, requires, together with a perfect accord in the one faith, complete submission and obedience of will to the Church and to the Roman Pontiff, as to God Himself."—"*The Great Encyclical Letters of Pope Leo XIII,*" *p. 193. New York: Benziger Bros., 1903.* He further says:
"We hold upon this earth the place of God Almighty."—*Id., p. 304.*

We have now seen from authentic Catholic sources, that the pope arrogates to himself the "place of God Almighty," the office of Christ on earth, and the prerogative of the Holy Spirit, as sole teacher of the faithful, and the interpreter of the Holy Scriptures. What more is needed to fulfill the prediction of 2 Thessalonians 2: 3, 4, and the prophecies of the Antichrist?

All Agreed on Antichrist

Up to the close of the Reformation God's people were generally agreed that the Papacy was the Antichrist foretold in prophecy. The Waldenses taught it. (See page 122.) About 1384 A. D. John Wycliffe wrote a book against the papal system entitled: "Of Antecrist and His Meynee." In fact, the English Reformers,—Tyndale, Cranmer, Latimer, and Ridley,—all agreed in pointing to the Papacy as the Antichrist. John Huss of Bohemia, in his "De Anatomia Antichristi," did the same. Turning to Germany we find Dr. Martin Luther strong in his convictions on this subject. He says:

"The Pope is . . . the true Antichrist, of whom it is written, that he sitteth in the temple of God, among the people where Christ is worshiped. . . .

"But Papists want to divert this passage from themselves, and they say that Christ and Paul speak about the temple at Jerusalem, and that Antichrist shall sit there and rule; that will not do. . . . It cannot be understood otherwise than of the new spiritual temple, which he says we are.

"There shall the Pope sit and be honored, not above God, but above all that is called God. . . . So also we see it before our eyes, that many princes and the world regard his law higher and more than the commandments of God. . . . Cannot this rightly be termed exalting and honoring Antichrist above God?"—*"Luther's Church Postil," "Gospels," 25th Sunday after Trinity, par. 24, 25, Part 2, pp. 734, 735. Stavanger, Norway: 1862.*

Luther further declares:

"Therefore, let whosoever will doubt, God's word and the proper divine worship convinces me sufficiently that the Pope is the Antichrist, and the ecclesiastical orders are his disciples, which deceive the whole world."—*Id., Part 1, p. 379.*

"I hope that the last day is at the door. Things could not become worse than the Roman see makes it. It suppresses the commandments of God, it exalts its own commandments above God's. If this is not Antichrist, then some one else must tell what it is."—*"Luther's Reformatory Works," p. 280. Copenhagen: 1883.*

"The Pope is the real Antichrist."—*Id., p. 278.*

Dr. Charles H. H. Wright, in speaking of the Bible prophecy of "antichrist," says:

"In all ages of the Church, from the days of Gregory the Great down to the present, men have pointed to the Papacy as the fulfillment of the prophecy. That interpretation is set forth in the Homilies of the Church of England and by all the Reformed Churches. The interpretation, however, has been ignored or rejected by critics, for reasons which need not be specified. It can, however, stand all the tests of criticism."—

"*Daniel and His Prophecies,*" p. 168. London: 1906. (*See also Catholic Encyclopedia,* Vol. I, p. 561, art. "*Antichrist.*")

Jesuits Undermine the Truth

The Rev. Joseph Tanner, B. A., says:

"So great hold did the conviction that the Papacy was the Antichrist gain upon the minds of men, that Rome at last saw she must bestir herself, and try, by putting forth other systems of interpretation, to counteract the identification of the Papacy with the Antichrist.

"Accordingly, towards the close of the century of the Reformation, two of her most learned doctors set themselves to the task, each endeavouring by different means to accomplish the same end; namely, that of diverting men's minds from perceiving the fulfilment of the prophecies of the Antichrist in the papal system. The Jesuit Alcasar devoted himself to bring into prominence the *Preterist* method of interpretation, . . . that the prophecies of Antichrist were fulfilled before the Popes ever ruled at Rome, and therefore could not apply to the Papacy. On the other hand the Jesuit Ribera tried to set aside the application of these prophecies to the papal power by bringing out the *Futurist* system, which asserts that these prophecies refer properly not to the career of the Papacy, but to that of some future supernatural individual, who is yet to appear, and to continue in power for three and a half years. Thus, as Alford says, the Jesuit Ribera, about A. D. 1580, may be regarded as the Founder of the Futurist system in modern times.

"It is a matter for deep regret that those who hold and advocate the Futurist system at the present day, Protestants as they are for the most part, are thus really playing into the hands of Rome, and helping to screen the Papacy from detection as the Antichrist. It has been well said that 'Futurism tends to obliterate the brand put by the Holy Spirit upon popery.' More especially is this to be deplored at a time when the papal Antichrist seems to make an expiring effort to regain his former hold on men's minds. Now once again, as at the Reformation, it

is especially necessary that his true character should be recognized, by all who would be faithful to 'the testimony of Jesus.'"
—"*Daniel and the Revelation,*" *pp. 16, 17. London: Hodder and Stoughton, 1898.*

To undermine the work of the Reformers, these Jesuits, Alcasar and Ribera, gathered a mass of material from the writings of the Church Fathers concerning Antichrist. This gave their works the appearance of scientific research, which appealed to many Protestant leaders. (An example of this can be seen in Encyclopædia Biblica, art. "Antichrist.") But statements from the Church Fathers which speak of the coming of Antichrist as an event *then* in the future, could be no proof for Ribera's "futurist" theory, for the reign of the papal Antichrist was then still in the future. The 1260 years of papal persecution, called the Dark Ages, had not yet begun when these Fathers wrote. The theories of Ribera and Alcasar were diametrically opposed to each other, and yet both were taught as Catholic truths, taken from the Church Fathers. From this we see how untrustworthy are these sources. Dr. Adam Clarke is evidently right when he says of the Fathers:

"We may safely state, that there is not a *truth* in the most orthodox creed, that cannot be proven by their authority; nor a *heresy* that has disgraced the Romish Church that may not challenge them as its abetters. In points of *doctrine*, their authority is, *with me*, nothing. The Word of God alone contains my creed."—*Commentary on Proverbs 8.*

Bible Prophecy of Antichrist Is Plain

The prophecies of the Bible regarding Antichrist are so plain that even Roman Catholics cannot evade them all. The seventh chapter of Daniel foretells the rise of four world empires, which the Douay Bible explains to be "the Chaldean, Persian, Grecian, and Roman empires." The Roman Empire was broken up into ten smaller kingdoms between the years 351 and 476 A. D. And among them there should grow up another power, symbolized by a "little horn." Of this the Douay Bible says: "*Another little horn.* This is commonly understood of Antichrist." Daniel 7: 7, 8. The Papacy is the only power that came up just at that time, and which fits all the specifications of the symbol.

We have seen on page 195 how clearly the Papacy is pointed out in 2 Thessalonians 2: 3-7. This prophecy states that the apostolic church would be gradually "falling away" until a "man" would exalt himself to take the place of God in the church. This "mystery of iniquity" was already at work in Paul's day, but something was holding it back. (Vs. 6, 7.) As long as the Roman Empire was heathen, and persecuted the Christians, there was no incentive to join the church for worldly gain; but during the time of Constantine the church became popular, and the worldly ambitious struggled for the highest ecclesiastical offices, because of the great honor and emolument connected with them; and when finally the Roman State was abolished, the bishop of Rome seated himself upon the throne of the Cæsars. It was therefore heathen Rome that had to "be taken out of the way," before the papal Antichrist could come into power. Speaking of this point the Catholic Encyclopedia says: "The impediment is the Roman Empire; the main event impeded is the 'man of sin.'"—*Vol. I, p. 560, art. "Antichrist."*

The Douay Bible says: "The Roman Empire, . . . was first to be destroyed, before the coming of Antichrist."—*Note on 2 Thessalonians 2: 3.*

Two Points Made Clear

There were two arguments used against the position taken by the Reformers which have puzzled many:

(1) It was claimed that the Apostle John used two distinctions: "*an* Antichrist" to designate the false teachers of his day, and "*the* Antichrist," referring to some superhuman monster of Jewish extraction that would appear just before Christ's second coming. But on this point Dr. C. H. H. Wright truthfully remarks: "St. John, the only New Testament writer who employs the term, makes no distinction whatever between 'an Anti-

christ' and 'the Antichrist.' That distinction was in the main an invention of the learned Jesuit interpreters."—"*Daniel and His Prophecies,*" *p. 165. London: 1906.*

(2) The second objection was that while "the Antichrist" would deny the incarnation, for he would deny that "Christ is come in the flesh" (2 John 7), the pope does not deny this, therefore he cannot be the Antichrist. This argument has seemed so logical and conclusive that Protestants, to a large extent, have given up the Protestant doctrine that the Papacy is Antichrist, and have ceased to *protest.*

This argument, however, is based on a misunderstanding, caused by overlooking one word in the text. Antichrist was not to deny that Christ had come in flesh, but was to deny that He had "come in *the* flesh," in "*the same*" kind of flesh, as the human race He came to save. (See 1 John 4:3; 2 John 7, and Hebrews 2:14, 17.) On this vital difference hinges the real "truth of the gospel." Did Christ come *all the way down* to make contact with the fallen race, or only part way, so that we must have saints, popes, and priests intercede for us with a Christ who is removed too far from fallen humanity and its needs to make *direct contact with the individual sinner?* Right here lies the great divide that parts Protestantism from Roman Catholicism. In order to understand this point clearly, let us briefly consider the gospel of Christ.

THE GOSPEL OF CHRIST VERSUS THE GOSPEL OF ROME

Through sin man has separated himself from God, and his fallen nature is opposed to the divine will; therefore he cannot by his own effort live a godly life, nor can he change his own heart. (Isaiah 59:1; Romans 8:7; Jeremiah 13:23; John 15:5.) Only through Christ, our Mediator, can man be rescued from sin, and again be brought into connection with the source of purity and power.

But in order to become such a connecting link Christ had to partake both of the divinity of God and of the humanity of man, so that He with His divine arm could encircle God, and with His

The Antichrist

human arm embrace man, thus connecting both in His own person. In this union of the human with the divine lies the "mystery" of the gospel, the secret of power to lift man from his degradation. "Great is the mystery of godliness: *God* was manifest in *the* flesh." 1 Timothy 3: 16. The "mystery," or secret of power to live a godly life in *human* flesh, was manifest in the life of Jesus Christ while on earth. (And "Christ in you" is the secret of power to conquer sin. Colossians 1: 27.)

But mark! It was fallen man that was to be rescued from sin. And to make contact with him Christ had to condescend to take *our* nature upon Himself (not some higher kind of flesh). "Forasmuch then as the children are partakers of flesh and blood, *He also Himself likewise took part of the same.* . . . Wherefore in *all* things it behooved Him to be made like unto His brethren." Hebrews 2: 14, 17. This text is so worded that it cannot be misunderstood. Christ "took part of the *same*" flesh and blood as ours; He came in "*the*" flesh. To deny this is the mark of Anti-Christ. (1 John 4: 3; 2 John 7.) To bridge the gulf that sin has made, Christ must be one with the Father in divinity, and one with man in humanity, and thus connect again earth with heaven.

God revealed this truth to the Patriarch Jacob that lonely night at Bethel. When he feared that his sins had cut him off from heaven, God showed him that mystic Ladder, connecting earth with heaven, which Christ explained to be "the Son of man." (Genesis 28: 12; John 1: 51.) Modernism has tried to cut off the upper part of this ladder by denying Christ's divinity; while the Roman Catholic Church cuts off the lower rounds by teaching that the Virgin Mary was born without sin, and that therefore Christ did not take upon Himself our kind of flesh and blood, but holy flesh, so far above us that He does not make contact with our humanity. For this reason the poor sinner cannot come to Him directly, they say, but must come through Mary, saints, popes, and priests, who will mediate for him. This has opened the floodgate for all the idolatry of the Catholic

Church. Here is this "dogma" presented in authentic Catholic works:

"'We define that the Blessed Virgin Mary in the first moment of her conception . . . was preserved free from every taint of original sin.'

"Unlike the rest of the children of Adam, the soul of Mary was never subject to sin."—*"Faith of Our Fathers," Cardinal Gibbons, pp. 203, 204. Baltimore: 1885.*

The Sainted Doctor Alphonsus de Liguori says:

"The merits of Jesus, shall be dispensed through the hands and by the intercession of Mary."—*"Glories of Mary," p. 180, New Revised Edition. New York: P. J. Kenedy and Sons, 1888.*

"God has chosen to bestow no grace upon us but by the hands of Mary."—*Id., p. 180.*

"Whoever asks and wishes to obtain graces without the intercession of Mary, attempts to fly without wings."—*Id., p. 189.*

"Mary is all the hope of our salvation."—*Id., p. 195.*

"Thou art the only advocate of sinners."—*Id., p. 129.*

"All those who are saved, are saved solely by means of this divine mother; . . . the salvation of all depends upon preaching Mary."—*Id., pp. 19, 20.*

"We ask many things of God and do not obtain them; we ask them from Mary and obtain them."—*Id., p. 150.* Much more could be cited.

A Protestant may ask if the merits of Christ's sacrifice on the cross are not sufficient, so that we can receive grace directly from Him. To this the Catholic Church answers:

"The merits and virtue of the sacrifice of the cross are infinite; but that virtue and these merits must be applied, and this can only be done by certain means."—*"Doctrinal Catechism," S. Keenan, p. 129. New York: Kenedy and Sons, 1846.*

"The priest has the power of the keys, or the power of delivering sinners from hell, of making them worthy of paradise, and of changing them from the slaves of Satan into the children of God. And God himself is obliged to abide by the judgment of His priests. . . . 'The Sovereign Master of the universe only follows the servant by confirming in heaven all that the latter decides upon earth.'"—"*Dignity and Duties of the Priest,*" St. Alphonsus de Liguori, pp. 27, 28. New York: Benziger Brothers, 1888.

We now have before us the only means of salvation in the Roman Catholic gospel, as presented by men of unquestionable authority among them. This throws light on the reason why the Catholic priest has such a hold on his people. They dare not oppose him, because he represents their only means of contact with heaven. Cut off from the church, they feel they are lost; for they do not know of a Christ who has come all the way down to the lost sinner's side, to whom they can come personally and receive forgiveness through grace alone. The divine ladder has been cut off, and Mary, saints, and priests have been substituted. But the Bible knows of only "one Mediator," Jesus Christ. (1 Timothy 2: 5; Psalm 49: 7, 8.)

But we have not yet gone to the depth of this substitute "mystery." Let us now take the next step. Having removed the living Christ from contact with the sinner, they had to substitute something else to satisfy the longing of the human heart for the indwelling presence of Christ. And that substitute is the "Sacrifice of the Mass." The Roman church teaches that the priest in the mass changes the little wafer into the real Christ, which they then fall down and worship, after which they eat Him, believing that they become partakers of Christ and receive the forgiveness of sin. Thus they have substituted a man-made Christ for a living Christ. Liguori says:

"If the person of the Redeemer had not yet been in the world, the priest, by pronouncing the words of consecration, would produce this great person of a Man-God. 'O wonderful dignity of the priests,' cries out St. Augustine; 'in their hands, as in the womb of the Blessed Virgin, the Son of God becomes incarnate.' Hence priests are called the parents of Jesus Christ. . . .

"Thus the priest may, in a certain manner, be called the creator of his Creator. . . . 'He that created me without me is Himself created by me!'"—"*Dignity and Duties of the Priest,*" pp. 32, 33.

"In obedience to the words of his priests—*Hoc est Corpus Meum*—God himself descends on the altar, . . . he comes wherever they call him, and as often as they call him, and places himself in their hands. . . . They may, if they wish, shut him up in the tabernacle; . . . they may, if they choose, eat his flesh, and give him for the food of others."—*Id., pp. 26, 27.*

Then priest and people worship the Christ thus created:
"Elevating a particle of the Blessed Sacrament, and turning towards the people, he [the priest] says: 'Behold the Lamb of God, behold Him who taketh away the sins of the world.'

"And then says three times: Lord, I am not worthy that Thou shouldst enter under my roof; but only say the word, and my soul shall be healed. . . .

"This pure and holy Sacrament. Who livest and reignest forever and ever. Amen."—"*The Key of Heaven,*" *Right Rev. J. Milner, D. D., approved by Cardinal Gibbons, pp. 126, 127. Baltimore: J. Murphy and Co., 1898.*

In the following quotation the Catholic Church explains why she believes this worship of the wafer (host) is not idolatry:

"Now turn for a moment to the Catholic altar. The holy Sacrifice of the Mass is being offered up. The bell has given the signal that the most solemn and awful moment of consecration is at hand. As yet there is only bread in the hand of the priest, and wine in the chalice before him. To worship these lifeless elements would be the grossest idolatry. But suddenly, amid the silence of the breathless multitude, the priest utters the divine life-giving words of consecration; and that which was bread and wine, is bread and wine no longer, but the true Body and Blood of our Lord Himself. It is that same Body that was born of the Blessed Virgin Mary, that died for us upon the cross, that was raised again to life, and that even now sits at the right hand of God the Father. . . .

"Now in this mystery the power of the creation appears as much as in the mystery of the incarnation."—"*The Holy Mass: The Sacrifice for the Living and the Dead.*" *M. Muller, pp. 174, 175. New York: 1876.*

Pastor Charles Chiniquy, a former Catholic priest, says: "No words can give any idea of the pleasure I used to feel when alone, prostrated before the Christ I had made at the morning mass, I poured out my heart at His feet. . . . I may say with truth, that the happiest hours I ever had, during the long years of darkness into which the Church of Rome had plunged me, were the hours I passed in adoring the Christ whom I had made with my own lips. . . .

"In fact, the Roman Catholics have no other Saviour to whom they can betake themselves than the one made by the consecration of the wafer. He is the only Saviour who is not angry with them, and who does not require the mediation of virgins and saints to appease His wrath."—"*Fifty Years in the Church of Rome*," *chapter 17, pars. 29, 31.*

In the thirty-sixth chapter of his book Pastor Chiniquy tells how he was led to question seriously this worship of Rome's wafer-god, the "host." "In the spring of 1840 . . . Father Daule [an old, blind priest, was residing with him at Beauport, Quebec.] One morning when the old priest was at the altar, saying his mass, [and had just changed the wafer into the real Christ, and was reaching for it, it was gone. He called to Chiniquy] with a shriek of distress: 'The Good God has disappeared from the altar. He is lost!' [Chiniquy, remembering how often rats had tried to get the wafer while he himself had officiated there, knew what had happened, and in his consternation replied:] 'Some rats have dragged and eaten the Good God!' [The sorrow of the old priest knew no bounds, but Chiniquy declared:] 'If I were God Almighty, and a miserable rat would come to eat me, I would surely strike him dead.'"—*Id., chapter 36, pars. 7, 13, 24.*

But Catholics deny that the Papacy is Antichrist, for, say they, Antichrist is to come in the last days. To this we answer: It is true that both Paul and John speak of the activity of Antichrist at the time of Christ's second coming, but they also speak of its already having begun in their day. (1 John

2:18; 2 Thessalonians 2:7.) There is a beautiful harmony in this when we look at it in the light of Revelation 13:3, 5, 10 and 17:8, where it is stated that this power will continue forty-two prophetic months, or twelve hundred sixty literal years, after which it is "wounded to death" and lies dormant for a time, till its deadly wound is healed, and all the world will again follow it in wonder and admiration, and finally it will be destroyed at Christ's second coming. So the Antichrist of the last days is simply the Papacy restored to power. See "Romanism and the Reformation," by H. Grattan Guinness, F. R. G. S., and "The Papacy," by Dr. J. A. Wylie.

"The Romanists themselves shame you in their clear-sighted comprehension of the issues of this question. Cardinal Manning says, '*The Catholic Church is either the masterpiece of Satan or the kingdom of the Son of God.*' Cardinal Newman says, '*A sacerdotal order is historically the essence of the Church of Rome; if not divinely appointed, it is doctrinally the essence of antichrist.*' In both these statements the issue is clear, and it is the same. Rome herself admits, openly admits, that *if she is not the very kingdom of Christ, she is that of antichrist.* Rome declares she is *one* or *the other.* She herself propounds and urges this solemn alternative. You shrink from it, do you? *I accept it.* Conscience constrains me. History compels me. *The past, the awful past, rises before me.* I see THE GREAT APOSTASY, I see the desolation of Christendom, I see the smoking ruins, I see the reign of monsters; I see those *vice-gods*, that Gregory VII, that Innocent III, that Boniface VIII, that Alexander VI, that Gregory XIII, that Pius IX; I see their long succession, I hear their insufferable blasphemies, I see their abominable lives; I see them worshiped by blinded generations, bestowing hollow benedictions, bartering lying indulgences, creating a paganized Christianity; I see their liveried slaves, their shaven priests, their celibate confessors; I see the infamous confessional, the ruined women, the murdered innocents; I hear the lying absolutions, the dying groans; I hear the cries of the victims; I hear the anathemas, the curses, the thunders of the interdicts; I see the racks, the dungeons, the stakes; I see that inhuman Inquisition, those fires of Smithfield, those butcheries of St. Bartholomew, that Spanish Armada, those unspeakable dragonnades, that endless train of wars, that dreadful multitude of massacres. *I see it all, and in the name of the ruin it has wrought in the Church and in the world*, in the name of the truth it has denied, the temple it has defiled, the God it has blasphemed, the souls it has destroyed; in the name of the millions it has deluded, the millions it has slaughtered, the millions it has damned; with holy confessors, with noble reformers, with innumerable martyrs, with the saints of ages, *I denounce it as the masterpiece of Satan, as the body and soul and essence of antichrist.*"—"*Romanism and the Reformation*," H. Grattan Guinness, pp. 158, 159. London: 1891.

The Time of the End

THE book of prophecy was to be closed up and sealed till "the time of the end." "But thou, O Daniel, shut up the words, and seal the book, even to the time of the end: many shall run to and fro, and knowledge shall be increased." Daniel 12: 4. The question was then asked: "How long shall it be?" And the answer was given: "It shall be for a time, times, and an half; and when he shall have accomplished to scatter the power of the holy people, all these things shall be finished." V. 6, 7.

We have seen (pp. 52-60) that the "time, times, and an half," during which the papacy should scatter God's true followers, began in 538 A. D., and ended in 1798 A. D. And as "the time of the end" begins when this period "shall be finished." it is plain that "the time of the end" began in 1798 A. D. And at that time "many shall *run* to and fro, and knowledge shall be increased." Daniel 12: 4. And it is remarkable how knowledge has been increased since 1798, not only in the prophecies, but also in general, as we shall presently see. But we must answer one question first. Some ask why God wanted to give important prophecies, and then keep them sealed up for so many centuries. There is a reason.

The prophecies give solemn warnings against the papal power. If these prophecies had been fully understood during the Dark Ages, when the Roman Catholic Church burned all books she thought were damaging to her, those prophecies would have suffered the same fate. Therefore God spoke in symbolic language, and placed the keys to those symbols where they would not be found till the Papacy lost its power, when God would impress the minds of His people where to find the keys. No one who locks his house will leave the key in the door, but he puts it where only members of his family know where to find it. Just

The Time of the End

so the Lord did with His prophecies. (The keys to prophetic symbols are given on page 34.) When these prophecies were to be opened at "the time of the end," their message would have to go quickly to earth's remotest bounds. (Revelation 14: 6, 7; Romans 9: 28.) And as this could never have been accomplished without the modern printing press, and the more speedy means of travel and communication, the Lord set in motion those spurs in the human breast that led to new discoveries. During the 1260 years of papal supremacy, people did not dare to think freely, or independently of the lines of education established by the Church. (See p. 127.) Galileo's trial by the Inquisition in 1623 will serve as an example of how advancement in science and invention was opposed by the church of Rome. But when in 1798 the Papacy lost its power, its downfall broke the shackles, and unloosed the world's genius, so that invention followed invention in quick succession.

Table of Inventions

1. Gas for lighting purposes - - - - - 1798
2. Cast-iron plows - - - - - 1800
3. Steel pens for writing - - - - - 1803
4. First locomotive - - - - - 1804
5. First steamboat - - - - - - 1808
6. Steam printing press - - - - - 1811
7. Passenger cars for trains - - - - - 1825
8. Kerosene for lighting purposes - - - 1825
9. Matches - - - - - - - 1829
10. Mowing machine, reaper - - - - 1833
11. First electric motor - - - - - 1834
12. Telegraph - - - - - - - 1837
    First message: "What hath God wrought!" - 1844
13. Photography - - - - - - 1839
14. Submarine telegraph cable - - - - 1851
15. Typewriter - - - - - - 1868
16. Telephone - - - - - - - 1876
17. Phonograph - - - - - - 1877

18. Electric railway - - - - - - 1879
19. Linotype - - - - - - - 1885
20. Automobile - - - - - - - 1893
21. Wireless telegraphy - - - - - 1895
22. Aeroplane, first successful flight - - - 1903
23. Radio broadcasting - - - - - 1921
24. Television - - - - - - - 1926
25. Pushbutton elevator - - - - - 1934
26. Airplane bombsight - - - - - 1940

Prophecy had decreed that in the day of God's preparation for finishing His work on earth, "knowledge shall be increased"; and when His hour struck for the giving of His last warning message, nothing could stop it. We read: "The chariots shall be with flaming *torches* in the day of His *preparation*. . . . The chariots shall *rage* in the streets, they shall justle one against another in the *broad ways:* they shall seem like torches, they shall run like the lightnings." Nahum 2: 3, 4.

How could any one give a better description of modern railroads and automobiles? Even the coming of the Zeppelin and the airplane is foretold in the Bible: "Who are these that fly as a cloud, and as the doves to their windows?" Isaiah 60: 8. The simile is striking, for doves and airplanes both need landing places. This prophecy speaks of a time when "darkness shall cover the earth, and gross darkness the people," while God's glorious light is shining upon His faithful servants. (Verses 1, 2.) This was never more true than now. The book of prophecy, that had been closed for centuries, is now opened to God's people. (Daniel 12: 4, 10; Revelation 5: 1-9; 10: 1, 2, 8-11; 22: 6, 7, 16.) Light is now shining from the throne of God upon *them*, while evolution, infidelity, spiritism, and Roman Catholic superstitions are enveloping the world in the grossest of spiritual darkness, and crime is at its high tide. Thinking people are everywhere scanning the horizon to detect some prophetic message from heaven that will cast light on the present chaos.

William T. Ellis, in an article entitled, "Why Don't the

Churches Settle Things?" which appeared in the *Saturday Evening Post*, of February 12, 1921, points out this fact in a striking manner. He says:

"There never before was a greater interest in religion in America than today—or a smaller interest in the churches. This is the paradox of our times. . . .

"Ever since the war began, the country has been listening for a clear trumpet note from some prophet of the living God. In vain." He then speaks of "the church's reproach of having failed in her prophetic function." After relating the concern of two business men on this point he says:

"That incident brings me squarely up against one of the most uncomfortable, perplexing and tragic situations in connection with this entire theme of the strange spiritual stirrings of the race today. Many clergymen seem scarcely aware of what is going forward beneath the surface of life. Many experts upon religion, who are the ministers of the gospel, have seemingly failed to hear 'the sound of a going in the tops of the mulberry trees.' Otherwise we should find them gathering with agony of soul in protracted sessions of prayer. . . .

"Morbid minds could easily persuade themselves that there is a present visitation of blindness upon the teachers of religion."

D. L. Moody says:

"If God did not mean to have us study the prophecies, He would not have put them into the Bible. . . . About one third of the Bible is prophetical. . . .

"The return of the Lord to this earth is taught in the New Testament as clearly as any other doctrine in it. . . . Whoever neglects this has only a mutilated gospel. . . . Yet I was in the church fifteen or sixteen years before I ever heard a sermon on it. . . . I can see a reason for this; *the Devil does not want us to see this truth,* for nothing would wake up the church so much. The moment a man realizes that Jesus Christ is coming back again to receive His followers to Himself, this world loses its hold upon him."—"*The Second Coming of Christ,*" *pp. 17, 18*

A Message for Our Times

GOD knows the future, and He has a set "time there for every purpose and for every work." (Acts 15: 18; Ecclesiastes 3: 1, 17.) He has also pledged Himself to "do nothing" that vitally concerns this world "but He revealeth His secret unto His servants the prophets" beforehand (John 15: 14, 15; Psalm 25: 14; Amos 3: 7), and then He holds His servants responsible for warning the world (Ezekiel 33: 1-8). They are watchmen on the walls of Zion, who should be able to read the signs on God's prophetic clock, so they can tell the time and give the warning at the hour of crisis (Isaiah 21: 11, 12; 2 Peter 1: 19; Romans 13: 11; Matthew 16: 2, 3); and when God's hour strikes, He has His agencies in readiness to carry His message to the world.

Before the world was destroyed by the Flood, Noah warned the people for one hundred twenty years (Genesis 6: 3-13, 22; 2 Peter 2: 5); before the destruction of Sodom, Lot gave the warning message to that wicked city (Genesis 19: 12-14); and before Christ's first coming, John the Baptist heralded the coming of the Messiah (Luke 1: 13-17). Then why should not so important an event as Christ's second coming be given proper notice, and a warning message be sent to prepare the world for its final destruction?

It is true that the world in general has never received favorably any of God's warning messages in former ages, and Christ declares that His final warning will not be heeded any more than His warnings sent through Noah and Lot. (Luke 17: 26-30.) Yet the message must be given though there are but few who receive it. Here is Christ's message for our days:

"I Jesus have sent Mine angel to testify unto you these things in the churches." Revelation 22: 16. "Behold, I come quickly: blessed is he that keepeth the sayings of the prophecy

A Message for Our Times

of this book." V. 7. Here we see that the message to be given just before Christ's second coming is found in the "book" of Revelation. This is specifically given in chapter 14, verses 6-14. Here is presented "the everlasting gospel," connected with the warning that "the hour of His judgment is come," and an appeal for a return to the loyal worship of the Creator, combined with a warning against the worship of the "beast and his image," and against taking "his mark." Those who receive this message are characterized by the fact that they "keep the commandments of God, and the faith of Jesus." Revelation 14: 6-13. The very next scene is the Son of man coming on the cloud to reap the harvest of the earth, and "the harvest is the end of the world." Verses 14-16 and Matthew 13: 39.

The people who give this message to the world must therefore know what is meant by "the beast," "his image," and "his mark." This we find clearly presented in Revelation 13. Let us study this chapter.

The Beast with Ten Horns

John "saw a beast rise up out of the sea, having seven heads and ten horns, and upon his horns ten crowns." Revelation 13: 1. The fact that it had "ten horns," the same as the fourth beast of Daniel 7: 7, 23, 24, identifies it as a Roman power (see pages 34, 35). The next question to settle will be whether this is Rome in its pagan or its papal state. The ten horns represent the ten European kingdoms into which the Roman Empire was divided between A. D. 351 and 476. On this beast the horns are crowned (Revelation 13: 1), showing that the empire had been divided, and the rulers of those ten kingdoms were already crowned. (Compare Revelation 12: 3.) But the Roman Empire became Christianized (Catholic) long before it was divided. The beast of Revelation 13: 1-10 therefore represents papal Rome.

The dragon with ten horns (Revelation 12: 3), which represents pagan Rome, gave to the beast "his power, and his *seat*, and great authority." Revelation 13: 2. The "seat" of the

Roman Empire was the city of Rome. How was this given to the Papacy? Francis P. C. Hays (Roman Catholic) says:

"When the Roman Empire became Christian, and the peace of the Church was guaranteed, the Emperor left Rome to the Pope, to be the seat of the authority of the Vicar of Christ, who should reign there independent of all human authority, to the consummation of ages, to the end of time."—"*Papal Rights and Privileges,*" *pp. 13, 14. London: R. Washbourne, 1889.*

Alexander C. Flick, Ph. D., Litt. D., says:

"The removal of the capital of the empire from Rome to Constantinople in 330, left the Western Church practically free from imperial power, to develop its own form of organization. The Bishop of Rome, in the seat of the Cæsars, was now the greatest man in the West, and was soon forced to become the political as well as the spiritual head."—"*The Rise of the Mediæval Church,*" *p. 168.*

"And meekly stepping to the throne of Cæsar, the vicar of Christ took up the scepter to which the emperors and kings of Europe were to bow in reverence through so many ages."— *Rev. James P. Conroy, in "American Catholic Quarterly Review," April, 1911.*

But let us consider the other marks used by the Holy Spirit to point out this power. It cannot be a local government, confined to a certain country, for "all that dwell upon the earth shall worship him." Revelation 13: 8. And it must be a religious, rather than a civil, power; for it concerns itself with the "worship" of the people. V. 4, 8. "There was given unto him a mouth speaking great things," and he was "to make war with the saints, and to overcome them" (Revelation 13: 5, 7), just as the "little horn" of Daniel 7: 8, 21, 25. (See pp. 34-48.) All this could apply to no other power than the Papacy.

The Number 666

The Scripture gives us still another earmark of this power. We read: "Here is wisdom. Let him that hath understanding count the number of the beast: for it is the number of a man;

A Message for Our Times

and his number is Six hundred threescore and six." "The number of his name." Revelation 13: 17, 18. The note below the eighteenth verse in the Douay, or Catholic, Bible says: "Six hundred sixty-six. The numeral letters of his name shall make up this number."

CATHOLIC AUTHORITIES

In our examination of this subject we shall first consult Roman Catholic authorities to ascertain what sacred title they apply to the pope to denote his official position and authority. Any one at all familiar with authentic Catholic authors knows that their paramount and constant claim for the pope is that Christ appointed St. Peter to be His vicar, or representative on earth, and that each succeeding pope is the lawful successor of St. Peter, and is therefore the "*Vicar of the Son of God*" on earth. This official title in Latin (the official language of the Catholic Church) is "*Vicarius Filii Dei.*" We find this title used officially in Roman Catholic canon law, from medieval times down to the present. In the earliest collection of canon law we read:

"*Beatus Petrus in terris Vicarius Filii Dei videtur esse constitutus.*"—"*Decretum Gratiani,*" *prima pars, dist. xcvi.* Translated into English this would read: "Blessed Peter is seen to have been constituted vicar of the Son of God on the earth."— "*Decretum of Gratian,*" *part 1, div. 96, column 472, first published at Bologna about 1148, and reprinted in 1555. Translation by Christopher B. Coleman, Ph. D., in "The Treatise of Lorenzo Valla on the Donation of Constantine," p. 13. New Haven: Yale University Press, 1922.*

The Catholic Encyclopedia says of Gratian: "He is the true founder of the science of canon law."—*Vol. VI, art.* "*Gratian,*" *p. 730.*

The same Catholic authority says: "The 'Decretum' of Gratian was considered in the middle of the twelfth century as a *corpus juris canonici,* i.e. a code of the ecclesiastical law then in force."—*Id., Vol. IV, art.* "*Decretals,*" *p. 671.*

It further states: "It must be admitted that the work of Gratian was as near perfection as was then possible. For that reason it was adopted at Bologna, and soon elsewhere, as the textbook for the study of canon law. . . . While lecturing on Gratian's work, the canonists labored to complete and elaborate the master's teaching."—*Id., Vol. IX*, art. "*Law, Canon*," pars. "*D*" and "*E*," *p. 62*.

Different popes added their own decrees to the collection of Gratian, as the following quotation will show:

"Thus by degrees the *Corpus Juris Canonici* took shape. This became the official code of canon law for Western Europe during the Middle Ages, and was composed of six books, namely, the *Decretum* of Gratian (about 1150), the *Decretals* of Gregory IX (1234), the *Sextus* of Boniface VIII (1298), the *Clementines* of Clement V (1313), the *Extravagantes* of John XXII (about 1316), and the *Extravagantes Communes*, which contained laws made by succeeding popes."—"*The Papacy*," *Rev. C. Lattey, S. J., page 143. Cambridge, England: 1924.*

After the Council of Trent, Pope Pius V had this "Canon Law" revised.

"Pius V appointed (1566) a commission to prepare a new edition of the 'Corpus Juris Canonici.' This commission devoted itself especially to the correction of the text of the 'Decree' of Gratian and of its gloss. Gregory XIII ('Cum pro munere,' 1 July, 1580; 'Emendationem,' 2 June, 1582) decreed that no change was to be made in the revised text. This edition of the 'Corpus' appeared at Rome in 1582, *in œdibus populi Romani*, and serves as examplar for all subsequent editions."—*Catholic Encyclopedia, Vol. IV*, art. "*Corpus Juris Cononici*," *pp. 392, 393.* It was reprinted verbatim in 1613 and 1622.

This is the standard text of canon law for the whole Roman Catholic Church. Pope Gregory XIII wrote July 1, 1580, in his preface to this corrected edition:

"We have demanded care in rejecting, correcting, and expurgating. . . . The Decree itself, without the glossæ, exists now entirely freed from faults and corrected, . . . as much the

A Message for Our Times

one without the glossæ as the entire one with the glossæ . . . all recognized and approved . . . this body of canonical law firmly grounded and incorrupted according to this model printed at Rome by Catholic typographers. . . . We wishing to proceed opportunely, so that this canonical law thus expurgated, may come restored to all the faithful . . . kept perpetually *integrid* and incorruptible, *motu proprio*, and from our certain knowledge, and from the plenitude of the apostolic power to all and singly in the dominion of our sacred Roman Church."—*Preface to Corpus Juris Canonici, Gregorii XIII, Pontif. Max. Auctoritate; in editions of 1582, 1613, 1622, and 1879.*

Of this corrected "Corpus," or canon law, "published in 1582 . . . by order of Gregory XIII," and established by his authority, we read:

"The text of this edition, revised by the *Correctores Romani*, a pontifical commission established for the revision of the text of the 'Corpus Juris,' has the force of law."—*Catholic Encyclopedia, Vol. IV, art. "Decretals, Papal," p. 672, par. 3.*

Notice that this revised edition of canon law "has the force of law." In this canon law, which Pope Gregory XIII had corrected by "the *plenitude of the apostolic power*," so that it is "entirely freed from faults," we find the same statement: "*Beatus Petrus in terris vicarius Filii Dei esse videtur constitutus.*"—"*Corpus Juris Canonici, Gregorii XIII, Pontif. Max. Auctoritate,*" *Distinctio 96, Column 286, Canon Constantinus 14, Magdeburg, 1747.*

"Moreover, custom has even given to several apocryphal canons of the 'Decree' of Gratian the force of law."—*Catholic Encyclopedia, Vol. IV, art. "Corpus Juris Cononici," p. 393.*

In "*Corpus Juris Canonici Emendatum et Notis Illustratum Gregorii XIII. Pont. Max.*," "*Lvgdvn, MDCXXII*," or "the Canon Law of Pope Gregory XIII, of 1622," with the Pope's own "Preface," in which he assures us of its being without flaw, we find the same: "*Beatus Petrus in terris Vicarius Filii Dei esse videtur constitutus.*"—*Column 295.*

We cannot see how any consistent Catholic can deny the

authenticity of this title without denying the infallibility of the pope. What more authority can they desire?

Before going further let us apply the rule laid down in the Catholic Bible for counting the number of his name. It says: "The numeral letters of his name shall make up this number."—*Note under Revelation 13: 18.* In Bible times they did not use figures. We can still see on dials of old clocks, in numbers given above chapters in the Bible, and in dates inscribed on cornerstones, certain numerical values given to some of the letters. In Latin, I stands for 1, V for 5, X for 10, L for 50, C for 100, D for 500, and M for 1,000. Originally we had no U, but V was used for U, and V is often used for U today on public buildings, such as "Pvblic Library," and our W is still written as a double V, not as a double U.

```
V =   5
i =   1
c = 100
a =   0
r =   0
i =   1
u =   5
s =   0
F =   0
i =   1
l =  50
i =   1
i =   1
D = 500
e =   0
i =   1
    ———
    666
```

The next Catholic authority we shall quote is F. Lucii Ferraris, who wrote "a veritable encyclopedia" in Latin, of which several editions have been printed by the papal church at Rome. The American Catholic Encyclopedia says of Ferraris's great work that it "will ever remain a precious mine of information."—*Vol. VI, p. 48.* From this unquestionable Catholic authority we shall first quote its Latin statement, and then give the English translation:

"*Ut sicut Beatus Petrus in terris vicarius Filii Dei fuit constitutus, ita et Pontifices eius successores in terris principatus potestatem amplius, quam terrenæ imperialis nostræ serenitatis mansuetudo habere videtur.*" ("As the blessed Peter was constituted Vicar of the Son of God on earth, so it is seen that the Pontiffs, his successors, hold from us and our empire the power of a supremacy on the earth greater than the clemency of our earthly imperial serenity.")—"*Prompta Bibliotheca canonica juridica moralis theologica*" etc., *Vol. VI, art. "Papa," p. 43. Printed by the Press of the Propaganda, Rome: 1890.*

A Message for Our Times

Henry Edward Cardinal Manning of England, an extensive Roman Catholic writer, of high esteem in his church, applies the same title to the pope, only using it in its English translation. He says of the popes:

"The temporal power in the hands of St. Gregory I was a fatherly and patriarchal rule over nations not as yet reduced to civil order. In the hands of St. Leo III it became a power of creating empires. In the hands of St. Gregory VII it was a scourge to chasten them. In the hands of Alexander III it was a dynasty, ruling supremely, in the name of God, over the powers of the world. . . . So that I may say there never was a time when the temporal power of the Vicar of the Son of God, though assailed as we see it, was more firmly rooted throughout the whole unity of the Catholic Church.

"It was a dignified obedience to bow to the Vicar of the Son of God, and to remit the arbitration of their griefs to one whom all wills consented to obey."—"*The Temporal Power of the Vicar of Jesus Christ,*" *pp. 231, 232, second edition. London: Burns and Lambert, 1862.*

The same year, this book was translated and published in Italian, with the sanction of the church attached to it. The title "Vicar of the Son of God" appears on pages 234 and 235 of that edition.

Philippe Labbe, "a distinguished Jesuit writer on historical, geographical, and philological questions" (Catholic Encyclopedia, Vol. VIII, pp. 718, 719), in his historical work "Sacrosancta concilia ad regiam editionem exacta," Vol. I, page 1534 (Paris: 1671), uses "Vicarius Filii Dei" as the official title of the pope.

Coming down to our own times, we shall call to the witness stand a modern advocate of the Roman Catholic cause. *Our Sunday Visitor*, of Huntington, Ind., in its issue of April 18, 1915, gives clear testimony in this case. We quote it in full:

"What are the letters supposed to be in the Pope's crown, and what do they signify, if anything?

"The letters inscribed in the Pope's mitre are these: *Vicarius*

Filii Dei, which is the Latin for Vicar of the Son of God. Catholics hold that the Church which is a visible society must have a visible head. Christ, before His ascension into heaven, appointed St. Peter to act as His representative. Upon the death of Peter the man who succeeded to the office of Peter as Bishop of Rome, was recognized as the head of the Church. Hence to the Bishop of Rome, as head of the Church, was given the title 'Vicar of Christ.'

"Enemies of the Papacy denounce this title as a malicious assumption. But the Bible informs us that Christ did not only give His Church authority to teach, but also to rule. Laying claim to the authority to rule in Christ's spiritual kingdom, in Christ's stead, is not a whit more malicious than laying claim to the authority to teach in Christ's name. And this every Christian minister does."—"*Our Sunday Visitor*," *April 18, 1915, thirteenth question under "Bureau of Information," p. 3.*

Later, when Roman Catholic authorities discovered that Protestants were making use of the foregoing statements to identify the Papacy with the antichristian power of Revelation 13:18, they attempted to repudiate the contents of their former article. But that article was not written by some contributor to their paper; it appeared in the "Bureau of Information," for which the *editorial staff was responsible*. And on page two of that paper appeared *sanctions for the editor* from Pope Pius X, dated May 17, 1914; from the Apostolic Delegate, John Bonzano, dated April 27, 1913; and from J. H. Alerding, Bishop of Fort Wayne, Ind., dated March 29, 1912. If statements made under such high authorities are not trustworthy, we would respectfully ask if their present denials are any more so?

To one versed in Catholic teaching and practice, there is nothing uncommon in such denials, where the interest of the Church is at stake. Cardinal Baudrillart's quotation on pages 64 and 245 of this book shows that some Catholic authors "ask permission from the Church to ignore or even deny" some historical facts, which they "dare not" face; and we read in "History of the Jesuits," by Andrew Steinmetz, Vol. 1, p. 13, that their accredited histories in common use, 'with permission of authority,' [are] veiling the subject with painful dexterity."—*London: 1848.*

We shall here refer to one other similar denial. In the Roman Catholic paper, *Shepherd of the Valley*, there appeared an article by the editor, in which he stated: "If Catholics ever attain, which they surely will, though at a distant day, the immense numerical majority in the United States, religious liberty, as at present understood, will be at an end." A Protestant lecturer, who made use of this quotation, was bitterly arraigned in a double-column front-page article in the *Catholic Standard and Times* for his false statements regarding Catholics; for, it pointed out, if he had finished the quotation with the words which followed, "so say our enemies," it would have reversed its meaning. The incident would have passed off at the expense of the Protestant lecturer, had not the *Western Watchman* of July 24, 1913, continued the quotation still further, declaring:

"'The whole quotation should read: 'If Catholics ever attain, which they surely will, though at a distant day, the immense numerical majority in the United States, religious liberty, as at present understood, will be at an end. So say our enemies; so say we.'"—*Quoted in "Protestant Magazine," October, 1913, p. 474.*

Why those who tried to deny their former statements should leave out the words, "so say *we*," is very evident. But what can we think of those who publicly *deny facts* to screen their church from unfavorable public opinions, unless they act from the motive that "the end justifies the means," and that "heretics" have no moral right to facts which they would misuse. (See also pages 64 and 65 of this book.)

We shall therefore continue to believe that the editors of *Our Sunday Visitor*, in its issue of April 18, 1915, page three, were perfectly honest and well informed on the subject, and that the later denials are of the same class as those mentioned above.

Our Sunday Visitor in the aforementioned quotation makes use of *Vicarius Filii Dei* and "Vicar of Christ" as synonymous terms, and Cardinal Manning does the same in his book, "Temporal Power of the Pope." It cannot, therefore, be maintained, as some do, that *Vicarius Christi* is the only mode of spelling used as the title of the pope, although the shorter rendering is used more often for brevity's sake. In fact *Vicarius Christi* is composite in its origin, *Vicarius* being Latin, while *Christi* is Latinized from the Greek. It would hardly seem probable that learned Romanists would adopt such a composite title to the exclusion of the pure, dignified, Latin title, *Vicarius Filii Dei*, which has been in use among them for centuries.

Of late, Catholic apologists have argued that the "name of the beast" in Revelation 13: 17, 18 is a personal name of a single individual, such as Nero, and not the official title of a series of men, as that of the popes would be. But this would be entirely out of harmony with the context, for how could *one man* make war with God's people, and overcome them in every country, so that he would have power "over all kindreds, and tongues, and nations"? Revelation 13: 7. Then, too, that power was to continue forty and two months (v. 5), which those apologists claim to be literal. But how could *one man* accomplish such a world task in forty-two literal months?

These forty-two months are twelve hundred and sixty prophetic days (Revelation 11: 2, 3), and in prophecy a day stands for a year (Ezekiel 4: 6). (Even Catholics acknowledge that a day in prophecy stands for a year. See note under Daniel 9: 24-27 in the Douay Bible. Father Reaves says: "The prophet's weeks are, by all interpreters of the Holy Scriptures, understood to include years for days."—*"Bible History," p. 345.*) The forty-two months, or twelve hundred and sixty days, of Revelation 13: 5 are therefore twelve hundred and sixty years, during which this power was to continue. But would not that period be quite a long time for one man to live? This attempt made by Roman apologists to screen the Papacy from being detected as the antichristian power of Revelation 13 appears too shallow to be seriously asserted by men who have made a thorough study of Bible prophecy.

Testimony of Eye-Witnesses

That the title, *Vicarius Filii Dei*, has been employed elsewhere than in Roman Catholic canon law is also asserted by Rev. B. Hoffman:

"*To Whom It May Concern:*

"This is to certify that I was born in Bavaria in 1828, was educated in Munich, and was reared a Roman Catholic. In 1844 and 1845 I was a student for the priesthood in the Jesuit College in Rome.

"During the Easter service of 1845, Pope Gregory XVI wore a triple crown upon which was the inscription, in jewels, *Vicarius Filii Dei*. We were told that there were one hundred diamonds in the word *Dei;* the other words were of some other kind of precious stones of a darker color. There was one word upon each crown, and not all on the same line. I was present at the service, and saw the crown distinctly, and noted it carefully.

"In 1850 I was converted to God and to Protestantism. Two years later I entered the Evangelical Church ministry, but later in life I united with the Presbyterian Church, of which I am now a retired pastor, having been in the ministry for fifty years.

"I have made the above statement at the request of Elder D. E. Scoles, as he states that some deny that the pope ever wore this tiara. But I know that he did, for I saw it upon his head."

"Sincerely yours in Christian service,
 (Signed) "B. Hoffman.
"Webb City, Mo., Oct. 29, 1906."
—"*Review and Herald,*" *Dec. 20, 1906.*

The author of this book has photostats of the papal passport held by Rev. B. Hoffman, and of a signed letter from him stating the same facts as are given in the above statement. His testimony is confirmed by that of M. De Latti and others.

Statement of M. De Latti to D. E. Scoles.—"M. De Latti ... had previously been a Catholic priest, and had spent four years in Rome. He visited me when I was pastor in St. Paul, Minn. ... He stated that he had often seen it [the crown with this inscription] in the museum of the Vatican, and gave a detailed and accurate description of the whole crown. ...

"De Latti ... said the first word of the sentence was on the first crown of the triple arrangement, the second word on the second part of the crown, while the word *Dei* was on the lower division of the triple crown. He also explained that the first two words were in dark-colored jewels, while the *Dei* was composed of diamonds entirely."—*D. E. Scoles, in "Review and Herald," Dec. 20, 1906.*

Statement of Thomas Whitmore.—"'Some time ago, an English officer happening to be at Rome, observed on the front of the mitre which the pope wore at one of the solemnities, this inscription: "*Vicarivs Filii Dei.*" It instantly struck him—perhaps this is "the number of the beast." He set to work: and when he had selected all the numerals, and added them up, he found, to his great astonishment, that the whole amounted to precisely six hundred and sixty-six. What stress is to be laid on this I cannot say.

"'Vicarivs	Filii	Dei
V 5	I 1	D 500
I 1	L 50	I 1
C 100	I 1	—
I 1	I 1	501
V 5	—	112
—	53	53
112		—
		666

"Thus it will be seen, that by taking from the title 'Vicarivs Filii Dei' [Vicar of the Son of God], the letters which are commonly used as numerals, they make up the number of the

A Message for Our Times

beast."—"*A Commentary on the Revelation of St. John the Divine,*" *p. 231.* Boston: 1856.

Testimony of Dr. H. Grattan Guinness.—"An English officer of high rank, who in the year 1799, by a special favor, was given the opportunity, while in Rome, to get a close view of the Pope's jewels and precious things, discovered thereby, that the papal tiara bore this inscription: 'Vicarivs Filii Dei.'

"When you take out the Latin letters, which have numeral value, and which still are used to represent numbers, and which are: V, I, C, L, and D, these letters form the number given below. In these Latin words there are two V's, which letter denotes 5, six I's denoting 1, one C, which denotes 100, one L, which denotes 50, and one D, which denotes 500, thus: $V,V = 10$; $I,I,I,I,I,I = 6$; $C = 100$; $L = 50$; and $D = 500$, the sum 666."—"*Babylon and the Beast,*" *p. 141;* quoted in "*Kyrkans Strid och Slutliga Seger,*" *Professor S. F. Svensson, pp. 126, 128.* Stockholm: 1908.

OTHER PROTESTANT WITNESSES

Robert Fleming, V. D. M., wrote a book entitled "Apocalyptical Key. An Extraordinary Discourse on the Rise and Fall of the Papacy." It was published in London, 1701, 1703, and 1929. In the 1929 edition, p. 48, we read that an "explication may be found in the title which the Roman pontiff has assumed, and which is inscribed over the door of the Vatican, 'Vicarius Filii Dei' (Vicar of the Son of God). In Roman computation this contains the number 666, as will be seen below.

"V 5	F 0	D . . . 500
I 1	I 1	E . . . 0
C 100	L 50	I . . . 1
A 0	I 1	—
R 0	I 1	In all 666."
I 1		
V 5		
S 0		

Testimony of R. C. Shimeall

"It is to be observed as a singular circumstance, that the title, *vicarivs filii dei* (Vicar of the Son of God), which the Popes of Rome have assumed to themselves, and caused to be inscribed over the door of the Vatican, exactly makes the number of 666, when deciphered according to the numeral signification of its constituent letters, thus:

Vicar	of the Son	of God	
V I C A R I V S	F I L I I	D E I	added to-
5 1 100 1 5	1 50 1 1	500 1	gether thus:

V	5
I	1
C	100
A	0
R	0
I	1
V	5
S	0
F	0
I	1
L	50
I	1
I	1
D	500
E	0
I	1
	666"

—"*Our Bible Chronology, Historic and Prophetic, Critically Examined and Demonstrated,*" *R. C. Shimeall, p. 180. New York: A. S. Barnes and Co., 1867.*

Appended to the above is a footnote, giving the author's reply to a correspondent:

"Answer to a Querist. . . .

"Sir,—In answer to your observation and queries, permit me to say—the things I have asserted are stubborn, clear facts, not mere suppositions or fancies.

"The inscription in question, was actually written over the door of the Vatican at Rome, in express Latin words and characters, as inserted in this publication, viz., VICARIVS FILII DEI; and those Latin words and characters contain Latin numerals to the amount of 666, exactly corresponding with the number of the beast.

"With respect to the supposition you have conjured up, that the Pope might be called *Vicarius Christus*, or *Vicarius Christus Filii Dei* (a sort of gibberish that is neither Latin, German, nor English), it is a matter I have nothing to do with. Mr. D. may adopt these or any other fancies to amuse himself, and to screen the head of his holiness, but when he has done all, this question will still remain to be answered: Have those inscriptions ever appeared over the door of the Vatican at Rome?

"As to Mr. D's attempting to obscure the number of the beast 666, contained in the numerals of the words VICARIVS FILII DEI, by objecting to a V; however the Pope or his emissaries may be obliged to him for his kind exertions on their behalf, yet I presume neither of them will condescend to appear his humble fool in Latin, for the sake of sheltering themselves under his ignorance of the Latin alphabet and the ancient inscriptions."—*Id., p. 180.*

Dr. S. T. Bloomfield gives us the following rule for finding the number:

"It means the number which is made up by reducing the numeral power of each of the letters of which the name is composed, and bringing it to a sum total."—"*Greek Testament with English Notes,*" *Note on Rev. 13: 17, Vol. II, p. 175.*

Samuel Hanson Cox, D. D.—"Can they [Protestants] accord to the present dominant Gregory, the pompous titles which he claims—VICARIUS FILII DEI, *Vestra Sanctitas, Servus Servorus Domini*, with other profane and blasphemous appellations without end?"—*Introduction to Bower's "History of the Popes," Vol. I, p. x. Philadelphia: 1847.*

The fact that some may have seen a crown at the Vatican which did not have the above inscription does not disprove the statements of the men who saw the crown that has the inscription; for according to a copyrighted news report from Milan, Italy, dated December 11, 1922, and published in the Des Moines (Iowa) *Register*, December 12, 1922, the pope has five crowns, the last one made being decked with two thousand precious stones. The important part is not that the inscription *Vicarius Filii Dei* is on the pope's tiara, but that it is the official title of the popes, that it designates their official position, and is given to them at their coronation, just as the head of the United States government is called "President," without it therefore being necessary for him to wear that title on his hat.

Mr. H. S. Weaver, of Baltimore, Md., wrote to James Cardinal Gibbons, of the same city, under date of January 18, 1904, inquiring:

"Does the inscription, 'Vicarius Filii Dei,' appear on the crown or mitre of the pope, or has it at any time in the past appeared on the crowns or mitres of any of the popes?"

"Yours sincerely,
(Signed) "H. S. Weaver."

To this letter the Cardinal answered through his secretary, as follows:

"Baltimore, Md., Jan. 26, 1904.
"Mr. H. S. Weaver.
"Dear Sir:

"In reply to yours of 18th inst., I beg to say that I can not say with certainty that the words, 'Vicarius Filii Dei,' are on the pope's tiara. But the words are used by the cardinal who imposes the tiara at the coronation of a pope.

"Yours truly,
(Signed) "Wm. T. Russell, Secretary."

The New Catholic Dictionary says:

"Tiara, papal crown. . . . It is placed on his head at his Coronation by the second cardinal-deacon, with the words: 'Receive the tiara adorned with three crowns and know that thou art Father of princes and kings, Ruler of the world, Vicar of our Saviour Jesus Christ.'"—*The New Catholic Dictionary*, art. "Tiara," p. 955.

We have already seen that Catholics have several free translations into English of the Latin title, "Vicarius Filii Dei." Some try to find in the Greek word *Lateinos*, or the Latin Empire of the Papacy, a fulfillment of Revelation 13:18 (see "Bishop Newton on the Prophecies," pp. 548-550), but there is no need of going to the Greek. For while it is true that the apostles used mostly the Aramaic and the Greek, Latin was the official language of Rome, the world empire at that time. The Romans everywhere used Latin, all their laws were written in that language, and Latin has remained the official language of the Papacy to this day. The apostle was prophesying of a strictly Latin power, whose language was in use in his day, and it is quite common for Bible writers to borrow foreign words and phrases belonging to the subjects of which they are speaking. (John 19:20; Revelation 9:11; 16:16.)

Then, too, the power represented by Revelation 13:1-10, 17, 18, must not only have the name indicated, but must also fulfill all the other specifications in this prophecy, and the Papacy does this. M. James Durham, Professor of Divinity in Glasgow (1658), says:

"He that hath all the characters of Antichrist's doctrine, and hath a name which, in the numeral letters, makes up 666, he is Antichrist. But to the Pope both these do agree."—"*A Commentary Upon the Book of Revelation*," *Rev. 13:18, p. 491. Glasgow: 1680.*

The United States In Prophecy

A Beautiful Picture

WE HAVE now seen that "the first beast" of Revelation 13: 1-10 represents the Papacy, and that it received its "deadly wound" in 1798, when the Papal States had been abolished, Rome declared a republic, and Pope Pius VI taken a prisoner into France where he died in "captivity," August 19, 1799. (Revelation 13: 3, 10.) The prophet then sees "another beast coming up." Verse 11. Knowing that a "beast" in prophecy represents a "kingdom" (Daniel 7: 23) we must conclude that a new nation was to come up about 1798. In 1754 John Wesley, in his "New Testament with Explanatory Notes," applied the beast of Revelation 13: 1-10 to the Papacy, and then wrote the following note under the eleventh verse:

"Another . . . beast. . . . But he is not yet come, though he cannot be far off; for he is to appear at the end of the forty-two months of the first beast. And he had two horns like a lamb—a mild, innocent appearance."—*P. 427.*

In locating this new nation let us notice the following points in this prophecy:

(1) When the prophet saw the papal beast go "into captivity" (Revelation 13: 10), he "beheld another beast" "like a *lamb*" "*coming up.*" Verse 11. A lamb is not full grown. This nation, therefore, would be coming up, and not be full grown in 1798, when the papal beast went into captivity.

(2) While the four beasts of Daniel 7: 3, and the first beast of Revelation 13: 1, all came up from "the *sea*," which in prophecy means "peoples, and multitudes" (Revelation 17: 15), the second beast of Revelation 13: 11 came "up out of the *earth*," indicating that, while the former kingdoms arose in countries populated with peoples and multitudes, this latter nation was to rise in new territory, not formerly occupied.

The United States in Prophecy

(3) The dragon of Revelation 12, and the first beast of Revelation 13, both had crowns, but this beast had none, which would indicate that it was to be a republic, having no crowned head.

(4) It would exercise its power *"before"* the papal beast (verse 12), showing that it is not a Catholic nation, nor counted as part of the papal confederacy, therefore it would naturally be a Protestant nation to begin with.

(5) It would be a *great* nation, for it was equal in *power* to the Papacy. Verse 12.

(6) And yet its principles were to be lamblike, mild (verse 11), or as the Danish and German have it: "Like *the* lamb,"—Christlike. And Christ advocated two great principles: First, *separation of church and state.* He said: "Render therefore unto Cæsar the things which be Cæsar's, and unto God the things which be God's." Luke 20: 25. That is, keep the two separate. Second, *religious liberty.* He said: "If any man hear My words, and believe not, I judge him not." John 12: 47. "Judge not, that ye be not judged." Matthew 7: 1.

It is evident that only one nation answers to all these specifications: the United States of America. It became an independent nation in 1776, and was not full grown in 1798, having only thirteen states, compared with forty-eight now. Its peaceful growth and principles of liberty answer also to the predictions of this prophecy.

The words *"coming up"* used in Revelation 13: 11 mean to "spring up, as plants."—*T. S. Green's Lexicon, p. 9.* And G. A. Townsend says: "The history of the United States was separated by a beneficent Providence far from this wild and cruel history of the rest of the continent, and, like a silent seed, we grew into empire."—*"The New World Compared with the Old," p. 635. Hartford: 1870.*

The principles of Romanism had taken such deep root in the human heart that although the Puritans had come to this country to seek liberty of worship for themselves, they soon established a state religion, and persecuted dissenters most bitterly.

In several of the Colonies good citizens were put in the stocks for not going to church on Sunday; they were mercilessly whipped, or even put to death, for differing from the established religious belief.

Many of the nobler minds had grown tired of political tyranny and religious bigotry, and determined to throw off both yokes in one stroke. On June 7, 1776, Richard Henry Lee introduced a resolution in the Continental Congress at Philadelphia, Pa., declaring, "That these United Colonies are and of right ought to be free and independent States, that they are absolved from all allegiance to the British Crown, and that all political connection between them and the state of Great Britain is and ought to be totally dissolved." A committee, consisting of Thomas Jefferson, Benjamin Franklin, John Adams, Roger Sherman, and Robert R. Livingston, was appointed to draft a formal Declaration, which was penned by Mr. Jefferson, and on June 28, Congress proceeded to consider it. The discussion that followed was a tremendous struggle. On July 2, Lee's resolution was voted, and finally at 2: 00 P.M., July 4, 1776, the Declaration of Independence was voted, and the bell in the tower of Independence Hall, where they were assembled, rang out the joyful news. This bell bore the now prophetic inscription, "Proclaim liberty throughout all the land unto all the inhabitants thereof." Leviticus 25: 10.

"In all the colonies, indeed, the Declaration was hailed as the passing away of the old world and the birth of the new."— *"Great Events of the Greatest Century," R. M. Devens, p. 29.*

The noble men who framed the Declaration did not ask for toleration. They understood the fundamentals of true liberty, and declared:

"We hold these truths to be self-evident, that all men are created equal; that they are endowed by their Creator with certain unalienable rights; that among these are life, liberty, and the pursuit of happiness. That to secure these rights, governments are instituted among men, deriving their just powers from the consent of the governed." Sacred truths these are, written in Independence Hall. "Within that temple was born a nation, in whose destiny were wrapped the interests of Liberty and of Civilization to the end of time."—*Id., p. 31.*

The Federal Constitution, adopted September 17, 1787, and ratified by the several states between December 7, 1787 and May 29, 1790, has this statement in its preamble: "We, the people of the United States, in order to . . . secure the blessings of liberty to ourselves and our posterity, do ordain and establish this Constitution for the United States of America."

Still some friends of religious liberty, who had so long suffered persecution, feared that the Constitution did not sufficiently safeguard liberty of conscience, and they wrote to George Washington in regard to it. The following is his reply, dated August 4, 1789:

"If I could have entertained the slightest apprehension that the Constitution framed by the convention where I had the honor to preside might possibly endanger the religious rights of any ecclesiastical society, certainly I would never have placed my signature to it; and if I could now conceive that the general government might ever be so administered as to render the liberty of conscience insecure, I beg you will be persuaded that no one would be more zealous than myself to establish effectual barriers against the horrors of spiritual tyranny and every species of religious persecution. For, you doubtless remember, I have often expressed my sentiments that any man, conducting himself as a good citizen and being accountable to God alone for his religious opinions, ought to be protected in worshiping the Deity according to the dictates of his own conscience."—"*History of the Baptists,*" *Thomas Armitage, D. D., LL. D., pp. 806, 807. New York: 1890.*

A month later, September 23, 1789, the first ten Amendments to the Constitution, also called the Bill of Rights, were approved by Congress. By December 15, 1791, they had been ratified by ten states, and were declared in force. The first Amendment reads:

"Congress shall make no law respecting an establishment of religion, or prohibiting the free exercise thereof; or abridging the freedom of speech or of the press; or the right of the people peaceably to assemble, and to petition the government for a redress of grievances."

In the prophecy this beast "had two horns like a lamb." Dr. Alexander Cruden gives many examples in his Concordance to show that "the Scripture mentions the horn as the symbol of strength."—*Art.* "*Horn,*" *p. 291.* And the real strength of this republic has been its two great principles: civil and religious liberty—a state without a king, and a church without a pope. G. A. Townsend, speaking of the real secret of power in this country, says:

"'In view of this unparalleled progress and combination, what are the little toys with which we vex ourselves in Europe? What is this needle gun, we are anxious to get from Prussia, that we may beat her next year with it? Had we not better take from America the principle of liberty she embodies, out of which have come her citizen pride, her gigantic industry, and her formidable loyalty to the destinies of her Republican land?'"—"*The New World Compared with the Old,*" *p. 462.*

The secret of our power at home, and our influence abroad, was the citizens' love for, and enthusiastic devotion to, their country, which guaranteed liberty to all, instead of oppression by taxation and religious despotism, as had been the rule in former ages.

As the principles of liberty and the inherent equality of all men, enunciated in the Declaration of Independence, and in the first Amendment to the Federal Constitution, spread in Europe, people became awakened to their God-given rights. Mr. Townsend says:

"Since America was discovered she has been a subject of revolutionary thought in Europe. . . . Out of her discovery grew the European reformation in religion; out of our Revolutionary War grew the revolutionary period of Europe."—*Id., pp. 462, 463.*

The prophet saw these two powerful horns on the lamblike

The United States in Prophecy

beast, and thinking men today have also caught the vision of their power in the world.

A SAD CHANGE

We wish we could close the picture here, and leave its unmarred beauty lingering in our minds; but, sad to say, there is another chapter to it that must be read. The prophet continues: "He spake as a dragon." Revelation 13:11. A nation speaks through its laws. This prophetic statement, therefore, reveals that a great change in policy is to come over our beloved country. The "dragon" is a symbol of pagan Rome, that persecuted the early Christians during the first three centuries. (Revelation 12: 1-5, 11.) And a similar persecution will be inaugurated against the "remnant" church, for we read: "The dragon was wroth with the woman [church], and went to make war with the remnant of her seed, which keep the commandments of God, and have the testimony of Jesus Christ." Revelation 12: 17. And he has "great wrath, because he knoweth that he hath but a short time." Verse 12. Here we see what is meant by speaking "as a dragon," and we also see upon whom this persecution will come; namely, upon commandment-keepers.

This prophecy also reveals what influence will be brought to bear upon our lawmakers and people to produce this sad change. We have already seen that "the first beast" of Revelation 13: 1-10 represents the Papacy, and by reading the eleventh and twelfth verses we see that the effort of the lamblike beast will be to cause "the earth and them which dwell therein to *worship the first beast,* whose deadly wound was healed." That is: The whole trend is Romeward, therefore it must be Rome that is working in disguise to bring about such a trend. And now as to the facts in the case. We quote the following from Roman Catholic sources:

At the Centennial Conference of American Catholics, held in Baltimore, November, 1890, Archbishop Ireland said:

"Catholics of the United States are called . . . to make America Catholic. . . . The church triumphant in America,

Catholic truth will travel on the wings of American influence, and with it encircle the universe."—"*The Pope and the New Era,*" *pp. 222, 223. London: W. T. Stead, 1890.*

A letter from Rome, dated October 14, 1894, says: "The United States of America, it can be said without exaggeration, are the chief thought of Leo XIII. .... A few days ago, on receiving an eminent American, Leo XIII said to him: 'But the United States are the future; we think of them incessantly.' . . . That is why Leo XIII turns all his soul, full of ideality, to what is improperly called his American policy. It should be called his Catholic universal policy."—"*Catholic Standard and Times*" (*Philadelphia*), *November 3, 1894; quoted in "Protestant Magazine," October, 1913, p. 441.*

The report of "the third Washington conference" says:

"Our purpose is to make America dominantly Catholic."— "*The Mission Movement in America,*" *issued from the Catholic University, Washington, D. C., June, 1909.*

"It seems to me that the main support of Protestantism comes from the United States and England. . . . If we put an end to this effort in England and the United States by making these nations predominantly Catholic, we will have removed the chief obstacle to the conversion of the world to the true faith. . . . A vigorous effort in the United States at this time will reduce the opposition to an insignificant condition. . . . In the course of another century, the [Protestant] sects will be a study for the historian and antiquarian along with Arianism."— *Extract from a letter in "The Missionary" (Roman Catholic), Washington, D. C.: May, 1910; quoted in "Protestant Magazine," Vol. II, p. 22.*

This Catholic movement has already made such progress in England, that, with a little careful manipulation, its leaders anticipate very little opposition in the future. (See "History of the Romeward Movement in the Church of England," London: 1900, and "The Secret History of the Oxford Movement," London: 1899, both by Walter Walsh; and "The Oxford Movement in America," by Rev. C. E. Walworth, New York: 1895;

also "The Jesuits and the British Press," by Michael J. F. McCarthy).

Now the "Catholic Action" is focused on America, not in an antagonistic way, but quietly, in wisely planned, systematically organized, and well directed efforts along numerous lines, so as to gain favor among Protestants, and not to be suspected as propaganda. And, remarkable as it may sound, Protestant leaders and people are totally asleep on the Catholic question, even more so than the Huguenots were in France before the St. Bartholomew's Massacre.

Dr. E. Boyd Barrett, for many years a Jesuit, and still a Roman Catholic, as far as the author knows, has the following to say about the plans of his church:

"In theory, Catholic Action is the work and service of lay Catholics in the cause of religion, under the guidance of the bishops. In practice it is the Catholic group fighting their way to control America."—"*Rome Stoops to Conquer,*" *p. 15. New York: 1935.*

"The effort, the fight, may be drawn out. It may last for five or ten years. Even if it last for twenty—what is twenty years in the life of Rome? The fight must be fought to a finish—opposition must be worn down if it cannot be swept away. Rome's immortal destiny hangs on the outcome. That destiny overshadows the land.

"And in the fight, as she has ever fought when battles were most desperate in the past, Rome will use steel, and gold, and silvery lies. Rome will stoop to conquer."—*Id., pp. 266, 267.*

In a communication from Vatican City, published in the Saint Paul *Pioneer Press,* November 4, 1936, we read:

"Pope Pius feels that the United States is the ideal base for Catholicism's great drive. . . .

"The Catholic Movement, Rome's militant organization numbering millions all over the world, will be marshaled direct from Rome by Monsignor Pizzardo—next to Pacelli the Holy See's shrewdest diplomat and politician—instead of by the local bishops as before. The priest's education is to be thoroughly revised and modernized—with special attention to modern propaganda methods. In addition there will be established in each country a central bureau, responsible only to Rome, to combat red agitation with every political weapon available. . . . The church must fight, and at once.

"Coughlin has shown us the way of getting at the modern man. He has embarrassed us by showing and using the political power of the church so openly. . . . We know how to tackle America today, and that is our most important problem at the moment.

"Pacelli is contacting the American cardinals and leading Catholic personalities, . . . to explain the Vatican's plan for the new crusade. . . . The Catholic political organizations in the large cities, like Tammany Hall, will give the church a good lever. Those contacts are also being carefully inspected by the pope's minister.

"The Vatican itself resembles a general staff headquarters preparing plans and arms for a big offensive. Since the time of the Counter-Reformation, churchmen say, no such extensive reorganization of personnel and propaganda methods has been undertaken. The whole world-wide net of Catholic organizations and sub-organizations is being contacted directly from Rome and cleared for action. The church is to be adjusted to modern political, social, and cultural conditions."—*P. 10, col. 3, 4, used by permission.*

This article speaks of Eugenio Cardinal Pacelli, then papal secretary of state, coming from the Vatican to effect the above mentioned reorganization. He toured the United States "in a chartered airplane." *Christian Science Monitor* says: "The visit of a high Roman prelate to the United States on the eve of an election is as unprecedented as it is delicate."—*Oct. 2, 1926.*

This Catholic plan of conquest was well understood years ago. An illustration in *Harper's Weekly* of October 1, 1870, pictured the pope pointing to America as "The Promised Land."

Making America Catholic

THE Roman hierarchy knew that the older Protestants, who had read about the persecutions of the Dark Ages, and who knew some of the inside workings of the papal church, would never become Catholics. Rome's hope lay in capturing the younger generation. If the Papacy could cover up those dark pages of its history, when it waded in the blood of martyrs, and could appear in the beautiful modern dress of a real champion for liberty, as a lover of science, art, and education, it would appeal to the American youth, and the battle would be won.

The Jesuits, who through years of experience in Europe, have become experts in molding young minds, are now establishing schools everywhere, that are patronized by thousands of Protestant youth. They have also undertaken the delicate task of Romanizing the textbooks of our public schools, and books of reference, in order to cover up their past, and to whitewash the Dark Ages. That Romanists desire to cover up their past record of bloody persecution is acknowledged by that honorable Roman Catholic author, Alfred Baudrillart, Rector of the Catholic Institute of Paris. After giving a frank statement of the many persecutions of which his church is guilty, he says in the words of Mgr. d'Hulst:

"'Indeed, even among our friends and our brothers we find those who dare not look this problem in the face. They ask permission from the Church to ignore or even to deny all those facts and institutions in the past which have made orthodoxy compulsory.'"—"*The Catholic Church; the Renaissance and Protestantism,*" *Alfred Archeveque Cardinal Baudrillart, pp. 183, 184.*

ROMANIZING TEXTBOOKS

In the first place, all general histories used in our public schools and high schools had to be revised to eliminate every trace of the objectionable features from their pages. Plain historical facts of the Middle Ages,—such as the popes' interference with public government (as in the case of Henry IV, Emperor of Germany, A. D. 1077, and King John of England, A. D. 1213); the persecution of Waldenses, Albigenses, and Huguenots; the Inquisition; the sale of indulgences; and the Reformation,—all had to be eliminated or rewritten so as to exonerate the Papacy, and brand its opponents simply as political offenders and revolutionists, who suffered at the hand of the civil government, instead of being persecuted by the Church for their religion.

Such radical changes could never have been accomplished so quietly if Protestantism had not been asleep. At times it became necessary to create public sentiment against a certain textbook through newspaper articles written by some learned Catholic professor, and then pressure was brought to bear on school boards to eliminate it, substituting for it a Romanized book. Thus Swinton's "Outlines of History" was thrown out of the schools, and "Anderson's History" was blacklisted, but later revised according to Catholic wishes, and brought back to take the place of Swinton's. Myers's "Medieval and Modern History" was also censored. At first the author refused to change it, claiming "history is history," but later it was revised and came into quite general use for a time. Not all of this was done in the dark. As one example of protest we refer the reader to Senate Document on Public Hearing before the United States Committee on Education and Labor, Friday, February 15, 1889, and Friday, February 22, 1889, on "Senate Resolution No. 86:* Proposing an Amendment to the Constitution of the United States Respecting Establishment of Religion and Free Public Schools," which unmasks some of this work. We shall now point out two of the vital changes made in our textbooks:

(1) The Catholic Church will never acknowledge the Reformation of the sixteenth century as a *reform*, but brands it as a "revolt" against the authority of the pope, and as a "revolu-

---

* "Liberty," Vol. V, No. 3, Third Quarter. 1910 pages 30-32.

tion." A sure earmark, therefore, of all Romanized textbooks is the fact that they never speak of the Reformation as a work of reform but as "the Protestant Revolt," "the Protestant Revolution," "the so-called Reformation," or "what is called the Reformation." Let any one look it up in the schoolbooks used by his children, and see for himself.

To give the readers who may not have seen the textbooks used in our schools today an idea of what the Protestant children are taught, we shall take the "History of Western Europe," by Professor J. H. Robinson, as an example. It has the following chapters on the Reformation of the sixteenth century: chapter 24, "Germany Before the Protestant Revolt"; chapter 25, "Martin Luther and His Revolt Against the Church"; chapter 26, "Course of the Protestant Revolt in Germany"; chapter 27, "The Protestant Revolt in Switzerland and England." Chapter 25 says: "As Luther became a confessed revolutionist, he began to find friends among other revolutionists and reformers."— *P. 393*. Chapter 28 takes up the effort of the Catholics to destroy the Reformation by a counterreform, by the work of the Jesuits, and the bloody persecution of Protestants in Spain, in the Netherlands, and France. This chapter is entitled: "The Catholic Reformation," and yet it comes the farthest from deserving the title of reformation of all the above-mentioned chapters. In these Romanized textbooks the historical facts of the Middle Ages are entirely reversed. The way the last-mentioned chapter extols the Jesuits shows who has put their stamp on the book. Senator Thomas E. Watson truthfully says:

"In the public schools the Catholics have stealthily introduced textbooks written by Jesuits; and your children are being taught that the Roman church was misunderstood in the past; that its doctrines are not fatal to humanity and gospel religion; that its record is not saturated with the blood of innocent millions, murdered by papal persecutors, *and that there never was such a monstrosity as the alleged sale of papal pardons of sins.*

"Educate youth in this Catholic way, and the consequences are logical."—"*Roman Catholics in America Falsifying History* and *Poisoning the Minds of Protestant School Children,"* p. 5. Thompson, Ga.: 1928.

SALE OF INDULGENCES

Histories used in the public schools in the United States up to the year 1900 were opposed by the Roman Catholic Church on the ground that they were not stating the truth about "indulgences." These histories simply stated that Martin Luther began the Reformation by opposing Tetzel's sale of indulgences, which is a historical fact.

"An Introduction to the History of Western Europe," by Professor J. H. Robinson, says:

"It is a common mistake of Protestants to suppose that the indulgence was forgiveness granted beforehand for sins to be committed in the future. There is absolutely no foundation for this idea."—*P. 391. Ginn and Co.: 1903.*

This statement is copied on page 311 in "A General History of Europe," by Robinson, Breasted, and Smith, a textbook quite generally used of late. We shall leave it with the reader to judge whether such statements actually represent the Protestant conception of "indulgences," or whether they are part of a program to cover up historical facts; and we would respectfully ask: Are not American youth entitled to know the unvarnished facts of history?

The historical facts about "indulgences," gathered from unquestionable sources, are found on pages 162-172 of this book. It is here shown that the idea of "indulgences" had so degenerated between the eleventh and the sixteenth centuries, that they were actually sold for money. Tetzel's "Indulgences" read: I "absolve thee . . . from all thy sins, transgressions and excesses . . . and I restore thee . . . to that innocence and purity which thou possessedst at baptism; so that, when thou diest, the gates of punishment shall be shut, and the gates of the paradise of delight shall be open."—*Coxe's "House of Austria," Vol. I, p. 385. London: George Bell and Sons, 1906.*

REVISING BOOKS OF REFERENCE

The next step in the papal plan was to revise all books of reference, such as encyclopedias, dictionaries, and larger historical works, so as to mold the minds not only of pupils but also of teachers and of preachers. An example of this is seen in the revision of the New International Encyclopedia. The editor of the *Catholic Mirror* (at that time the official organ of Cardinal Gibbons), in a lengthy editorial, dated October 28, 1905, tells of how the publishers of that Encyclopedia cooperated with the Jesuits in revising it. He quoted the following letter from the Rev. Thomas J. Campbell, S. J., which he had just received:

"Dodd, Mead and Co. sent their representatives to us, and not only expressed a desire to avoid misstatements in their encyclopedia, but asked for some one to excise whatever might be offensive. . . . Mr. Conde B. Pallen took the matter in hand, and was afforded full liberty to revise and correct not only the topics which dealt professedly with Catholic subjects but those also which might have even an indirect bearing on them. . . . The firm has done all in its power to make it acceptable to Catholics."—*Quoted in "Liberty," Vol. V, No. 3, pp. 34, 35. Washington, D. C., 1910.*

After this was done, every effort was made to get this New International Encyclopedia into the hands of all Protestant ministers in this country, who were unaware of its Romanized features. Its molding influence was soon seen in the striking similarity in viewpoint (on many subjects) between the Roman theology and that of the Protestant pulpit and press, and this is becoming more so now after practically all encyclopedias have been Romanized. Even Webster's Dictionary has not been allowed to speak its old familiar truths any more. We read:

"Time was when complaint was common that injustice was done to the Catholics in 'Webster's Dictionary.' There is no room for such a thing in the new 'Webster's International Dictionary,' issued by G. and C. Merriam Co., Springfield, Mass., because Vicar-General Callaghan, of the diocese of Little Rock,

has revised and edited everything appertaining to the church."
—"*Freeman's Journal*" of New York, May 28, 1892. Since then a Catholic official has been regularly connected with the editorial staff, whenever a new revision was made, as can be seen in the preface of later editions.

Suppose, in the next encyclopedia, we ask brewery officials to edit everything pertaining to temperance and the liquor question, and ask the officials of Wall Street to edit all that pertains to capital and labor, would we then get a more correct and unbiased representation of these subjects? We ask why, then, should Roman Catholic officials edit everything pertaining to the Protestant controversy with Rome?

At the First American Catholic Missionary Congress, held at Chicago, November 17, 1908, Dr. William McGinnis outlined the program of the International Catholic Truth Society for making America Catholic: (1) by Romanizing our schoolbooks, (2) by revising our books of reference, (3) by controlling the daily press, (4) by capturing the libraries. He said in part:

"A few years ago the publishers of an encyclopedia in twelve volumes entered the office of the Truth Society and said: 'We realize there are many misstatements and errors regarding things Catholic in this work, but we put the whole edition in your hands and will accept every correction you make and every addition which you wish to insert.' . . . So, likewise, one of the largest publishing houses of the United States, a house that supplies perhaps one third of the textbooks used in the public schools of America, asked that certain books might be examined and erroneous statements and unjust charges against the Church be corrected. . . . And we are happy to say that in practically every case these misrepresentations of the Church that otherwise would have gone into the minds of millions of children were courteously corrected by gentlemanly authors."—"*The Two Great American Catholic Missionary Congresses*," pp. 427, 428. Chicago: J. S. Hyland and Co., 1914.

Many Protestant parents would not send their children to Catholic parochial schools, but they will allow them to be taught

Making America Catholic 249

the same thing from Romanized textbooks, without any protest! We ask, What made the afore-mentioned publishers so anxious to have the Catholics revise the public schoolbooks and encyclopedias, which they intended to publish? Why did they not go to some Protestant organization to have the books revised? Was it because Protestants are not educated? Certainly not! But these publishers knew from experience, that, unless the books were Romanized, Catholic societies would stir up such opposition against their use, that it would result in financial loss to the publishers. Dr. McGinnis tells the secret when he relates how he had urged the Knights of Columbus to "wake up" and "form a committee," to examine the "histories of education in use in high schools and normal schools." He says: "The spirit of Knighthood was not dead in that Council, the subject was investigated, the book I had quoted from was the textbook of the class, and, after much discussion, it was removed from the curriculum of the school."—*Id., pp. 423, 424.*

Any one who will take the trouble to examine the textbooks used in our public schools before 1900, and compare them with those used after this Romanizing propaganda began, will discover the fact that the Romanizing features have been introduced *gradually* into a series of textbooks, the one taking the place of the other as fast as the public could assimilate the Catholic sentiments and phraseology, and the same is true regarding books of reference.

Muzzling the Public Press

Dr. McGinnis also spoke of their plans regarding the daily papers. He said: "We may consider briefly the program of the International Catholic Truth Society in reference to two great agencies in the formation of the minds and hearts of the great American people,—the press and the public libraries.

"Our daily press . . . mold[s] the thought and influence[s] the will of the country. . . . We do demand that the great Catholic Church, in her saving doctrines and in her marvelous activities, should be brought more prominently before the American public."—*Id., p. 419.*

Dr. McGinnis further stated that arrangements had been made with the Vatican for Catholic reporters all over the world to furnish material for the "Truth Society" to be used in the daily press, and then he says:

"With a membership of two or three thousand scholarly, zealous priests and laymen, and the headquarters of the Society acting as a clearing house, calumnies would not remain unanswered, misstatements of doctrines would be corrected."—*Id., pp. 420, 421.*

"We realize, moreover, that refutations and corrections, valuable though they be, are not sufficient. We want to carry the campaign a little farther. We want to make of the press of this country a positive agency in the dissemination of Catholic ideas. . . . We are now furnishing on the first and third Sundays of each month one column or a column and a half of positive Catholic matter to daily papers. . . . But the 'Notes and Comments' . . . deal with such topics as the conversion of some distinguished scholar, the life work of a recently deceased Catholic who was eminent in the domain of physical science, archeological discoveries bearing upon Christian doctrine, important congresses abroad. . . . If the demands of our people prove that the new feature is appreciated, the 'service' will become weekly, and it will bring light and sympathy for things Catholic to many millions of readers."—*Id., pp. 421, 422.*

"The *demands*" must have proved successful, for instead of this "new feature" appearing weekly, articles and notes seem to appear almost daily. Though it is legitimate for religious denominations to make use of the public press, for them to muzzle the freedom of the press is not legitimate! When large religious organizations parade their great number of adherents and bring pressure to bear on the press, threatening nonsupport if the other side appears in its columns, while they monopolize them with their own propaganda, such organizations lose the respect of thinking people.

CAPTURING THE PUBLIC LIBRARIES

At the before-mentioned Catholic Congress plans were also laid for making the public libraries agencies in their propaganda. Dr. McGinnis says:

"Another force, second only to the school and the press in shaping the thoughts of the nation, is the public library system of the United States. . . . I ask why, in the name of the God of truth, is the great Catholic Church excluded from the shelves of the public libraries of the United States? . . . Create a strong, legitimate demand for Catholic literature, and the public libraries will meet the demand."—*Id., pp. 422, 423.*

But how did that Congress propose to "create" this strong "demand" for Catholic books? Here is their scheme: They will supply their people with lists of books to be asked for at the libraries, and when several hundred or thousand people have called for the same books, it will create a demand.

"The demand for such literature must be brought to the public libraries. We wish to emphasize the fact that the demand must be made in good faith—the books are called for at the library because the man wants to read them. The International Catholic Truth Society will supply general and special lists of books, and the Spiritual Director . . . will . . . designate appropriate works for individual members. From this widespread bona fide demand for Catholic works at public libraries three results will follow. [It will help the members.] Their work will be instrumental in placing these books within the reach of the great non-Catholic American public, who will thus have some opportunity to find out what the Church's doctrines and practices really are, and finally the increased circulation of such literature will be a well-deserved and much-needed stimulus to Catholic writers."—*Id., p. 424.* See also "*Catholic Digest*," *March, 1937, pp. 126, 127,* and "*America,*" *September 13, 1913, pp. 547, 548.*

Mr. Michael J. F. McCarty, of England, gives us some interesting facts regarding a similar work done by Jesuits in England. He says that they suppress books of Protestant authors, and bring to the front those of Catholics, and as a result of this systematic work, he says:

"Many Protestant authors are forced to speak favorably and kindly of Romanism. . . . The publication of books containing friendly allusion to Protestant Christianity has almost ceased in England, [while the other kind of books] floods the country."—*"The Jesuits and the British Press,"* p. 52. Edinburgh and London: 1910.

But, in addition to this, the Jesuits always have a man, either a priest or a layman, on the committee of almost every public library in Great Britain.

"The Jesuits' man comes provided with two lists, a black list, which includes every well-known book, ancient and modern, adverse to Romanism; and a white list of new books especially favorable to Romanism which he submits beforehand to the librarian, and eventually succeeds in getting placed in the library."—*Pp. 50, 51.*

It is quite evident from our investigation of the facts that the Jesuits are the same in America as in England. Besides this, the few remaining books from the days when it was not so unpopular to state the unvarnished facts about medieval history have been diminishing in number by being worn out or purposely destroyed.

Censorship of Books

Those who write histories today have more source matter on ancient history, but less on medieval, than historians had four hundred years ago; for after the Reformation had fully aroused the papal church to action, her emissaries, especially the vigilant Jesuits, searched out and destroyed every evidence that was damaging to her. When Bishop Gilbert Burnet, D. D., prepared to write his "History of the English Reformation," he became surprised, while searching among court records and public registers, to find so much missing, till he finally discovered the cause. He says:

"In the search I made of the Rolls and other offices, I wondered much to miss several commissions, patents, and other writings, which by clear evidence I knew were granted, and yet none of them appeared on record.

"But as I continued down my search to the fourth year of Queen Mary, I found in the twelfth roll of that year, a commission which cleared all my former doubts, and by which I saw what was become of the things I had so anxiously searched after. We have heard of the expurgation of books practiced in the Church of Rome; but it might have been imagined that public registers and records would have been safe; yet lest these should have been afterwards confessors, it was resolved they should then be martyrs; for on the 29th of December, in the fourth year of her reign, a commission was issued out under the great seal to Bonner, Bishop of London, Cole, Dean of St. Paul's, and Martine, a doctor of the civil law, [which commanded the destruction of] divers compts, books, scrolls, instruments. . . .

"When I saw this, I soon knew which way so many writings had gone."—"*History of the Reformation of the Church of England,*" *2-vol. ed., Vol. I, Preface, p. xiii. London: 1880.*

Let no one, therefore, say that statements in older histories are not true because we cannot now find sources to prove them.

The reader may not know that back of all this activity stands the Roman Curia, one department of which is the Sacred Congregation of the Index, which meets at Rome on stated days to decide what books are forbidden, and to make lists of them, called "The Index of Prohibited Books."* The writer has examined two editions of this "Index," one early edition, and their latest one of 1930 by Pope Pius XI. Some books are permanently forbidden, while others are forbidden until certain corrections are made in them, which explains the revisions of our schoolbooks, for the "Index" says:

"Can. 1396. Books condemned by the Holy See are prohibited all over the world and in whatever language into which they may have been translated.

---

* See "Romanism and the Republic," by Isaac J. Lansing, pp. 221-223. Pope Benedict XV, on March 25, 1917, transferred this work to the "Supreme Sacred Congregation of the Holy Office."—"*Index of Prohibited Books,*" *p. xxxi.*

"Can. 1397, Sec. 1. It is the duty of all the faithful, particularly of clerics, or those holding high positions and noted for their learning, to denounce any book, they may consider dangerous, to the local Ordinaries, or to the Holy See. . . .

"Sec. 3. Those to whom such denunciations are made are bound in conscience not to reveal the names of the accusers.

"Sec. 4. Local Ordinaries, either directly themselves, or through the agency of capable priests, are in duty bound to keep a close watch on the books that are published, or sold, within their territory. . . .

"Can. 1398, Sec. 1. The condemnation of a book entails the prohibition, without especial permission, either to publish, to read, to keep, to sell, to translate it, or in any way to pass it on to others.

"Sec. 2. A book which has been prohibited in any way may not be republished, unless, after the necessary corrections have been made."—"*Index*," *of 1930, pp. xvi, xvii. Vatican Polyglot Press.*

The Catholic Encyclopedia has this to say about the "Censorship of Books": "In general, censorship of books is a supervision of the press in order to prevent any abuse of it.

"The reverse of censorship is freedom of the press."—*Vol. III, p. 519.*

This "supervision of the press" extends also to articles written in magazines and newspapers, and among the special organizations working in this field is the International Catholic Truth Society, and the Catholic International Associated Press. Reporting the Louisville federation convention of the latter, Michael Kenny, S. J., in *America* (a Jesuit weekly) for August 31, 1912, says of their Catholic Press Bureau:

"We have it in our power to compel our papers, the thinking machines of the people, to tell the truth and refrain from transmitting slanders on Catholic matters. We can prevent the wells at which the people drink from being poisoned. We can, following the lead of the Austrian Catholic Congress, establish a

Catholic International Associated Press,* and to accomplish this object every Catholic of the right spirit, reading in the daily papers calumnies of our religion and the most brazen justification of the robber bands who drive our religious from their homes and confiscate their property, should be willing to contribute a tithe of his possessions. All this and more can be accomplished by federated action. . . . Marching shoulder to shoulder with the spirit of soldiers on the battlefield at the call of the Church, we can successfully combat the organizations of her enemies and make this an era of Catholic manhood."— *"America," August 31, 1912, p. 486, article by M. Kenny, S. J.*

As a result of this organized effort no newspapers in the United States will accept any news that reflects unfavorably on the Catholic Church or its propaganda in this country, while news unfavorable to Protestants is printed.

---

* *The Register* (Roman Catholic), Denver, Colo., April 3, 1938, announced the formation of the United Catholic Organizations' Press Relations Committee, to keep vigilant oversight over newspapers and magazines.

Americanism Versus Romanism

SOME say: What of it! Are not Roman Catholics as good as Protestants? Yes, certainly they are. As individuals there is no distinction before the law, and as neighbors they are loved and respected. We, however, are not speaking of individuals, but of a *church* organization that claims certain rights of jurisdiction in *civil* affairs, and whose avowed principles are diametrically opposed to liberty of speech, liberty of press, and religious liberty in general, as understood by the founders of this republic and incorporated into its fundamental laws. This we shall now prove (1) from official Catholic documents, (2) from the actual application of their principles to civil governments.

Official Catholic Documents

Pope Leo XIII, in an encyclical letter, *Immortale Dei*, November 1, 1885, outlines "the Christian constitution of states," by saying that "the state" should profess the Catholic religion, and that the Roman pontiffs should have "the power of making laws." "And assuredly all ought to hold that it was not without a singular disposition of God's providence that this power of the Church was provided with a civil sovereignty as the surest safeguard of her independence."

He says of the Middle Ages: "[then] church and state were happily united."—"*The Great Encyclical Letters of Pope Leo XIII,*" pp. 113, 114, 119. Benziger Bros., 1903.

"Sad it is to call to mind how the harmful and lamentable rage for innovations which rose to a climax in the sixteenth century, . . . spread amongst all classes of society. From this source, as from a fountain-head, burst forth all those later tenets of unbridled license. . . . .

"Amongst these principles the main one lays down that as all men are alike by race and nature . . . that each is free to think on every subject just as he may choose. . . . In a society grounded upon such maxims, all government is nothing more nor less than the will of the people. . . .

"And it is a part of this theory . . . that every one is to be free to follow whatever religion he prefers, or none at all if he disapprove of all. . . .

"Now when the state rests on foundations like those just named—and for the time being they are greatly in favor—it readily appears into what and how unrightful a position the Church is driven. . . . They who administer the civil power . . . defiantly put aside the most sacred decrees of the Church. . . .

"The sovereignty of the people . . . is doubtless a doctrine . . . which lacks all reasonable proof."—*Id., pp. 120-123.*

The theory "that the church be separated from the state," Pope Leo further calls a "fatal error," "a great folly, a sheer injustice," and "a shameless liberty."—*Id., pp. 124, 125.*

In his next encyclical letter, of June 20, 1888, he calls it "the fatal theory of the need of separation between Church and state," "the greatest perversion of liberty," and "that fatal principle of the separation of Church and state."—*Id., pp. 148, 159.*

In his letter of January 6, 1895, he says: "It would be very erroneous to draw the conclusion that in America is to be sought the type of the most desirable status of the Church, or that it would be universally lawful or expedient for state and church to be, as in America, dissevered and divorced. . . . She would bring forth more abundant fruits if, in addition to liberty, she enjoyed the favor of the laws and the patronage of the public authority."—*Id., pp. 323, 324.*

Among the many authorities that could be cited, we have chosen that of Pope Leo XIII, because he is not a medieval, but a modern, exponent of papal doctrines, which no Roman Catholic would deny. Any one familiar with the phraseology of the Declaration of Independence and the Federal Constitution cannot help but see in the expressions of Pope Leo a *declared opposition* to the fundamental principles upon which our government is founded. He urges his followers not to be content with attending to their religious duties, but "Catholics should extend their efforts beyond this restricted sphere, and give their attention to national politics."—*Id., p. 131.*

"It is the duty of all Catholics . . . to strive that liberty of action shall not transgress the bounds marked out by nature and the law of God; to endeavor to bring back all civil society to the pattern and form of Christianity which We have described. . . . Both these objects will be carried into effect without fail if all will follow the guidance of the Apostolic See as their rule of life and obey the bishops."—*Id., p. 132.*

"Especially with reference to the so-called 'Liberties' which are so greatly coveted in these days, all must stand by the judgment of the Apostolic See."—*Id., p. 130.*

In his encyclical letter of January 10, 1890, on "The Chief Duty of Christians as Citizens" (id., pp. 180-207) he urges all Catholics to put forth *united* action in politics in order to change the governmental policies so as to bring them into harmony with papal principles. He says:

"As to those who mean to take part in public affairs they should avoid . . . leading the lives of cowards, untouched in the fight. . . .

"Honor, then, to those who shrink not from entering the arena as often as need calls, believing and being convinced that the violence of injustice will be brought to an end and finally give way to the sanctity of right and religion."—*Id., pp. 199-201.*

They are urged to support (in elections) only those men who will stand by the principles of union of church and state:

"The Church cannot give countenance or favor to those whom she knows to be imbued with a spirit of hostility to her; who refuse openly to respect her rights; who make it their aim and purpose to tear asunder the alliance that should, by the very nature of things, connect the interests of religion with those of the state. On the contrary, she is (as she is bound to be) the upholder of those who are themselves imbued with the right way of thinking as to the relations between church and state, and who strive to make them work in perfect accord for the common good. These precepts contain the abiding principle by which every Catholic should shape his conduct in regard to public life. In short, where the Church does not forbid taking part in public affairs, it is fit and proper to give support to men of acknowledged worth, and who pledge themselves to deserve well in the Catholic cause, and on no account may it be allowed to prefer to them any such individuals as are hostile to religion. . . .

"Whence it appears how urgent is the duty to maintain perfect union of minds."—*Id., p. 198.*

"Union of minds, therefore, requires, together with a perfect accord in the one faith, complete submission and obedience of will to the Church and to the Roman Pontiff, as to God himself."—*Id., p. 193.*

"The political prudence of the Pontiff embraces diverse and multiform things; for it is his charge not only to rule the Church, but generally so to regulate the actions of Christian citizens. . . . The faithful should imitate the practical political wisdom of the ecclesiastical authority."—*Id., p. 202.*

"But if the laws of the state are manifestly at variance with the divine law, containing enactments hurtful to the Church, . . . or if they violate in the person of the supreme Pontiff the authority of Jesus Christ, then truly, to resist becomes a positive duty, to obey, a crime."—*Id., p. 185.*

"If, then, a civil government strives . . . to put God aside, . . . it deflects woefully from its right course and from the injunctions of nature. Nor should such a gathering together and association of men be accounted as a commonwealth, but only as a deceitful imitation and make-believe of civil organization."—*Id., p. 181.*

These are the exact statements of Pope Leo XIII, taken from his authentic records, published by the Catholics under the seal of the Church; and they show that the Papacy stands for the same principles today as it did in the Dark Ages. How truthfully the Pontiff says: "And in truth, wherever the Church has set her foot, she has straightway changed the face of things."—*Id., p. 107.*

A letter from the Vatican outlining the plans of Pope Leo XIII respecting the United States was published in the *New York Sun,* July 11, 1892, and contains the following significant statement:

"What the church has done in the past for others, she will now do for the United States. . . . He [the pope] hails in the United American States, and in their young and flourishing church the source of new life for Europeans. . . . If the United States succeed in solving the many problems that puzzle us, Europe will follow her example."—"*New York Sun,*" *July 11, 1892; quoted in "Liberty," 1907, No. 4, p. 10.*

How remarkably this coincides with the prophetic prediction: "His deadly wound was healed: and all the world wondered after the beast." Revelation 13: 3. Yes, it is true that "as America, the land of religious liberty, shall unite with the Papacy in forcing the conscience and compelling men to honor the false sabbath, the people of every country on the globe will be led to follow her example."—"*Testimonies," Vol. VI, p. 18.* This country led the world from despotism to liberty, and it will lead the way back.

The doctrine of Pope Leo XIII is the doctrine of the Catholic Church, and it is taught in her schools in the United States. One of their schoolbooks, "Manual of Christian Doctrine, by a Seminary Professor," printed by J. J. McVey, Philadelphia, 1915, and carrying the sanction of the Catholic Censor and the seal of the Church, has this to say concerning the "Relations of Church and State":

"Why is the Church superior to the state?

"Because the end to which the Church tends is the noblest of all ends.

"What right has the pope in virtue of his supremacy?

"The right to annul those laws or acts of government that would injure the salvation of souls or attack the natural rights of citizens.

"What then is the principle obligation of the heads of states?

"Their principle obligation is to practice the Catholic religion themselves, and, as they are in power, to protect and defend it.

"Has the State the right and the duty to proscribe schism or heresy?

"Yes, it has the right and the duty to do so.

"May the state separate itself from the Church?

"No, because it may not withdraw from the supreme rule of Christ.

"What name is given to the doctrine that the state has neither the right nor the duty to be united to the Church to protect it?

"This doctrine is called *Liberalism*. It is founded principally on the fact that modern society rests on liberty of conscience and of worship, on liberty of speech and of the press.

"Why is Liberalism to be condemned?

"Because it denies all subordination of the state to the Church."—*Pp. 131-133.*

We respectfully ask: With such avowed principles taught in Catholic schoolbooks, would it be safe to allow Romanized textbooks to be used in our public schools?

Pope Paul IV sets forth this same papal doctrine. We read:

"On February 15, 1559, appeared the Bull *Quum ex apostolatus officio* of which the most important heads are these:

"(1) The Pope as representative of Christ on earth has complete authority over princes and kingdoms, and may judge the same.

"(2) All monarchs, who are guilty of heresy or schism, are irrevocably deposed, without the necessity of any judicial formalities. They are deprived forever of their right to rule, and fall under sentence of death. If they repent, they are to be confined in a monastery for the term of their life, with bread and water as their only fare.

"(3) No man is to help an heretical or schismatical prince.

The monarch guilty of this sin is to lose his kingdom in favor of rulers obedient to the Pope."—"*Life and Times of Hildebrand,*" *Arnold Harris Mathews, D. D., p. 288. London: 1910.*

Later papal encyclicals show the same attitude toward Protestants. Here is a sample from the encyclical of Pope Pius X. Speaking of the Reformation of the sixteenth century, it says:

"That tumult of rebellion and that perversion of faith and morals they called reformation and themselves reformers. But, in truth, they were corrupters, for undermining with dissensions and wars the forces of Europe, they paved the way for the rebellions and the apostasy of modern times, in which were united and renewed in one onslaught those three kinds of conflict, hitherto separated, from which the Church has always issued victorious, the bloody conflicts of the first ages, then the internal pest of heresies, and, finally, under the name of evangelical liberty, a vicious corruption and a perversion of discipline unknown perhaps in mediæval times."—"*Encyclical Letter of Our Most Holy Lord Pius X,*" *quoted in Supplement to "The Tablet," June 11, 1910, p. 950. London: England.**

Application of Papal Principles to Civil Government

The Jesuits in this country endeavor to make us believe that it is not within the pope's domain to "meddle with the civil allegiance of Catholics" or to interfere with a ruler's governing of his subject and that, should any pope "try such interference, he would be going beyond the limits of his proper authority; Catholics would be under no obligation to obey him—nor would they obey him."—"*The Pope and the American Republic,*" *by J. E. Graham, p. 3.* But it is understood that this is only "mission" literature written for the American people, who can best be won by such sentiments, and that it does not apply to Catholic countries; nor will it apply to our own when conditions here can be changed.

---

* For further evidences that the Papacy claims the right of interfering with the affairs of civil governments, see "The Middle Ages," Henry Hallam, LL.D., F.R.A.S., Vol. I, chap. 7, Parts I, II.

King Henry IV Versus Pope Gregory VII

We do not suppose that such writers have forgotten the claims of so many popes that civil magistrates are not exempt from the rule of Christ, or from the governing power of His Vicar, and that "the church never changes." Nor can any well-read man have forgotten that Pope Gregory VII on the twenty-second of February, 1076, excommunicated Henry IV, "forbade him to govern Germany and Italy, dispensed all his subjects from the oath of allegiance they had taken to him, and forbade every one to obey him as a king."—"*Life and Times of Hildebrand,*" *A. H. Mathews, D. D., p. 109. London: 1910.* Pope Gregory VII wrote the following letter on September 3, 1076:

"To All the Faithful in Germany, Counselling them to Choose a New King:

"Gregory . . . to all the . . . bishops, dukes, counts, and all defenders of the Christian faith dwelling in the kingdom of Germany . . . Henry, king so-called, was excommunicated . . . he was bound in bondage of anathema and deposed from his royal dignity, and that every people formerly subject to him is released from its oath of allegiance. . . .

"Let another ruler of the kingdom be found by divine favor, such an one as shall bind himself by unquestionable obligation to carry out the measures we have indicated."—"*Records of Civilization Sources and Studies,*" *edited under the auspices of the Department of History, Columbia University,*" *Vol. XIV, pp. 105-107.*

Any person who had any dealing with the excommunicated king became thereby himself excommunicated. If the king did not secure release from this "band" within a year, he was to lose his kingdom and be put to death, or if he repented after the year passed he would be imprisoned in a monastery, and fed with bread and water till his death, and this finally became his fate. Henry had to set out across the dangerous Alps in midwinter. "The cold was intense, and there had been heavy falls of snow, so that neither men nor horses could advance in the narrow road alongside precipices without running the greatest risks. Nevertheless, they could not delay, for the anniversary of the King's excommunication was drawing near." The men walked, and the queen was placed in "a kind of sledge made of oxhide, and the guides dragged [it] the whole way." At last they arrived at Canossa, where the pope temporarily abode.

"Then, in the penitent's garb of wool, and barefoot, the King appeared before the walls of the fortress. He had laid aside every mark of royalty, and, fasting, he awaited the pleasure of the Pope for three days. The severity of the penance was enhanced by the coldness of the season. Bonitho speaks of it as a 'very bitter' winter, and says that the King waited in the courtyard amid snow and ice. Even in the presence of Gregory there were loud murmurs against his pride and inhumanity."—*"Life and Times of Hildebrand," pp. 126-128.* At last through the intercession of others the pope admitted the king and released him of the excommunication, January 28, 1077.

Pope Gregory VII himself acknowledged the whole proceeding with evident satisfaction in a letter to the princes of Germany, dated January 28, 1077, in the following words:

"At length he came in person with a few followers to the town of Canossa where we were staying. Not a sign of hostility or boldness did he show. All his royal insignia he laid aside, and, wretchedly clad in woolen garments, he stood persistently for three long days with bare feet before the gate of the Castle. Constantly and with many tears he implored the apostolic mercy for help and consolation until he had moved all who were within hearing to such pity and depth of compassion that they interceded for him with many prayers and tears. They expressed wonder at the unusual hardness of our heart, and some even insisted that we were exercising, not apostolic severity, but the ferocious cruelty of a tyrant."—*"Parallel Source Problems in Medieval History," F. Duncalf, Ph. D., and A. C. Krey, M. A., p. 89. New York and London: 1912.*

And yet the pope had the audacity to extract from the humiliated king the promise of a meeting among the princes of Germany, where "the pope as judge" was to decide whether

Henry was to be "held unworthy of the throne according to ecclesiastical law" or not. (Id., p. 51.) And finally the pope excommunicated Henry the second time, March 7, 1080, and a new king, Rudolph of Suabia, was elected, the pope sending him a costly crown. Civil war ensued, which deluged Germany in blood, and Rudolph, the king of the papal party, was slain. This is not an isolated case.

"When, in the year 1119, Calixtus excommunicated Henry V, the Pope also solemnly absolved from their allegiance all the subjects of the Emperor."—"*Life and Times of Hildebrand,*" *p. 284.*

OTHER POPES MEDDLE IN POLITICS

On May 24, 1160, Pope Alexander III excommunicated Frederic Barbarossa, "and released his subjects from their allegiance." Pope Innocent III "deposed and reinstated princes and released subjects from their oaths" as if he were a universal ruler. In 1208 he placed the whole kingdom of England under "interdict," excommunicated King John in 1209, and deposed him in 1212, releasing all his subjects from their allegiance to him, and invited King Philip of France to occupy England in the name of the pope. John was finally forced to surrender the kingdom into the hands of the pope, to be returned to him as a fief. The barons, displeased with such transactions, forced the king to sign the "Magna Charta," a document of liberty. But the pope declared it null and void.

"The Emperor Frederick II was excommunicated by Gregory IX; his subjects were released from their allegiance, and he was deposed by Innocent IV [in 1245]. Boniface VIII, who meddled incessantly in foreign affairs, [explained the pope's] two swords [to mean, that the temporal sword of] the monarch is borne only at the will and by the permission of the Pontiff."—*Id., p. 286.*

MODERN RULERS WALK THE ROAD TO CANOSSA

One more example of a later date may be of interest. For centuries France had been under the controlling power of the

Papacy, and in the Revolutionary period she attempted to shake off the shackles. But, the fetters were so strong and the chains so heavy, that she found herself unable to do so, till finally the Association Law of 1901 and the Separation Law of 1905 granted religious liberty to all denominations alike. Rome, however, does not want liberty, but sole control, and so her thunderbolts were hurled against the "injustice" of France, till the impression was created that Rome was fighting for "liberty." It is the same old story. The Papacy always feels oppressed where it is not given a free hand to control. F. T. Morton (member of the Massachusetts bar) says:

"It is *not* in defense of religious liberty the pope is attacking the French republic, but because the republic has placed all religious bodies alike under the regime of religious liberty, equality, and toleration, and this he calls the law of oppression." —"*The Roman Catholic Church and Its Relation to the Federal Government,*" *p. 110. Boston: 1909.* See also "Papal Attack on France," in the *Nineteenth Century Magazine,* April, 1909, and "Papal Aggression in France," in *Fortnightly Review,* October, 1906.

In a Catholic booklet, Rev. J. T. Roche, LL. D., says of the French law:

"Three hundred million dollars' worth of property has been swept away by a single legal enactment, because the French laity did not have an influential, efficient, and vigorous press to protest against this colossal injustice. The Cardinal Archbishop of France a few weeks ago made the statement, that if one tenth of the money put into churches and religious institutions, had been expended on their Catholic press, this property would never have been confiscated. This utterance has been well borne out by the results already achieved in Germany. That country today has over two hundred Catholic daily papers, and a great number of weekly and monthly periodicals. It has a great lay society, the Volksverein, which devotes its energies to the upbuilding of the press. . . . From end to end of the country, the people are kept in touch with what is going on in governmental as well as church circles. There is unity of thought and action. . . . It has become a universally accepted axiom amongst us, that the church in any country is no stronger or weaker than its official press."—"*The Catholic Paper*," *pp. 9, 10; printed by "Catholic Register and Canadian Extension." Toronto, Can.: 1910.*

Attorney F. T. Morton quotes the following from newspaper clippings concerning a mass meeting of nearly 8,000 Catholics, held in Brooklyn, N. Y., Feb. 3, 1907, to protest against the Separation Law of France: "Even Bismarck had to pass on his way to a metaphorical Canossa."—"*The Roman Catholic Church," p. 114. Boston: 1909.*

The Roman Catholic weekly, *The Tablet*, of London, March 21, 1914, pp. 440, 441, has an article on "French Catholics and the General Elections," which we wish we had space to copy in full, as it shows the way leaders in the Roman church instruct her people, and marshal them in mass in times of elections. We quote:

"'Catholics have had their duty in this matter long ago placed before them by the *Pope*: to unite together under their Bishops on the platform of religion.' . . .

"'Catholics above all things' was to be their motto.

"The only purpose was to form a vast association of Catholic citizens to act together for ends which he summed up as follows:—'What we want is religious peace (1) by the revision of the laws which have attacked our liberties, and (2) by an understanding between the State and the Head of the Catholic Church.' . . .

"In accordance with these principles it was determined to constitute at once a Committee to multiply organizations which would group Catholics together for this work, and that action should be taken as far as possible in the forthcoming electoral struggle.

"The call to united action thus sounded finds a strong re-enforcement in the pastorals of the Bishops. Thus Cardinal Andrieu, Archbishop of Bordeaux, has reminded his flock that they should use their votes, and that in doing so they are bound in conscience to vote only for those candidates who shall have promised to respect the rights of God and the Church. 'Those,' declares His Eminence, 'who decline to make this promise are undeserving of your confidence, and if, from fear or from self-interest, you vote for them, you make yourselves responsible before God and men for the harm that may be done by their sectarianism to our religion and to our country.'

"Cardinal Dubillard, Archbishop of Chambery, has written in the same sense. Even still stronger is the note struck in a Joint Pastoral issued by the six Bishops of the Province of Bourges. They open by declaring that with the elections in view it is their right and their duty to speak about them to their people, who are under an obligation, not only to vote, but to vote right. 'To vote is not an indifferent, because it is a political, act, for politics cannot escape from Christian morality or claim independence seeing that conscience is binding in public as well as in private life.' . . .

"Catholics have gone to the ballot as individuals, disunited and without a programme. This time they should unite on behalf of the interests of religion. Now more than ever before united action is necessary *sub vexillo Christi*. . . . The Bishops proceed to lay down the line of conduct to be followed by Catholic electors: to refuse to vote for all candidates who shall take their stand on the laws described as secular and intangible; to vote unhesitatingly and without *arriere pensee* [mental reservation] for every Catholic candidate—Republican, Royalist, or Imperialist—because he is a Catholic, and determined above all to defend and demand the rights of God and of the Church; to vote for those Liberal candidates who give a satisfactory pledge to support the Catholic claims. From this it will be seen that the laymen's movement is in full accord with the directions of the Bishops."—*Pp. 440, 441.*

Now, as the Roman Catholic Church rests one of its main propositions on the fact that it is the same the world over, and never changes, and seeing that it is governed in every

Americanism Versus Romanism

country by the same rules of the Roman Curia, with the pope at its head, we know that the same regulations apply to the United States as to the Republic of France. As an illustration of this fact we find that, when the Poles of Milwaukee, Wis., in their city election of 1912, voted the Socialist ticket, the Roman Catholic paper, *Western Watchman*, of April 11, 1912, commented thus: "We are sorry for the Poles. It is a shame that their clergy have them not under better control."—*Quoted in "Protestant Magazine," December, 1913, p. 568.* When Mr. T. J. Carey of Palestine, Texas, in a letter to Archbishop John Bonzano, the Papal Delegate, of Washington, D. C., dated June 10, 1912, asked: "Must I as a Catholic surrender my political freedom to the Church?" the Archbishop answered in a letter dated June 16, 1912: "You should submit to the decisions of the Church even at the cost of sacrificing political principles."—*Frontispiece in "Protestant Magazine," August, 1913.* Many other incidents could be cited if space permitted.

Let no one, therefore, claim that the Catholic Church is not active in politics. As a sequel to this Catholic Action in France, we read in the *Minneapolis Journal*, December 7, 1920, in the report of a sermon by Dr. P. B. Donally, O. M. I. (Catholic) of London, England, preached at the Pro-Cathedral in Minneapolis, the following significant words:

"'The Church, Christ's Masterpiece.' . . . Amid the universal crash of nations, thrones, and doctrines, she is the one moral force that remains standing.

"Protestant England sends its ambassador to the Pope of Rome. Lutheran Germany, through her representative at the Vatican, seeks light and counsel from the Vicar of Christ. And the infidel government of France has walked the road to Canossa."

We have seen the reason why the Republic of "France has walked the road to Canossa"; namely, through the activities of Catholic bishops, and their organizations, in elections. As sure as that same power is operating in other countries, they too will walk the road to Canossa. What a delight it seems for the leaders of the Roman church to look back to the grand scene at Canossa, and see a mighty king standing with bare feet in snow and cold for three days, begging the pope to allow him to rule his own country. This is the Roman ideal, it appears. We could continue this subject by relating Rome's fight against government officials of Spain, Mexico, etc., bringing its activities in politics up to date, but space forbids. To sum up: Rome is unchanged in principle, and will do today what it did in the Middle Ages, whenever opportunity offers itself.

The World War gave the Papacy a new hold on the nations of Europe. Mr. Michael Williams, an eminent Catholic editor, says: "Before the World War . . . there were few national representatives at the Vatican." But now "a spiritual movement such as the world has not seen since the Crusades or the conquest of the Roman Empire by the earlier members of the same church [has taken place]. In that movement the laity are participating in close co-operation with the ecclesiastical leaders."—"*Current History Magazine,*" *Aug., 1926.* And what a change has taken place!

"A total of thirty-one countries now maintain official diplomatic relations with the Vatican. . . . To this number it is expected here both France and the United States will be added. . . .

"As a consequence the Vatican is today in diplomatic relations not only with all of the great Catholic countries of the world and most of the Protestant nations, but it has succeeded in entering into semi-official relations with several of the great nations with other religions, such as Turkey, Japan, and China."
—*By mail from Rome, printed in Minneapolis "Tribune," April 10, 1921.*

Such pressure was brought to bear on the smaller nations not having diplomatic relations with the Vatican, that Latvia felt the need of having a "pull" there too. "The papal authorities agreed to extend their recognition to Latvia and to make Riga the seat of a Roman Catholic archbishop, provided the government of Latvia would turn over to the archbishop the Cathedral of Riga. Though the cathedral had been in the con-

Americanism Versus Romanism 271

tinuous possession of the Lutherans for more than three hundred years, the government accepted the condition of the Vatican."—*Bishop Edgar Blake, in New York "Christian Advocate," Sept. 23, 1926.*

Now the Vatican is strongly urging the United States to begin diplomatic relations with the Holy See. We read in a *New York Herald-Tribune–Minneapolis Journal* cable for April 15, 1934:

"*Rome, April 14.*—The 'preparation' by President Franklin D. Roosevelt of a favorable public opinion now appears to be considered at the Vatican . . . of a resumption of diplomatic relations between the United States and the Holy See. . . . The Roosevelt administration has progressed from a merely friendly attitude to a definite willingness to dispatch a minister to the Holy See as soon as the American public—and especially Congress—can be put into the frame of mind to accept the step.

"The frequent and amiable contacts of the President and Archbishop Cicognani, Apostolic Delegate to Washington, are said to have done much to prepare the ground, but at the Vatican the greatest hope is pinned to the clear-cut assurance which Postmaster General James A. Farley gave the Pope when he was received last August."—*Minneapolis "Journal," April 15, 1934.*

What this diplomatic relation will cost this country in concessions to the Vatican, time alone will tell. We venture to say that it will be of a different nature from that of Latvia, and infinitely greater in its consequences! But Protestants seem to be so fast asleep that they do not even dream of danger. Dr. Samuel Hanson Cox says:

"Our greatest national dangers arise from our lamentable apathy; as this arises mainly from our ignorance. *While men slept*, says our Saviour, *the enemy sowed tares*. And if 'the price of liberty is eternal vigilance,' it ill becomes the heirs of such a boon, from such ancestors as ours, to lose or even to peril the freedom which was purchased by them at the cost of blood.

Nor will any thing like indifference suit the occasion. America expects every citizen, as Christ every Christian, to do his duty. And to omit this—on any pretense—is criminal. It is suiting and serving the enemy. It is servility and subserviency to the common foe. *Sleep on,* says Rome, *and we will have you!* We need do nothing, but only omit to do our duty, and we act for him; and our ruined posterity may remember only to accuse us, only to execrate our memories. Shall we then be indifferent, and so abet the interests of antichrist? What could we do more truly to favor the worst adversary of this most noble and desirable nation?"—"*The History of the Popes to A. D. 1758," Archibald Bower, Esq., with Introduction by Rev. Samuel Hanson Cox, D. D., p. xi of Introduction. Philadelphia: 1844.*

The Jesuits

THE "Society of Jesus," commonly called "the Jesuits," is a secret order of the Roman Catholic Church, founded August 15, 1534, by the Spaniard, Ignatius Loyola, and sanctioned by Pope Paul III, September 27, 1540. Loyola had received a military training, and when he later became an extreme religious enthusiast, he conceived the idea of forming a spiritual militia, to be placed at the service of the pope. The Jesuit T. J. Campbell says:

"They are called the Society or Company of Jesus, the latter designation expressing more correctly the military idea of the founder, which was to establish, as it were, a new battalion in the spiritual army of the Catholic Church."—*The Encyclopedia Americana, art. "Jesuits."*

Organization and Rules of the Society

Loyola organized his Company on the strictest military basis. Its General was always to reside at Rome, supervising from his headquarters every branch scattered over the world. Theodor Griesinger says:

"Its General ruled as absolute monarch in all parts of the world, and the different kingdoms of Europe, Asia, Africa, and America lay at his feet divided into provinces. Over each province was placed a provincial, as lieutenant of the general, and every month it was the duty of this provincial to send in his report to his General. . . . From these thousands of reports the General was in possession of the most accurate information regarding all that was going on in the world. Moreover, by means of the Father Confessors at the various Courts, he was initiated into all the secrets of these latter. [The officials] had to be careful to report nothing but the exact truth, [for] each one of them was provided with an assistant who was also in direct communication with the General, [who checked the reports of the one against the other.]"—"*History of the Jesuits,*" *p. 280. London: 1892.*

The Abbate Leone, after personal investigation, writes: "Every day the general receives a number of reports which severally check each other. There are in the central house, at Rome, huge registers, wherein are inscribed the names of all the Jesuits and of all the important persons, friends, or enemies, with whom they have any connection. In those registers are recorded . . . facts relating to the lives of each individual. It is the most gigantic biographical collection that has ever been formed. The conduct of a light woman, the hidden failings of a statesman, are recounted in these books with cold impartiality. . . . When it is required to act in any way upon an individual, they open the book and become immediately acquainted with his life, his character, his qualities, his defects, his projects, his family, his friends, his most secret acquaintances."—"*The Secret Plan of the Order,*" *with preface by M. Victor Considerant, p. 33. London: 1848.*

Similar registers are also found in the offices of the provincials, and in the "novitiate houses," so that when one Jesuit follows another in office, he has at his finger tips the fullest knowledge of the most secret lives of those for whom he is to labor, whether they are friends or foes. The Abbate Leone says of his secret investigation of this fact:

"The first thing that struck me was some great books in the form of registers, with alphabeted edges.

"I found that they contained numerous observations relative to the character of distinguished individuals, arranged by towns or families. Each page was evidently written by several different hands."—*Id., p. 31.*

Those who enter the Jesuit society spend two years of "noviceship," and then take the "simple vows." After several more years of intensive training, they take the fourth vow, by which they pledge themselves under oath to look to their General and their Superiors as holding "the place of Christ our

Lord," and to obey them unconditionally without the least hesitation.

The Jesuits being a secret order, they did not publish their rules. How then can we be absolutely sure about these regulations? Dr. William Robertson says:

"It was a fundamental maxim with the Jesuits, from their first institution, not to publish the rules of their order.* These they kept concealed as an impenetrable mystery. They never communicated them to strangers, nor even to the greater part of their own members. They refused to produce them when required by courts of justice." But during a lawsuit at Paris, in 1760, Father Montigny committed the blunder of placing the two volumes of their "Constitutions" (the Prague edition of 1757) in the hands of the French court. "By the aid of these authentic records the principles of their government may be delineated."—"*History of Charles the Fifth*," *Vol. II, p. 332.* (See also "*History of the Jesuits*," *Theodor Griesinger, pp. 435-439, 474-476.*)

The author was so fortunate as to have the privilege of carefully reading "The Constitutions of the Society of Jesus." He saw a Latin edition of 1558, and an English translation of it printed in 1838, together with the three Papal Bulls: 1. The Bull of Pope Paul III, given September 27, 1540, sanctioning "The Society of Jesus." 2. The Bull of Clement XIV, abolishing the "Society," July 21, 1773. 3. The Bull of Pius VII, restoring it, August 7, 1814. We shall now quote from "The Constitutions," thus presenting first-hand evidence of their Rules:

"It is to be observed that the intention of the Vow wherewith the Society has bound itself in obedience to the supreme Vicar of Christ without any excuse, is that we must go to whatever part of the world he shall determine to send us, among believers or unbelievers."—"*Constitutions*," *pp. 64, 65.*

"Displaying this virtue of obedience, first to the Pope, then to the Superiors of the Society . . . we . . . attend to his

---

* "The Constitutions" was preserved only in handwritten manuscripts, and allowed only to a few select members of the Society; and when these books finally were printed, they were not for the public.

voice, *just as if it proceeded from Christ Our Lord;* . . . doing wh'.ever is enjoined us with all celerity, with spiritual joy and perseverance; *persuading ourselves that everything is just; suppressing every repugnant thought and judgment of our own in a certain obedience.* . . . Every one . . . should permit themselves to be moved and directed under divine Providence by their Superiors just *as if they were a corpse,* which allows itself to be moved and handled in any way. . . . Thus obedient he should execute anything on which the Superior chooses to employ him."—*Id., pp. 55, 56.*

It is this *corpse-like obedience,* required of all its members, that has made the Jesuits such a power in the world. Rene Fulop-Miller in his book: "The Power and Secret of the Jesuits," commended by Father Friedrich Muckermann, leading Jesuit writer of Germany, and Father Alfonso Kleinser, S. J., and the *Deutsche Zeitung,* Berlin's leading Catholic organ, says:

"The Society of Jesus represented a company of soldiers. Where 'duty' in the military sense is concerned, as it is in the Society of Jesus, obedience becomes the highest virtue, as it is in the army. The Jesuit renders his obedience primarily to his superior . . . and he submits to him as if he were Christ Himself."—"*The Power and Secret of the Jesuits," pp. 18, 19.*

"So the Jesuits seek to attain to God through 'blind obedience.'

"Ignatius requires nothing less than the complete sacrifice of the man's own understanding, 'unlimited obedience even to the very sacrifice of conviction.'"—*Id., pp. 19, 20.*

He taught his Jesuit members by a complete "corpse-like obedience" to be governed by the following principle:

"'I must let myself be led and moved as a lump of wax lets itself be kneaded, must order myself as a dead man without will or judgment.'"—*Id., p. 21.*

"It was the obedience of the Jesuits that made it possible to oppose to the enemies of the Church a really trained and formidable army."—*Id., p. 23.*

"For, within a short time after the foundation of the order,

The Jesuits

the Jesuits were acting as spiritual directors at the courts of Europe, as preachers in the most remote primeval forests, as political conspirators, disguised and in constant danger of death; thus they had a thousand opportunities to employ their talents, their cleverness, their knowledge of the world, and even their cunning."—*Id., p. 26.*

Jesuits Decide on Their Mission

Loyola first planned to convert the Mohammedans of Palestine, but finding himself entirely unprepared for that work, and the road blocked by war, and finding, after his return to Paris, that the Protestant Reformation was turning the minds of men from the Roman church to the Bible, he resolved to undertake a propaganda of no less magnitude than the restoration of the Papacy to world dominion, and the destruction of all the enemies of the pope. The Jesuit T. J. Campbell says:

"As the establishment of the Society of Jesus coincided with the Protestant Reformation the efforts of the first Jesuits were naturally directed to combat that movement. Under the guidance of Canisius so much success attended their work in Germany and other northern nations, that, according to Macaulay, Protestantism was effectually checked. In England . . . the Jesuits stopped at no danger, . . . and what they did there was repeated in other parts of the world. . . . The Jesuits were to be found under every disguise, in every country.

"Their history is marked by ceaseless activity in launching new schemes for the spread of the Catholic faith.

"They have been expelled over and over again from almost every Catholic country in Europe, always, however, coming back again to renew their work when the storm had subsided; and this fact has been adduced as a proof that there is something iniquitous in the very nature of the organization."—*The Encyclopedia Americana, sixteen-volume edition, Vol. IX, art.* "*Jesuits." 1904.*

Loyola's plan of operation was to have his emissaries enter new fields in a humble way as workers of charity, and then begin to educate the children and youth. After gaining the good will of the higher classes of society, they would, through their influence, secure positions as confessors to the royal families, and advisers of civil rulers. These Jesuit Fathers had been skilfully trained to take every advantage of such positions to influence *civil rulers* and direct them in the interest of the Roman church, and to instill in them, that it was their sacred duty to act as worthy sons of the Church by purging their country from heresy. And when war against "heretics" commenced, the Jesuits would not consent to any truce till Protestantism was completely wiped out.

At the time Loyola and his "knights" took the field, the Protestant Reformation had swept over the greater part of Europe, and one country after another was lost to the Papacy. But in a short time the Jesuits had turned the tide. The Netherlands, France, and Germany were swept by fire and sword till the very strongholds of Protestantism were threatened. The Protestant countries were finally forced to combine in the Thirty Years' War to save themselves from being brought back by force under the papal yoke. (See "History of the Jesuits," T. Griesinger, Book II, chap. 2.)

The Abolition of the Jesuit Order

As long as this war of extermination was waged against Protestantism, the assistance of these daring "knights" was accepted, but when they continued to meddle in politics, and to gather the civil reins in their own hands, the Catholic princes at length became aroused to their danger, and complaints began to pour into the Vatican from various heads of Catholic states. Finally, Pope Clement XIV, after four years of investigation. felt compelled to abolish the Jesuit Order. In his "Bull of Suppression," issued July 21, 1773, he wrote, that repeated warnings had been given to the Society of "*the most imminent dangers, if it concerned itself with temporal matters, and which relate to political affairs, and the administration of government.*" It was "strictly forbidden to all the members of the society, *to interfere in any manner whatever in public affairs.*" Clement then cites eleven popes who "employed without effect all their efforts . . . to restore peace to the Church" by keeping the Jesuits out of "secular affairs, with which the company ought not to have interfered," as they had done "in Europe, Africa, and America." The Pope continues:

"We have seen, in the grief of our heart, that neither these remedies, nor an infinity of others, since employed, have produced their due effect, or silenced the accusations and complaints against the said society. . . . In vain [were all efforts.]" —"*Bull of Clement XIV,*" *in "Constitutions of the Society of Jesus," pp. 116, 117. London: 1838.*

"After so many storms, troubles, and divisions . . . the times became more difficult and tempestuous; complaints and quarrels were multiplied on every side; in some places dangerous seditions arose, tumults, discords, dissensions, scandals, which weakening or entirely breaking the bonds of Christian charity, excited the faithful to all the rage of party hatreds and enmities. Desolation and danger grew to such a height, that . . . the kings of France, Spain, Portugal, and Sicily,—found themselves reduced to the necessity of expelling and driving from their states, kingdoms, and provinces, these very companions of Jesus; persuaded that there remained no other remedy to so great evils; and that this step was necessary in order to prevent the Christians from rising one against another, and from massacring each other in the very bosom of our common mother the Holy Church. The said our dear sons in Jesus Christ having since considered that even this remedy would not be sufficient towards reconciling the whole Christian world, unless the said society was *absolutely abolished and suppressed,* made known their demands and wills in this matter to our said predecessor Clement XIII."—*Id., p. 118.*

"After a mature deliberation, we do, out of our certain knowledge, and the fulness of our apostolical power, *suppress and abolish the said company.* . . . We *abrogate* and *annul* its statutes, rules, customs, decrees, and constitutions, even though confirmed by oath, and approved by the Holy See. . . . We declare . . . the said society to be *for ever annulled and extinguished.*"—*Id., pp. 119, 120.*

"Our will and meaning is, that the suppression and destruction of the said society, and of all its parts, shall have an immediate and instantaneous effect."—*Id., p. 124.*

"Our will and pleasure is, that these our letters should *for ever and to all eternity be valid, permanent, and efficacious,* have and obtain their full force and effect. . . . Given at Rome, at St. Mary the Greater, under the seal of the Fisherman, the 21st day of July, 1773, in the fifth year of our Pontificate."—"*Bull for the Effectual Suppression of the Order of Jesuits.*" Quoted in "*Constitutions of the Society of Jesus,*" *p. 126.*

We now respectfully ask: Can any Roman Catholic doubt that the pope is telling the truth about the Jesuits? If he is telling the truth, can we be blamed for feeling that there is a Jesuit danger, after that society has been reinstated and has labored incessantly for more than a century, and is unchanged in principle?

When we reflect upon their past history, and remember that the Jesuits have been expelled from fifty different countries, seven times from England, and nine times from France, and from the Papal States themselves, there must be a reason why civil governments, Catholic as well as Protestant, have found it necessary to take such steps. Only in countries such as the United States, where they are allowed to carry on their work peaceably, we hear little of them. But some day Americans may wake up to find our present generation completely Romanized, and our boasted "liberty" a thing of the past. The prophet declares: "And through his policy also he shall cause craft to prosper in his hand; . . . and by *peace* shall destroy many." Daniel 8: 25. Any one desiring to know the historical facts should read the "History of the Jesuits," by T. Griesinger, and "The Roman Catholic Church," by F. T. Morton, pp. 167, 168.

"*The end justifies the means.*" This maxim is generally attributed to the Jesuits, and while it might not be found in just that many words in their authorized books, yet the identical

The Jesuits

sentiment is found over and over again in their Latin works. Dr. Otto Henne an Rhyn quotes many such sentiments from authorized Jesuit sources. We quote from him the following: "Herman Busembaum, in his 'Medulla Theologiæ Moralis' (first published at Frankfort-on-the-Main, 1650) gives this as a theorem (p. 320): *Cum finis est licitus, etiam media sunt licita* (when the end is lawful, the means also are lawful); and p. 504: *Cui licitus est finis, etiam licent media* (for whom the end is lawful, the means are lawful also). The Jesuit Paul Layman, in his 'Theologia Moralis,' lib. III., p. 20 (Munich, 1625), quoting Sanchez, states the proposition in these words: *Cui concessus est finis, concessa etiam sunt media ad finem ordinata* (to whom the end is permitted, to him also are permitted the means ordered to the end). Louis Wagemann, Jesuit professor of moral theology, in his 'Synopsis Theologiæ Moralis' (Innsbruck and Augsburg, 1762) has: *Finis determinat moralitatem actus* (the end decides the morality of the act)."—"*The Jesuits," pp. 47, 48. New York: 1895.*

"But the mischief is that the whole moral teaching of the Jesuits from their early days till now is but a further extension of this proposition, so redoubtable in its application."—*Id., pp. 49, 50.**

Rene Fulop-Miller says of the Jesuits:

"In actual fact, the Jesuit casuists deal with two forms of permissible deception: that of 'amphibology' and that of *reservatio mentalis*. 'Amphibology' is nothing else than the employment of ambiguous terms calculated to mislead the questioner; 'mental reservation' consists in answering a question, not with a direct lie, but in such a way that the truth is partly suppressed, certain words being formulated mentally but not expressed orally.

"The Jesuits hold that neither intentional ambiguity nor the fact of making a mental reservation can be regarded as lying, since, in both cases, all that happens is that 'one's neigh-

---

* See also "The Power and Secret of the Jesuits," Rene Fulop-Miller, pp. 150-156; and "The Secret Plan," the Abbate Leone, p. 155.

bor is not actually deceived, but rather his deception is permitted only for a justifiable cause.'"—"*The Power and Secret of the Jesuits,*" *pp. 154, 155.*

The Jesuit Gury gives examples of this; among others he says:

"Amand promised, under oath, to Marinus, that he would never reveal a theft committed by the latter. . . . But . . . Amand was called as a witness before the judge, and revealed the secret, after interrogation.

"He ought not to have revealed the theft, . . . but he ought to have answered: 'I do not know anything,' understanding, 'nothing that I am obligated to reveal,' by using a mental restriction. . . . So Amand has committed a grave sin against religion and justice, by revealing publicly, before the court, a confided secret."—"*The Doctrine of the Jesuits,*" *translated by Paul Bert, Member of the Chamber of Deputies, Professor at the Faculty of Sciences (in Paris), pp. 168, 169, American edition. Boston: 1880.*

Alphonsus de Liguori, the sainted Catholic doctor, says in "*Tractatus de Secundo Decalogi Præcepto,*" on the second [third] precept of the decalogue:

"One who is asked concerning something which it is expedient to conceal, can say, 'I say not,' that is, 'I say the word "not"'; since the word 'I say' has a double sense; for it signifies 'to pronounce' and 'to affirm': now in our sense 'I say' is the same as 'I pronounce.'

"A prisoner, when lawfully questioned, can deny a crime even with an oath (at least without grievous sin), if as the result of his confession he is threatened with punishment of death, or imprisonment, or perpetual exile, or the loss of all his property, or the galleys, and similar punishments, by secretly understanding that he has not committed any crime of such a degree that he is bound to confess.

"It is permissible to swear to anything which is false by adding in an undertone a true condition, if that low utterance can in any way be perceived by the other party, though its sense is not understood."—*The Latin text, and an English translation of the above statements are found in "Fifty Years in the Church of Rome," by Father Chiniquy, chap. XIII, and in "Protestant Magazine," April, 1913, p. 163.*

Violations of the sixth, seventh, eighth, and ninth commandments are justified by many leading Jesuit writers, according to many quotations from their books, cited in "The History of the Jesuits," by Theodor Griesinger, pp. 285-304, 478-488, 508-616, 670, 740; and in Gury's "Doctrines of the Jesuits," translated by Paul Bert; and in "The Jesuits," by Dr. Otto Henne an Rhyn, chap. V.

Theodor Griesinger quotes from eight prominent Jesuit authorities, who advocate that it is permissible to kill a prince or ruler who has been deposed by the pope. Here are a few samples:

"In the 'Opuscula Theologica' of Martin Becan, at page 130, the following passage occurs:

"'Every subject may kill his prince when the latter has taken possession of the throne as a usurper, and history teaches, in fact, that in all nations those who kill such tyrants are treated with the greatest honor. But even when the ruler is not a usurper, but a prince who has by right come to the throne, he may be killed as soon as he oppresses his subjects with improper taxation, sells the judicial offices, and issues ordinances in a tyrannical manner for his own peculiar benefit.'"

"With such principles Father Hermann Buchenbaum entirely agreed, and, in the 'Medulla Theologia Moralis,' permission to murder all offenders of mankind and the true faith, as well as enemies of the Society of Jesus, is distinctly laid down. This 'Moral Theology' of Father Buchenbaum is held by all the Society as an unsurpassed and unsurpassable pattern-book, and was on that account introduced, with the approval of their General, into all their colleges.

"Imanuel Sa says, in his aphorisms, under the word 'Clericus': 'The rebellion of an ecclesiastic against a king of the country in which he lives, is no high treason, because an ecclesiastic is not the subject of any king.' 'Equally right,' he adds further, 'is the principle that anyone among the people may kill an illegitimate prince; to murder a tyrant, however, is considered, indeed, to be a duty.'

"Adam Tanner, a very well known and highly esteemed Jesuit professor in Germany, uses almost the identical words, and the not less distinguished Father Johannes Mariana, who taught in Rome, Palermo, and Paris, advances this doctrine in his book 'De Rege' (lib. i., p. 54), published with the approbation of the General Aquaviva and of the whole Society, when he says: 'It is a wholesome thought, brought home to all princes, that as soon as they begin to oppress their subjects, and, by their excessive vices, and, more especially, by the unworthiness of their conduct, make themselves unbearable to the latter, in such a case they should be convinced that one has not only a perfect right to kill them, but that to accomplish such a deed is glorious and heroic.' . . .

"But most precise are the words of the work, so highly prized above all others by the Roman Curie, *Defensio Fidei Catholicæ et Apostolicæ* [Defence of the Catholic and Apostolic Faith]' of the Jesuit Suarez, which appeared in Lisbon in the year 1614, as therein it is stated (lib. vi, cap. iv, Nos. 13 and 14): 'It is an article of faith that the Pope has the right to depose heretical and rebellious kings, and a monarch dethroned by the Pope is no longer a king or legitimate prince. When such an one hesitates to obey the Pope after he is deposed, he then becomes a tyrant, and may be killed by the first comer. Especially when the public weal is assured by the death of the tyrant, it is allowable for anyone to kill the latter.'

"Truly regicide could not be taught by clearer words. . . . The sons of Loyola . . . declared that a more learned, or God-fearing book, had never appeared. . . . Indeed, from this time forth no Jesuit professor whatever wrote on moral theology, or any similar subject, without adopting the teaching of Suarez."—"*History of the Jesuits,*" *pp. 508-511.*

Can any one doubt that the Jesuits have faithfully carried

out this "Article of Faith," wherever they thought it advisable, when he reads of the many attempts upon the life of Queen Elizabeth of England; of the "Gunpowder Plot" to murder James I, and to destroy the "Houses of Parliament" in one blast; of the assassination of William, Prince of Orange; of the attempts upon his son, Maurice, Prince of Orange, and upon Leopold I of Germany, by agents of that Society? We could refer to the "Holy League" of 1576, sponsored by the Jesuits, for the purpose of uniting Catholic Europe to crush Protestantism, and the assassination of Henry III and Henry IV of France in the interest of that scheme. "The Jesuits were, indeed, the heart and soul of the Leaguist conspiracy."—*Id.*, *p. 210.* See also pp. 508-608.

If the political activities of the Jesuits, of which Pope Clement XIV complained so pathetically, are not a serious problem to civil governments, then why were the Jesuits expelled from so many states, Catholic as well as Protestant, as the following table shows? Francis T. Morton, Member of the Massachusetts Bar, gives the following:

"JESUITS EXPELLED FROM

"Saragossa	1555	Touron and Berne	1597
La Palinterre	1558	England again	1602
Vienna	1566	England again	1604
Avignon	1570	Denmark, Venice, etc.	1606
Antwerp, Portugal, etc.	1578	Venice again	1612
England	1579	Amura, Japan	1613
England again	1581	Bohemia	1618
England again	1584	Moravia	1619
England again	1586	Naples and Netherlands	1622
Japan	1587	China and India	1623
Hungary and Transylvania	1588	Turkey	1628
		Abyssinia	1632
Bordeaux	1589	Malta	1634
The whole of France	1594	Russia	1723
Holland	1596	Savoy	1724

Paraguay	1733	From entering Saxony	1831
Portugal Sept. 3,	1759	Portugal	1834
Prohibited in France	1762	Spain again	1835
France again	1764	Rheims (by the people)	1838
Spain, colonies, and Sicilies and Naples	1767	From entering Lucerne	1842
		Lucerne again	1845
Parma and Malta	1768	France again	1845
All Christendom, by bull of Clement XIV, July 21,	1773	Switzerland	1847
		Bavaria and Genoa	1848
		Papal States, by Pius IX, Sardinia, Vienna, Austria	1848
Russia	1776		
France again	1804		
Canton Grisons	1804	Several Italian States	1859
Naples again	1810	Sicily again	1860
France again	1816	Spain again	1868
Moscow, St. Petersburg, and Canton Soleure	1816	Guatemala	1871
		Switzerland	1871
Belgium	1818	German Empire	1872
Brest (by the people)	1819	Mexico (by the viceroy)	1853
Russia again	1820	Mexico (by Comonfort)	1856
Spain again	1820	Mexico (by Congress)	1873
Rouen Cathedral (by the people)	1825	New Granada since	1879
		Venezuela	1879
Belgium, schools	1826	Argentine Republic	1879
France, 8 colleges closed,	1828	Hungary	1879
Britain and Ireland	1829	Brazil	1879
France again	1831	France again	1880."

—"*The Roman Catholic Church and Its Relation to the Federal Government,*" *pp. 167, 168. Boston: 1909.*

Those who feel that the foregoing facts constitute no danger to American civil and religious liberty, would do well to remember that the Jesuits carry on an extensive educational program in this country, and that, according to their textbooks, their principles of civil government are diametrically opposed to the American ideas of separation of church and state. See their

"Manual of Christian Doctrine, by a Seminary Professor," pp. 131-133. Philadelphia: 1915.

The author has stated the foregoing facts, not because of any enmity towards Jesuits as individuals, nor to Catholics in general, but only from a feeling of responsibility to enlighten the American people regarding a public danger. We can truly love the persons, while we warn people against their dangerous tendencies. If we did not sincerely love everybody, we would not be true Christians. (Matthew 5: 43-48.) Jesus loves the sinner, while He hates his sins; and we must have the mind of Christ. (Philippians 2: 5; 1 Corinthians 2: 16.)

To those who wish to study this subject further we recommend the careful reading of the following books, besides those referred to in this chapter:

"History of the Jesuits," by Andrew Steinmetz, London, 1848; "History of the Jesuits," by G. B. Nicolini, London, 1854; "Secret Instructions of the Jesuits," translated from the Latin by W. C. Brownlee, D. D., New York, 1841; "The Footprints of the Jesuits," by R. W. Thompson; "The Jesuit Enigma," by E. Boyd Barrett; "The Programme of the Jesuits," by W. Blair Neatby, London, 1903; "Provincial Letters," by Blaise Pascal, New York, 1853; "History and Fall of the Jesuits," by Count Alexis de Saint-Priest, London, 1861; "Political Life of an Italian," by Francesco Urgos, Battle Creek, Mich., 1876; and "The Jesuit Morals, collected by a Doctor of the College of Sorbonne in Paris," translated into English, London, 1670.

The Mark of the Beast

IN REVELATION 13:16 the Apostle John has penned these significant words: "And he causeth all, both *small* and great, *rich* and poor, free and *bond*, to receive a mark in their right hand, or in their foreheads." What is this mark? It must be of great importance to understand this, for Jesus gives us a solemn warning against receiving the mark. (Revelation 22: 16; 14: 9, 10.) Some claim that it is the mark of the labor unions; but the "small" cannot belong to them, neither are the "rich," or capitalists, members of labor organizations. Others say this prophecy refers to the peculiar "handshake" of the Freemasons; but the "bond," or slave, and the "small," or children, cannot become members of that organization; and yet all these will receive the mark of the beast. (Revelation 13: 16.)

This mark must belong to religion, for it has to do with "worship" (Revelation 13: 12), and it must have originated with the Papacy, for it is "his mark" (Revelation 15: 2), and yet it must be something both Catholics and Protestants agree upon, for "all" will receive it (Revelation 13: 12, 16). It is something in which not only the people but also "the *earth*" on which they dwell, can show obedience. (Revelation 13: 12.) There is but one thing that answers to all these specifications; namely, Sunday-keeping. Sunday is a religious institution that originated with the Catholic Church, and yet Protestants agree to keep it, and we shall now show how the earth can have a part in receiving the mark.

God required "thy manservant," "thy stranger," and "thy cattle" to rest on His holy Sabbath (Exodus 20: 10); that is, no work should be allowed in a field of which we have control. And because the Jews did not obey this, the Lord declared: "I will scatter you among the heathen, . . . and your land shall be

The Mark of the Beast

desolate. . . . Then shall the land rest, and enjoy her Sabbaths; . . . because it did not rest in your sabbaths, when ye dwelt upon it." Leviticus 26: 33-35. And so the Jews were taken into captivity to Babylon for seventy years. (Jeremiah 17: 27; 2 Chronicles 36: 20, 21.) Generally speaking, the people of this world have not allowed the earth to rest on God's holy Sabbath for six thousand years, therefore He will lay it desolate for one thousand years, to give it the rest man has denied it. (Jeremiah 4: 23-25; Revelation 20: 1, 2.)

We have now seen that God wants the earth as well as the people to rest on His holy Sabbath. But the Roman Catholic Church has put herself on record as flatly denying God's claim. Father Enright declares:

"The Bible says: 'Remember the Sabbath day, to keep it holy,' but the Catholic Church says: 'No, keep the first day of the week,' and the whole world bows in obedience."—"*The Industrial American,*" *Harlan, Iowa, Dec. 19, 1889.*

When our government, under pressure from the churches, shall by law enforce the papal Sunday in open violation of God's command, so that the people rest on Sunday, and work their land on the Sabbath, then "*the earth* and them which dwell therein" will yield obedience to the papal power. (Revelation 13: 12.)

Some will ask how a *day* can be a mark in a person's forehead or hand. But we read in Exodus 13: 3, 4, 9 that a *day* can be "for a sign unto thee upon thine hand, and for a memorial between thine eyes." But some one will ask how this "mark" can be received by some only "in their right hand," while others receive it "in their foreheads." (Revelation 13: 16.) That is easy to see. Many people tell us: "We know that the seventh day is the right Sabbath, but we have to work on that day or lose our jobs." Such people have no Sunday-Sabbath in their mind, or forehead, because they do not believe in it; but their "hand" obeys it, and so they receive it in their hand. There are others who see the seventh day is the true Sabbath in the New Testament, but they love their old friends and their old ways more than the unpopular truth, and wish they did not have to obey it.

Now, as God cannot accept unwilling service, He will no longer impress them with the importance of obeying it. God's Spirit is grieved away, and another spirit steps in unnoticed and leads them against the truth. "Because they received not the *love* of the truth, . . . God shall send them strong delusion, that they should believe a lie." 2 Thessalonians 2: 10, 11. (We have an example of this in 1 Kings 22.) After rejecting the truth they become enthusiastic believers in the false sabbath, and thus they receive this mark "in their foreheads."

Who Receives the Mark?

On the other hand, people who have never heard the facts presented, but innocently keep Sunday, thinking it is the right day, are not receiving the mark of the beast by so doing, for God does not hold a person responsible for light that he has never had opportunity to hear or reject. Let us illustrate this fact:

An earnest Christian is the owner of a dry-goods store, and has sold a woman ten yards of cloth. Later she comes back with it, claiming that it is too short. He measures it again, and finds it full length, but, as she insists that it is short, he buys a new yardstick, and placing both side by side he finds his old one an inch short. In amazement he exclaims: "My grandfather was an earnest Christian, and he used this yardstick, and so did my godly father. They were unwittingly stealing, and died without repenting of their sin; they are lost!" He reflects a moment, then adds: "No! I saw them die triumphantly in Christ; they are saved. And I have had blessed seasons with Jesus during these twenty years I have used this old yardstick. If they could be saved using it, and I could serve God acceptably all these years, I will continue to use it hereafter!" But can he be saved while knowingly breaking one of God's commandments? He could have been saved, if his attention had not been called to it. But can he now continue to use the short yard measure and remain a true Christian?

Christ says: "If I had not come and spoken unto them, they had not had sin: but now they have no cloak for their sin"

(John 15:22); and Paul declares: "The times of this ignorance God winked at; but now commandeth all men everywhere to repent" (Acts 17:30). "Therefore to him that knoweth to do good, and doeth it not, to him it is sin." James 4:17. Seeing that God's law is His measuring rod, or standard for moral conduct, and that the Papacy has cut off part of it, so people innocently have followed a faulty rule, and Christ has not attributed this sin to His people till they had opportunity to know better. But when His last message of mercy is being heralded to the world, all are given their choice as to whom they will serve, and those who refuse to listen to His message are as responsible as though they had heard it. (Revelation 22:14; 14:12; Luke 11:31; Proverbs 28:9.)

All will admit that Christ has a perfect right to choose any "sign" He desires, and when He sets forth the Sabbath as the sign, or mark, of His authority and of His sanctifying power, we should accept it with pleasure. (Ezekiel 20:12, 20; 9:4-6.)

The Papacy Selects Its Flag

On the other hand the pope claims to be Christ's representative on earth, having authority to act in His name, so that "the sentences which he gives are to be forthwith ratified in heaven."—*Catholic Encyclopedia, Vol. XII, art. "Pope," par. 20, p. 265.*

Any one who makes counterfeit money tries to make it as near like the genuine as possible. And when Christ has chosen the Sabbath as His sign, the Papacy, in selecting a counterfeit sign, would naturally choose one as near like the genuine as possible, and so it took the very next day. And after having changed the day of rest from the seventh to the first day, the Papacy would naturally point to such a vital change in God's law as evidence of its power; for no one could validly change God's moral law without being authorized to act in Christ's stead.

Hence if, after we have carefully searched the New Testament, and found no command there for the change of the day, we still rely on the custom of the church by keeping the Sunday, we thereby acknowledge the authority of the church that made this change. The Roman Catholic Church sees this point, and uses it as a challenge to Protestantism, as the following quotations from Roman Catholic authorities will show:

Rev. Stephen Keenan says:

"*Q.*—Have you any other way of proving that the Church has power to institute festivals of precept?

"*A.*—Had she not such power, she could not have done that in which all modern religionists agree with her;—she could not have substituted the observance of Sunday, the first day of the week, for the observance of Saturday, the seventh day, a change for which there is no Scriptural authority."—"*Doctrinal Catechism,*" *p. 174. New York: P. J. Kenedy and Sons, 1846.*

Rev. Henry Tuberville, D. D., says:

"*Q.*—How prove you that the Church hath power to command feasts and holy-days?

"*A.*—By the very act of changing the Sabbath into Sunday, which Protestants allow of; and therefore they fondly contradict themselves, by keeping Sunday strictly, and breaking most other feasts commanded by the same Church.

"*Q.*—How prove you that?

"*A.*—Because by keeping *Sunday,* they acknowledge the Church's power to ordain feasts, and to command them under sin: and by not keeping the rest by her commanded, they again deny, in fact, the same power."—"*An Abridgment of the Christian Doctrine,*" *p. 58. New York: Kenedy, 1833.*

J. F. Snyder, of Bloomington, Ill., wrote Cardinal Gibbons asking if the Catholic Church claims the change of the Sabbath "as a mark of her power." The Cardinal through his Chancellor, gave the following answer:

"Of course the Catholic Church claims that the change was her act. It could not have been otherwise, as none in those days would have dreamed of doing anything in matters spiritual and ecclesiastical and religious without her. And the act is a mark

of her ecclesiastical power and authority in religious matters."
(Signed) "H. F. Thomas,
"Chancellor for the Cardinal."
"Nov. 11, 1895."

We will now let the Catholic Church tell *when* it changed the Sabbath day. Here is its answer:

"*Q.*—Which is the Sabbath day? *A.*—Saturday is the Sabbath day. *Q.*—Why do we observe Sunday instead of Saturday? *A.*—We observe Sunday instead of Saturday because the Catholic Church, in the Council of Laodicea (A. D. 336), transferred the solemnity from Saturday to Sunday."—"*Convert's Catechism,*" *Rev. P. Geiermann, p. 50. London: 1934. Sanctioned by the Vatican, Jan. 25, 1910.*

"The Catholic Church for over one thousand years before the existence of a Protestant, by virtue of her Divine mission, changed the day from Saturday to Sunday."—"*The Christian Sabbath," p. 29. Printed by the "Catholic Mirror," the official organ of Cardinal Gibbons, Baltimore, Md., 1893.*

Kindly notice how often Catholic authors refer to the fact that there is no Scripture proof for Sunday, but that it rests solely on the authority of the Catholic Church. Rt. Rev. John Milner says:

"The first precept in the Bible is that of sanctifying the seventh day: 'God blessed the *seventh day,* and sanctified it.' Genesis 2: 3. This precept was confirmed by God in the Ten Commandments: 'Remember the Sabbath-day, to keep it holy. The *seventh day* is the Sabbath of the Lord thy God.' Exodus 20. On the other hand, Christ declares that He is *not come to destroy the law, but to fulfill it.* Matthew 5: 17. He Himself observed the Sabbath: 'and, as His custom was, He went into the synagogue on the Sabbath day.' Luke 4: 16. His disciples likewise observed it after His death: '*They rested on the Sabbath day according to the commandment,*' Luke 23: 56. Yet with all this weight of Scripture authority for keeping the Sabbath, or seventh day, holy, Protestants of all denominations make this a *profane day,* and transfer the obligation of it to the *first day of the week,* or the *Sunday.* Now what authority have they for doing this? None whatever, except the *unwritten word,* or *tradition,* of the Catholic Church."—*"End of Religious Controversy," p. 89. New York: P. J. Kenedy, 1897.*

The Brotherhood of St. Vincent de Paul says:

"'The seventh day is the Sabbath of the Lord thy God; in it thou shalt not do any work.' (Exod. XX. 8, 9). . . . Such being God's command then, I ask again, Why do you not obey it? . . .

"You will answer me, perhaps, that you *do* keep holy the Sabbath-day; for that you abstain from all worldly business, and diligently go to church, and say your prayers, and read your Bible at home, every Sunday of your lives.

"But *Sunday is not the Sabbath-day,* Sunday is the *first* day of the week; the Sabbath-day was the *seventh* day of the week Almighty God did not give a commandment that men should keep holy *one day in seven;* but He named His own day, and said distinctly, 'Thou shalt keep holy *the seventh day*': and He assigned a reason for choosing this day rather than any other— a reason which belongs only to the seventh day of the week, and cannot be applied to the rest. He says, 'For in six days the Lord made heaven and earth, the sea and all that in them is, and rested on the seventh day; *wherefore* the Lord blessed the Sabbath-day and hallowed it.' Almighty God ordered that all men should rest from their labor on the seventh day, because He too had rested on that day: He did not rest on Sunday, but on Saturday. On Sunday, which is the first day of the week, He *began* the work of creation. . . . Gen. 2: 2, 3. Nothing can be more plain and easy to understand than all this; and there is nobody who attempts to deny it. . . . Why then do you keep holy the Sunday, and not Saturday?

"You will tell me that Saturday was the *Jewish* Sabbath, but that the *Christian* Sabbath has been changed to Sunday. Changed! but by whom? Who has authority to change an express commandment of Almighty God? When God has spoken and said, Thou shalt keep holy the seventh day, who shall dare

The Mark of the Beast   295

to say, Nay, thou mayest work and do all manner of worldly business on the seventh day; but thou shalt keep holy the first day in its stead? This is a most important question, which I know not how you can answer.

"You are a Protestant, and you profess to go by the Bible and the Bible only. . . . The command to keep holy the seventh day is one of the Ten Commandments; you believe that the other nine are still binding; who gave you authority to tamper with the fourth?

"We blame you not for making Sunday your weekly holyday instead of Saturday, but for rejecting tradition, which is the only safe and clear rule by which this observance can be justified."—"*Why Don't You Keep Holy the Sabbath-Day?*" *pp. 2-4, 8. London: Burns and Oates. Found also in "The Clifton Tracts," Most Rev. John Hughes, D. D.*

"That the Church has instituted the Sunday as the Lord's day instead of the Sabbath . . . shows forth her great power which she solemnly received from Christ."—"*Manual of the Catholic Religion," p. 186.*

Dr. Martin Luther and Melancthon felt the stinging force of this Catholic argument in proof of the power of the papal church, although they knew that the time had not then come for a Sabbath reform. Dr. Eck, disputing with Luther, said:

"If, however, the Church has had power to change the Sabbath of the Bible into Sunday and to command Sunday-keeping, why should it not have also this power concerning other days? . . . If you omit the latter, and turn from the Church to the Scriptures alone, then you must keep the Sabbath with the Jews, which has been kept from the beginning of the world."—"*Enchiridon," pp. 78, 79, 1533.*

Calling attention to this Roman Catholic assumption of authority, the Reformers said:

"They also point out, that the Sabbath is changed to Sunday, contrary as it seems, to the Ten Commandments; and there is no example over which they make more ado than the change of the Sabbath. Great, they assert, must be the power of the

Church, when it can grant release from one of the Ten Commandments."—"*The Augsburg Confession,*" *art. 28, in "Book of Concord," p. 79. (Norwegian ed., printed in Christiania, 1882.*)

At the great Council of Trent (1545-1563), which was called to determine the "doctrines of the Church in answer to the heresies of the Protestants" (Catholic Encyclopedia, Vol. XV, art. "Trent," p. 30), the question of the authority of the church over that of the Bible was decided in the following manner:

"Finally, at the last [session] opening on the eighteenth of January, 1562, their last scruple was set aside; the archbishop of Reggio made a speech in which he openly declared that tradition stood above Scripture. The authority of the church could therefore not be bound to the authority of the Scripture, because the church had changed Sabbath into Sunday, not by the command of Christ, but by its own authority. With this, to be sure, the last illusion was destroyed, and it was declared that tradition does not signify antiquity, but continual inspiration."—"*Canon and Tradition," Dr. J. H. Holtzman, p. 263. ("Source Book,"pp. 603, 604.*)

After the Jesuits were expelled from England in 1579 they determined to recapture that country, and at their school at Rheims, France, they translated their New Testament from the Vulgate Latin into English in 1582. (Their Old Testament was printed at Douay, 1609, so that their whole Bible has come to be called the Douay version.) In their English New Testament, translated from the Vulgate Edition of 1582, printed in New York, 1834, we read on page 413, note on the Apocalypse 1: 10:

"And if the Church had authority and inspiration from God, to make Sunday, being a work-day before, an everlasting holyday: and the Saturday, that before was holyday, now a common work-day: why may not the same Church prescribe and appoint the other feasts of Easter, Whitsuntide, Christmas, and the rest? For the same warrant she hath for the one she hath for the other."

Thus we see that the Roman Catholic Church always and

everywhere points to her change of the Sabbath as the *mark*, or evidence, of her having the power and inspiration from God to legislate in Christ's stead for His church on earth, and that this power is vested in the pope. Pope Leo XIII says: "We hold upon this earth the place of God Almighty." All must yield "complete submission and obedience of will to the Church and to the Roman Pontiff, as to God Himself."—"*Great Encyclical Letters*," *pp. 304, 193.* And Pope Gregory says of the power of the pope:

"Hence he is said to have a heavenly power, and hence changes even the nature of things, applying the substantial of one thing to another—can make something out of nothing—a judgment which is null he makes to be real, since in the things which he wills, his will is taken for a reason. Nor is there any one to say to him, Why doest thou this? For he can dispense with the law, he can turn injustice into justice by correcting and changing the law, and he has the fulness of power."—"*Decretals of Gregory*" (R. C.), *Book I, title 7, chap. 3. Gloss on the Transfer of Bishops.*

The Roman "Decretalia," an authentic work on Roman ecclesiastical law, says of the power of the pope:

"He can pronounce sentences and judgments in contradiction to the right of nations, to the law of God and man. . . . He can free himself from the commands of the apostles, he being their superior, and from the rules of the Old Testament.

"The pope has power to change times, to abrogate laws, and to dispense with all things, even the precepts of Christ."—"*Decretal, de Translat. Episcop. Cap.*"

"The Pope's will stands for reason. He can dispense above the law; and of wrong make right, by correcting and changing laws."—*Pope Nicholas, Dist. 96; quoted in "Facts for the Times," pp. 55, 56. 1893.*

"The Mark of His Name"

We have now seen that the pope claims to be the "Vicar of the Son of God" on earth; to have authority to act in His name.

And as proof for this claim he points to the fact that he has changed the Sabbath into Sunday. How conclusive! He must be authorized as Christ's "Vicar" in order to validly make such a vital change in God's moral law. That is imperative! The Sunday-Sabbath is therefore the proof or mark of his "vicarship"; it is "the mark of his name." Revelation 14: 11. When once a person has become aware of the wording of this text (Revelation 14: 11), it becomes impossible for him to exchange this explanation of either the "mark" or the "name" for some other. For the creation of the Sunday-Sabbath by the Papacy constitutes the mark, or proof, of the pope's being invested with authority to act as "Vicar of the Son of God." This "mark" and this "name" fit together as prepared by the divine hand of prophecy, and no others do. Catholics can therefore appeal to Protestants in the following way:

Sunday-keeping "not only has no foundation in the Bible, but it is in flagrant contradiction with its letter, which commands rest on the Sabbath, which is Saturday. It was the Catholic Church which, by the authority of Jesus Christ, has transferred this rest to the Sunday. . . . Thus the observance of *Sunday* by the Protestants is an homage they pay, in spite of themselves, to the authority of the Church."—"*Plain Talk About the Protestantism of Today,*" *from the French by Segur, p. 213. Boston: 1868.*

While God did not attribute this sin to His people in former ages, when they had not been enlightened on the subject, we are now approaching the final struggle between Christ and the restored Papacy, and it behooves us to show under which flag we have decided to stand. For example: In times of peace, no serious results would come to an alien in this country, if, on his holiday, he should hoist his native flag. But if our country was at war with his homeland, and he then should tear down the "Stars and Stripes," and trample on it, while he hoisted his own flag, it would be an entirely different matter. And so now, while Christ and Antichrist face each other in the last deadly struggle, it becomes a serious matter to hoist the enemy's flag, while

The Mark of the Beast

trampling on the blood-stained banner of Prince Emmanuel! The papal power was "to continue forty and two months" (Revelation 13: 5), and, as the Bible reckons thirty days to a month, this period would be 1260 prophetic days (Revelation 11: 2, 3). And a day in prophecy stands for a year. (Ezekiel 4: 6.) Thus we see that the papal supremacy would continue for 1260 years. We have already seen that this period began in 538 and ended in 1798 A. D. (See pp. 52-60.) At that time the pope, who had for centuries driven God's people "into captivity," was himself to "go into captivity," the prophet declared. (Revelation 13: 10.) And when the hour struck, to which God's prophetic clock had pointed for 1700 years, the pope had to "go into captivity." Rome was taken by the French on February 10, 1798, the Roman Republic proclaimed on the fifteenth, and on the night of the twentieth, Pope Pius VI was hurried off "into captivity," where he finally died at Valence, France, in 1799. Napoleon had previously given orders that no new pope was to be elected in his place. "No wonder that half Europe thought Napoleon's veto would be obeyed, and that with the Pope the Papacy was dead."—"*Modern Papacy*," *Joseph Rickaby, S. J., p. 1.*

But this prophecy also foretells its restitution. The prophet declares: "His deadly wound was healed; and all the world wondered after the beast." Revelation 13: 3. (Compare 17: 8.) A new pope (Pius VII) was elected March 14, 1800, and, as J. Rickaby further states:

"Yet since then, the Papacy has been lifted to a pinnacle of spiritual power unreached, it may be, since earliest Christian history."—*Id., p. 1.*

Especially since the days of Pope Leo XIII the healing of the "deadly wound" has been steadily progressing. On February 11, 1929, the pope once more became a civil ruler (a king). Some day he will attempt to assume his ancient authority over the nations of earth, and then the world will realize that the Papacy is unchanged in spirit, that it will do today just what it did in the Dark Ages.

We shall now see what God will do for those who have been faithful to Him in this time of apostasy, and have not deviated from His word, while the whole Christian world has gone astray. But let all remember that we cannot follow what is easy and popular, and expect to stand under God's protection. It was the ark of Noah—the object of so much scorn and derision from the world—that finally became the means of rescue to all who stood faithfully by it under taunt and ridicule. And so now. (Luke 17:26.) God always uses unpopular truths with which to test His people and gather out the honest in heart, and He will protect His own in the time of trouble.

They "shall abide under the shadow of the Almighty," safe "from the noisome pestilence." As a hen protects her brood in a storm, so "He shall cover thee with His feathers, and under His wings shalt thou trust: *His truth* shall be thy shield and buckler. Thou shalt not be afraid for the *terror by night* [night raids by airplanes]; nor for the arrow that flieth by day; nor for the pestilence that walketh in darkness; nor for the destruction that wasteth at noonday. A thousand shall fall at thy side, and ten thousand at thy right hand; but it shall not come nigh thee, . . . neither shall any plague come nigh thy dwelling." Psalm 91:1-10.

God will reveal that He still lives and reigns, and the world shall yet see that He puts a difference "between him that serveth God and him that serveth Him not" (Malachi 3:18), just as He did during the plagues of Egypt (Exodus 8:22, 23; 9:4; 10:23; Isaiah 4:5, 6). "His truth shall be thy shield and buckler." Psalm 91:4. (Compare John 17:17; Colossians 1:5; Psalm 119:142, 151.)

According to the new covenant promise, the Holy Spirit is to write the law of God in the heart of God's children. (Hebrews 8:8-10; 2 Corinthians 3:3.) But it must be put "into their mind" before it can be written "in their hearts" (Hebrews 8:10); and as they have been looking at a mutilated law, the missing part must be restored before the Holy Spirit can write it in their hearts. And so the message comes to "bind up the

The Mark of the Beast

testimony, seal the law among My disciples." Isaiah 8: 16. While the nations are moving toward Armageddon, while angels are about to release the winds of war but have been admonished to hold a little longer, another angel comes with the "seal of the living God," saying: "Hurt not the earth, . . . till we have sealed the servants of our God in their foreheads," so they shall be able to stand during the terrible time of trouble just ahead. (Revelation 6: 17; 7: 1-3). The Lord revealed the same scene to Ezekiel. He saw the destroyers coming, but a man clothed in linen (a symbol of purity, Revelation 19: 8) went before them to "set a mark upon the foreheads of" God's people, after which the destroyers were told to "slay utterly old and young, . . . but come not near any man upon whom is the mark." Ezekiel 9: 1-6. This mark, or sign, is the Sabbath. "I gave them My Sabbaths to be a sign between Me and them." Ezekiel 20: 12, 20.

As Christ viewed His people on the earth, and found them without "the seal of the living God," He commanded the winds of war to be held in check "till we have sealed the servants of our God in their foreheads. "Revelation 7: 1-3. They were God's servants, but lacked the seal. In Ezekiel 9: 4-6 and 20: 12, 20 it is called God's "mark," or "sign," while in Revelation 7: 1-4 it is called His "seal." God's "name" will be written in the foreheads of His people. (Revelation 14: 1.) In God's law His name is found only in the fourth commandment. The fourth commandment, which enjoins the keeping of the seventh-day Sabbath, is the seal of God which the Holy Spirit places in the minds and hearts of His people.

The day of wrath is fast approaching. God's people will need a shelter during Armageddon. But God will not do miracles to protect the willfully disobedient. The Lord is greatly grieved over the situation, and complains that His watchmen are not preparing the people "to stand in the battle in the day of the Lord." Ezekiel 13: 5. Compare Ezekiel 22: 26, 30; Isaiah 58: 1, 2, 12, 13; 56: 1-5, 10, 11; Hebrews 10: 26, 29. "But the Lord will be the hope of His people, and the strength of the children of Israel." Joel 3: 16.

The Image to the Beast

Early Efforts to Unite Church and State

IN HOLY Scripture Christ Jesus is repeatedly spoken of as the Lamb of God. Bible prophecy represents America by a similar symbol, which "had two horns like a lamb." The word of God informs us, however, that this peace-loving power, despite its lamb-like principles, eventually would say "to them that dwell on the earth, that they should make an *image* to the beast [the Papacy], which had the wound by a sword, and did live." Revelation 13: 14. The Papacy was formed by a union of church and state, which resulted in the persecution of dissenters. An "image," or "likeness," to the Papacy in America would be a union of church and state, or a co-operation between them, as in the days of papal Rome. And, seeing it is to be "an image to the beast," it cannot be the beast itself, but must be an effort started among Protestants, who desire the aid of the state to enforce some of their dogmas. For nearly three quarters of a century Protestant churches and civic organizations have been at work to create just such a relation between church and state in the United States.

In 1863, representatives of eleven Protestant denominations convened at Xenia, Ohio, and organized a federation, with the avowed purpose of placing the name of God in the Federal Constitution. This National Reform Association declared in Article II of its constitution:

"The object of this Society shall be to . . . secure such an amendment to the Constitution of the United States as will declare the nation's allegiance to Jesus Christ and its acceptance of the moral laws of the Christian religion, and so indicate that this is a Christian nation, and place all the Christian laws, institutions, and usages of our government on an undeniably legal basis in the fundamental law of the land."—"*American State*

Papers," William A. Blakely, p. 343. Washington, D. C.: 1911.

Their official organ: *The Christian Statesman*, (1888) points out their reason for such an amendment to the Federal Constitution in the following words:

"We need it to correct our most unfortunate attitude under the First Amendment, which restrains Congress from prohibiting the free exercise of any false religion."—"*Facts for the Times*," *p. 165*.

That is, the First Amendment to the Federal Constitution, which safeguards religious liberty, must be made null and void by their proposed amendment, just as the eighteenth amendment was nullified by the twenty-first.

Rev. M. A. Gault, a district secretary of the organization, said:

"Our remedy for all these malefic influences is to have the government simply set up the moral law, and recognize God's authority behind it, and *lay its hand on any religion that does not conform to it.*"—"*The Christian Statesman*," *Jan. 13, 1887*; quoted in "*Facts for the Times*," *page 166*.

Jonathan Edwards, another of their speakers, said:

"We want state and religion, and we are going to have it. . . . So far as the affairs of the state require religion, it shall be religion, the religion of Jesus Christ. . . . We use the word religion in its proper sense, as meaning a man's personal relation of faith and obedience to God. Now we are warned that to engraft this doctrine upon the Constitution will be oppressive; that it will infringe the right of conscience; and we are told that there are atheists, deists, Jews, and Seventh Day Baptists who would suffer from it. These all are, for the occasion and so far as our amendment is concerned, one class. . . . What are the rights of the atheist? . . . I would tolerate him as I would a conspirator."—"*Religious Liberty in America*," *C. M. Snow, pp. 266, 267*.

The Lord's Day Alliance is another organization working for the same ends. In their "Lord's Day Papers" (Milwaukee, Wis.), No. 117, p. 4, they say of those who do not sanction their propaganda for Sunday laws: "That anarchistic spirit that tramples on any law that one does not like needs to be completely crushed."

Joining Hands with Catholicism

The Federal Council of Churches of Christ in America has also interested itself along the same lines, and has co-operated more or less with the other two organizations. November 21, 1905, twenty denominations met in New York, and invited the co-operation of the Roman Catholic Church to help solve these civic questions. Another meeting was held in Chicago, December 4-9, 1912, where representatives of thirty-two denominations, having a constituency of nearly 18,000,000 people, met in council. *The Inter-Ocean* of December 7, 1912, reported:

"Federal Council Opens Its Doors to the Catholics

"Word Protestant Is Stricken from Committee Report on Object of Association of Churches.

"The Federal Council of Churches of Christ in America took one of the most important forward steps in its history when it adopted a resolution presented by the executive committee eliminating the word Protestant from the report of the committee, and virtually threw down the bars and invited the Roman Catholic Church of America to join the council, and lend its titanic strength toward solving the common problems of the church."—*Quoted in "Review and Herald," Jan. 9, 1913.*

A strong resolution for the enforcement of Sunday laws by civil government was then adopted.

In forming the Papacy during the fourth and fifth centuries the Catholic bishops, in conjunction with the state, enforced the pagan Sunday as one of the first steps in uniting church and state, thus producing what prophecy terms "the beast." And now in forming "an image to the beast" the Protestant and Catholic clergy will again make Sunday laws the entering wedge in their attempt to enforce religion by law, because Sunday legislation constitutes the neutral ground for co-operation between Catholics and Protestants, and in this work they seek each other's assistance. Rev. S. V. Leech, a Protestant Sunday advocate, said in an address at Denver, Colorado:

"Give us good Sunday laws, well enforced by men in local authority, and our churches will be full of worshipers. . . . A mighty combination of the churches of the United States could win from Congress, the state legislatures, and municipal councils, all legislation essential to this splendid result."—"*Homiletic Review*," November, 1892; quoted in "*American State Papers*," William A. Blakely, p. 732. Washington, D. C.: 1911.

Rev. Sylvester F. Scovel, a leading National Reformer, says:

"This common interest [in Sunday] ought to strengthen both our determination to work, and our readiness to co-operate with our Roman Catholic fellow citizens. . . . It is one of the necessities of the situation."—"*Views of National Reform, Series One*," Bible Students' Library, No. 3, pp. 85, 86. Oakland, Calif.: Jan. 15, 1889.

"Whenever they [the Roman Catholics] are willing to co-operate in resisting the progress of political atheism, we will gladly join hands with them."—"*Christian Statesman*," Dec. 11, 1884.

The Catholic Lay Congress, held in Baltimore, November 12, 1889, said:

"We should seek an alliance with non-Catholics for the purpose of proper Sunday observance."—*Quoted in "Religious Liberty in America*," C. M. Snow, pp. 283, 284.

When the great Federation of Catholic Societies was organized in 1906, they said:

"The Federation is a magnificent organization that is bound to root out prevailing and ruling national evils; a patriotic undertaking in which Catholic and non-Catholic may join hands."—"*The Catholic Union and Times*," Aug. 2, 1906; quoted in "*Signs of the Times*," July 8, 1908.

The following resolution was adopted by the Boston Archdiocesan Federation of Catholic Societies:

"We are unalterably opposed to any relaxation of the Sunday laws. Sunday is a day of rest to be devoted to the praise and service of God. We hold the safest public policy at present is to adhere to the rigid observance of the laws now safeguarding the sanctity of the Lord's day."—"*Boston Pilot,*" *official organ of Cardinal O'Connell, March 16, 1912.*

In 1910 forty-six Protestant denominations co-operated in an effort to reunite all the Christian churches in the world, and fifty-five commissions were appointed to attend a world's conference. They were to have been sent in September, 1914, to different countries to explain the plan, but the World War delayed it. Another effort was made in 1917, when delegates from "many denominations, including Protestant Episcopal, Baptist, Lutheran, and Presbyterian," met at Garden City, N. Y., where they received a letter from Cardinal Gasparri, Papal Secretary of State; and in 1919 three Episcopal bishops were sent to Rome to interview the pope on this question of church union, for Pope Benedict XV had already (1917) started a "move for reunited Christianity."

The daily papers reported in January, 1930, that a plan for a world federation of Lutheran churches was being worked on by a sub-committee of the National Lutheran Council at New York. Reports at that time stated the federated church would be headed by a world executive comparable in administrative respects to the Roman Catholic pope. *Decorah Posten* (Norwegian) for January 21, 1930, gives a similar report. So "federation" and "consolidation" are in the air.

Earnest Men See the Danger

God-fearing men in different denominations, who see the trend of the times, fear the consequences. Dr. A. C. Dixon says:

"The purpose of this 'Inter-church' movement seems to be to make a great ecclesiastical machine which will dominate all smaller bodies. It is an attempt to form a papacy without a pope; and, if evangelical truth is to be sacrificed or compromised, such a papacy without a pope will be no improvement upon the present ecclesiastical machine which has its center in Rome."— A front-page article in the "*Baptist Messenger*," *June 23, 1920. Oklahoma City, Okla.*

Dr. George A. Gordon, Pastor of Old South Church, Boston, says:

"The church was united once, the holy Catholic Church throughout the world, and what was it?—An ineffable tyrant, denying freedom over its whole broad domain, and crushing the intellect and the spirit into a dead uniformity. . . . Your one holy Catholic Protestant American Church would give me much uneasiness if it should come into existence tomorrow."— "*Review and Herald*," *May 11, 1913.*

How clearly these God-fearing men, and many others we could have quoted, see the trend of the Protestant church in forming "an image to the beast" and even seeking the aid of the Papacy in their efforts to form a "holy Catholic Protestant American Church," that could control the state as the papal church did during the Middle Ages!

As long as a church has a living connection with Christ, its true Head, and is loyal to His written word, she is supplied with divine power to do His bidding (Matthew 28: 18-20; Acts 1: 8; 5: 32; Romans 1: 16; John 1: 12), and feels no craving for the power of the state to enforce its teachings. But when apostasy has robbed it of its divine power, and the *power of love* (2 Corinthians 5: 14) has been exchanged for the *love of power*, it usually seeks the aid of the civil arm. All attempts to secure the enforcement of religion by civil laws is therefore a confession of apostasy from apostolic purity.

A Miracle-Working Power

Whenever God has sent a message of reform to prepare His people for some great crisis, the archenemy has always tried to counterfeit it. When Moses was sent to deliver Israel from Egypt, Jannes and Jambres withstood his message by counterfeiting his miracles. (Exodus 7: 10-13, 22; 8: 6, 7; 2 Timothy 3: 8, 9.) And so it was when the message of Christ's first coming was given. In these last days God has promised to send a message in the power and spirit of Elijah to prepare His people for "the coming of the great and dreadful day of the Lord." Malachi 4: 5.) The devil knows this, and so he will counterfeit this message. The prophet, in speaking of the United States, says: "He doeth great wonders, so that he maketh fire come down from heaven on the earth in the sight of men [as Elijah did]. And he deceiveth them that dwell on the earth by the means of those miracles which he had power to do in the *sight* of the *beast*, saying to them that dwell on the earth that they should make an image to the beast, . . . and he causeth all . . . to receive a mark in their right hand or in their foreheads." Revelation 13: 13-16. Thus we see that this country was to become a miracle-working power.

It was here in the United States that modern Spiritism originated in 1848. And it is working miracles. But what is the source of this miraculous power? We will let the leaders of Spiritism answer this question. In *Spiritten* [a Norwegian Spiritist periodical], for December 15, 1889, page 2, we read:

"Spiritism is the serpent in Paradise offering man to eat of the tree of knowledge of good and evil."

To understand this statement we must remember that God told man not to eat of this tree or he would "surely die," but Satan assured Eve: "Ye shall not surely die." Genesis 2: 17; 3: 4. And Spiritists have based their belief on the devil's words, claiming that people at death do not actually die, but simply pass into the spirit world. Moses Hull, a leading teacher and lecturer among them, makes this point clear. He says:

"A Truthful Snake. . . . In answer to the question, 'Who, then, are we to believe—God or Satan?' I answer, The facts, in every case in the Bible, justify us in believing Satan, he has ever been truthful; that is more than can be said of the other one. . . . It was not the devil, but God who made the mistake in the Garden of Eden. . . . It was God, and not the devil, who was a murderer from the beginning."—"*The Devil and the Adventists,*" *pp. 15, 16. Chicago: 1899.*

The Image to the Beast

I must ask pardon of the readers for quoting such blasphemous words, but the only fair way of revealing the true nature of Spiritism is to allow its followers to speak for themselves. In later years, however, Spiritism has changed its *face*, but not its *heart*, by professing Christianity; and in that garb has succeeded in getting into the churches. Some startling revelations have been unearthed of late years regarding the work of Spiritism in the different churches all over the world. Many in these churches have felt the emptiness of formalism, and have craved spiritual power, but have been unwilling to get it by the way of the cross. Humble confession, heartfelt repentance, and straightening up of wrongs done to neighbors is a road too narrow for many to walk; unpopular truths, which cut across their selfish path of ease, are unwelcome to them; but Spiritism in its Christian form offers the desired power without such sacrifices, and the easy road is accepted with eagerness by many. (Compare Mark 8: 34, 38; Acts 5: 32; Matthew 4: 3-10; 2 Thessalonians 2: 9-11; Matthew 24: 24.) They mistakenly accept spiritual power and miracles as evidence of their being right with God (Matthew 7: 21-23; Luke 9: 55), but God's children cannot thus prove whether a movement is true or false, for the enemy can work miracles. Judge I. W. Edmonds, a noted Spiritist, says of his daughter:

"She knows no other language than her own native tongue, the English, except a little French she learned in the girls' school; and yet she has talked in nine or ten different languages, often a whole hour at a time, with the same ease as a native. Quite often strangers in their native tongue hold conversation with their spirit friends through her."—*"Spiritualism Before the Judgment Seat of Science," p. 42.*

In the near future Spiritism will influence people in America to form a union of church and state. When this is accomplished, the Papacy will step in and take charge of it. Thus every effort to form this union is helping the Papacy to power. This is so strikingly pictured by the prophet Zechariah that we must take the space here to refer to it.

The Woman in the Ephah

The prophet saw "an ephah" (which is a fitting symbol of the business world) and "a woman that sitteth in the midst of the ephah." Zechariah 5: 7. A woman in prophecy symbolizes a church, and in the book of Revelation this woman is called "*the mother*" church, which is "drunken with the blood of . . . the martyrs of Jesus." It is also represented as "that great city" on "seven mountains." (Revelation 17: 5, 6, 9, 18.) M'Clintock and Strong says :"The city of Rome was founded . . . on the Palatine Hill; it was extended by degrees, so as to take in six other hills."—*Encyclopedia, art. "Rome."* This woman is said to be trading in all kinds of "merchandise": linen, silk, wine, flour, sheep, chariots, and souls of men. (Revelation 18: 12, 13.) A more striking picture of the Papacy could hardly be given, for no advantage in the business world escapes her vigilance. She always seeks to place her members in strategic government positions, and at advantageous labor posts.

The ephah, in which this prophetic woman sat, was covered with "a talent of lead," and when this cover was lifted the "wickedness" was seen, or, as the Septuagint has it: "This is the iniquity." (Zechariah 5: 7, 8.) And just so, when the Reformation of the sixteenth century pulled off the cover, "the mystery of iniquity" was seen in all its "wickedness." (2 Thessalonians 2: 7, 8.) But the prophet saw the cover placed back on again, and, through the efforts of Jesuits, this covering-up work is being accomplished. "Two women" are next seen who "lifted up the ephah between the earth and the heaven." (Zechariah 5: 8, 9.) That is, after the true nature of the papacy has been concealed, the miracle-working power of *Spiritism* in some *Christian form*, and fallen Protestantism (these two women) will raise the Papacy to the sky.

"Then said I to the angel that talked with me, Whither do these bear the ephah? And he said unto me, To build it an house in the land of Shinar: and it shall be established, and set there *upon her own base.*" Verses 10, 11. It was "in the land Shinar" that the former tower of Babel was built, as a man-made way to

The Image to the Beast

heaven, so as to avoid the judgment of God in case of another Flood. The builders called it "Babil," "Gate of God," but God called it "Babel," "Confusion." It was around this tower that the city of Babylon was built; and it stands as a synonym for a man-made way of salvation; and for this reason the Roman Catholic Church is called "BABYLON THE GREAT, THE MOTHER." Revelation 17:5. Even Cardinal Gibbons declares: "'Babylon,' from which Peter addresses his first epistle, is understood by learned annotators, Protestant and Catholic, to refer to Rome."—"*Faith of Our Fathers,*" *edition of 1885, p. 131; and p. 106 in "Eighty-third Revised Edition" of 1917.* It is natural, therefore, when the prophet speaks of the Papacy's being established "there upon *her own base*," that he should symbolically refer to it as "the land of Shinar," or Babylon. (Zechariah 5:10, 11.) Thus we see, that, through the coöperation of modernized Protestantism, and Christianized Spiritism, the Papacy will be brought back to power. This is so aptly stated by another author that we give the quotation here:

"When Protestantism shall stretch her hand across the gulf to grasp the hand of the Roman power, when she shall reach over the abyss to clasp hands with Spiritualism, when, under the influence of this threefold union, our country shall repudiate every principle of its Constitution as a Protestant and Republican government, and shall make provision for the propagation of papal falsehoods and delusions, then we may know that the time has come for the marvelous working of Satan, and that the end is near."—"*Testimonies,*" *Vol. V, p. 451.*

Then the "deadly wound" will be fully healed (Revelation 13:3), and in her restored relationship to the kings of the earth, the Papacy will exclaim in the pride of her power: "I sit a queen, and am no widow, and shall see no sorrow." Revelation 18:7. But, as pride and "a haughty spirit" go before a fall, her glorying will be short, for she shall "go into perdition." Verse 8; 17:8. Thus we can better understand the seven heads of the beast. The Papacy is said to be one "of the seven" heads, and yet it is "the eighth" (Revelation 17:11), because, as one of the seven it received its deadly wound, and when this is healed it comes back as the eighth in rotation, while in reality it is only one of the seven coming back to life and power. (Compare Revelation 13: 3 with 17: 8, 11.)

"THAT NO MAN MIGHT BUY OR SELL"

"And that no man might buy or sell, save he that had the mark." Revelation 13: 17. We have seen that the Papacy has adopted Sunday as "a mark of her ecclesiastical power and authority," and the Protestant organizations have also adopted this mark, as the following quotations show:

"This day [Sunday] is set apart for divine worship and preparation for another life. It is the *test* of all religion."—*Dr. W. W. Everts, in Elgin (Ill.) "Sunday Convention," November, 1887.*

"When the people, through their representative, legalize the *first day of the week* as a day of rest and of worship for those who choose so to observe it, it is a *sign* of the Christian nation."— *From a sermon reported in "Christian Oracle," January 12, 1893.*

The Puritans in the United States made Sunday "a sign between them and the heathen world around, and, to a large extent, it has continued to be a *mark of American religion* to the present day."—*Rev. J. G. Lorimer, in "Christian Treasury"; all quoted in "Signs of the Times," April 1, 1908.*

When these large religious organizations, that are so vitally interested in Sunday enforcement, combine in their efforts, it is not remarkable that they should attempt to deprive dissenters of their natural rights of attaining their livelihood, for we have seen that this combination is making "an image to the beast" (Revelation 13: 14-17); and the beast, or Papacy, did this very thing. At the Synod of Tholouse, A. D. 1163, it made the following decrees against Sabbath-keepers:

"The bishops and priests [were] 'to take care, and to forbid, under the pain of excommunication, every person from presuming to give reception, or the least assistance to the followers of this heresy, *which first began in the country of Tholouse*, whenever they shall be discovered. Neither were they to have any dealings with them in buying or selling; that by being thus deprived of the common assistance of life, they might be compelled to repent of the evil of their way. Whosoever shall dare to contravene this order, let them be excommunicated, as a partner with them in their guilt. As many of them as can be found, let them be imprisoned by the Catholic princes, and punished with the forfeiture of all their substance.'"

Stirred by this decree, King Ildefonsus of Arragon banished all Waldenses in 1194. "He adds: 'If any, from this day forwards, shall presume to receive into their houses, the aforesaid Waldenses and Inzabatati, or other heretics, of whatsoever profession they be, or to hear, in any place, their abominable preachings, or give them food, or do them any kind office whatsoever; let him know, that he shall incur the indignation of Almighty God and ours; that he shall forfeit all his goods, without the benefit of appeal, and be punished as though guilty of high treason."—"*History of the Inquisition,*" *Philip Limborch,*" *pp. 88, 89. London: 1816.*

That the "image to the beast" will actually duplicate the work of the Papacy also in this respect is seen from the following utterance, among many others we could quote: Dr. Bascom Robins, in a sermon on the "Decalogue," preached in Burlington, Kansas, Sunday, January 31, 1904, said:

"In the Christian decalogue the first day was made the Sabbath by divine appointment. But there is a class of people who will not keep the Christian Sabbath unless they are forced to do so. But that can be easily done. We have twenty million of men, besides women and children, in this country, who want this country to keep the Christian Sabbath. If we would say we will not sell anything to them, we will not buy anything from them, we will not work for them, or hire them to work for us, the thing could be wiped out, and all the world would keep the Christian Sabbath."

God, who knows the end from the beginning, has foretold that they would do this very thing, so "that no man might buy or sell, save he that had the mark." Revelation 13: 17. But will

God forsake His faithful children in this trying hour? Oh, no! "He that toucheth you toucheth the apple of His eye." Zechariah 2: 8. As a loving Father He will step forward to the protection of His children. (Psalm 103: 13.) And His enemies will find that "it is a fearful thing to fall into the hands of the living God." Hebrews 10: 31.

When the world refuses to permit God's people to "buy or sell," He will send drought and famine, so that the wicked will have little or nothing to sell, and will be unable to buy because their money will be worthless. The seven last plagues will be God's answer to man's challenge, as the ten plagues of Egypt were His answer to the haughty challenge of a Pharaoh against His message in ancient time. (Exodus 4: 22, 23; 5: 2.) With men suffering from sores and fever, and no water to drink, while the sun is scorching them with great heat (Revelation 16: 1-9), causing the most terrible drought the world has ever witnessed (Joel 1: 10-20), the earth will be in a deplorable condition (Isaiah 24: 1-6), and people "shall pass through it, hardly bestead and hungry: and it shall come to pass, that when they shall be hungry, they shall fret themselves, and curse their king, and their God". (Isaiah 8: 21, 22). And they will turn against the rich (James 5: 1-5), who will "cast their silver in the streets" to appease the angry mob, but "their gold shall be removed" (Ezekiel 7: 19). They hoarded millions, and cornered markets, while working people were suffering, till at last the storm has gathered around their well-filled palaces, and too late they make an attempt to save themselves from the long-pent-up wrath.

The laws that deprive God's people of their rights, and thus force them out of the cities, seem to them a calamity, and many surrender the truth to support their families. But what appears to be such a calamity is a blessing in disguise, for it drives them out of the cities in time to escape this terrible labor-revolution. Some day we shall find that no hardship comes to God's loyal children but what is absolutely necessary to their salvation. Those who make it their undeviating practice to put God's will first in all their plans and habits of living,

The Image to the Beast

can safely trust Him for the rest. (Matthew 6: 33; Philippians 4: 19; Isaiah 43: 2.) Driven from the cities, they flee to mountain fastnesses and solitary places, where angels supply their needs, as Elijah was fed. "Bread shall be given him; his waters shall be sure." Isaiah 33: 16. Oh, we have a wonderful God. "Blessed are all they that put their trust in Him." Psalm 2: 12.

God's loyal children will be fed by angels, while the world is starving. The fondest hopes of God's people will be realized: "Thine eyes shall see the king in His beauty: they shall behold the land that is very far off." Isaiah 33: 17, 18. No pen can describe that thrill of joy when we shall meet our dear Saviour and our loved ones, and be taken home to that beautiful land that knows no heartaches, no farewell scenes, no funeral trains. (John 14: 1-3.)

The great question for each one of us to settle is whether we will have our citizenship papers in order when King Jesus shall come to claim His own. The reader might ask what papers are required for citizenship in that kingdom. To answer that question satisfactorily, we must remember that *sin* has caused all the anguish, sorrow, and trouble in this world, and that God's heart of infinite love has been wrung with pain for suffering humanity. He has therefore decided that sin, with all its trail of woe, shall not be permitted to enter His eternal kingdom, and that all who enter that blissful home must part company with sin.

But sin is inbred in man, and forms a part of his very character, so that he cannot, by his own efforts, extricate himself from its toils. (Jeremiah 13: 23; Romans 7: 15, 18-24.) Christ, however, stands ready to free us from our sins. He will deliver us if we will let Him do it. (Matthew 1: 21; John 1: 12.) But He will not use force, even in things that are for our own good, for He has created man a free moral agent, and respects his choice. (Isaiah 1: 18; Revelation 22: 17; 1 John 1: 7, 9.) A complete surrender to Christ is therefore necessary, that He may change our desires, affections, and characters so we can enjoy the society of the pure and unselfish inhabitants of that happy land.

Index

Abbott, John S. C. 51
A. D. 538   52, 54, 57, 212, 299
A. D. 1798   57-60, 212, 234, 299
Adolphus, John 59
Albigenses 124-130, 244
Allix, Dr. Peter 113, 120, 121-123
Alps, a refuge for the persecuted 118
Ambassadors at the Vatican 270-271
Anderson, W. J. 176
Andrews, J. N. 98, 117, 125, 149
Antichrist 113, 196-211
  Bible prophecies of 202-203
  defined 196-197
  identified 197-200, 210-211, 233
  no distinction between an, and the 203-204
  origin of name 197
  Papacy is, Reformers taught 199
  time of his coming 197, 210, 211
Apostolic succession 26
Aquinas, Thomas 66
Arian controversy 36-37, 40, 44-49, 52
Armageddon 301
Armenians, Sabbath-keepers among 154
Armitage, Thomas 152, 237
Arnaud, Henri 120, 121
Astruc, Jean 29-30
Augsburg Confession 295-296
Augustine, mission to British Isles 138-140
Babylon of Revelation seventeen 118, 311
Bampfield, Dr. Thomas 144
Bang, A. Ch. 110
Baptist Church and Sabbath reform 174-177
Barrett, E. B. 241, 287
Baudrillart, Alfred 64, 224, 243
Beast, first, of Revelation thirteen 217-218, 226, 234, 235, 239, 312-313
  of Revelation seventeen 311
  two-horned 234, 235
Bede, Venerable 136
Belisarius 42-44, 47-49, 52
Bellesheim 138, 141
Belmont and Monod 53
Benedict, David 122, 125
Bethlehem Moravian Church Records 150
Bible, inspiration of 9-10
  Syriac 153, 154
  translation 13-16, 18-25, 128
"Bible on the Inquisitorial Rack" 32
Bibles, burned 15-16
Bill of Rights 152, 237-238
Bingham, Joseph 84
Blake, Edgar 271
Blakely, Wm. A. 152, 303, 305
Bloodshed over church elections 115-116
Bloomfield, S. T. 231
Bolce, Harold 30, 31
Bompiani, Sophia V. 119
Bonacursus 125
Books changed by Catholic Church 162, 243-249, 261
"Boston Post" 306

Bower, A. 47, 53, 165, 232, 272
Boycott, religious 312-314
Bruno, Joseph Faa di 26
Buchanan Claudius 154, 156, 157
E. S. 22
Burnet, Gilbert 252
Bury, J. B. 43, 47, 49
Butler, A. 138
"Cambridge Medieval History" 40, 43, 47, 49
Campbell, Alexander 93
  T. J. 273, 277
Canon law 219, 220, 221
Canossa 263-265, 269
Catechisms, extracts from 69, 292-293
Cathcart, Wm. 135, 136, 137
"Catholic Action" 241
Catholic Church, and higher criticism 33
  and the Bible 10-11, 14-25, 154, 199
  destroys records of early Christianity 125-126, 139, 140, 158, 212
  use of calumny by 123
  treachery by 130, 132-133, 262
"Catholic Encyclopedia" 17, 20, 21, 22, 27, 29, 50, 61, 63, 129, 164, 198, 203, 219, 220, 221, 223, 254, 291
Catholicism, delineation of 210-211
"Catholic Mirror" 69, 247
"Catholic Standard and Times" 240
"Catholic Union and Times" 305
"Catholic World" 69, 103
Celibacy, enforced, depraved priesthood 159
Celtic Church 118, 127, 134-143
  destroyed by Rome 139, 140
  learning of 134
Censorship, Jesuit, of publications and public records 252-255
Chafie, Thomas 101
Chambers, T. W. 78
"Change times and laws" 67-69
Chapman, Dom John 41, 42
Chillingworth, Wm. 27-28
Chiniquy, Charles, 209-210
  on cost of masses 163
Christ, nature of, Bible doctrine on 204
"Christian Oracle" 312
"Christian Register" 31
"Christian Science Monitor" 242
"Christian Statesman" 303, 305
Church and State, Catholic doctrine of 256-272
  united to form Papacy 302
Church of England and Sabbath reform 174
Clarke, Adam 202
Clement XIV, Pope 278-280
Clovis 46
Coleman, Ch. B. 219
Columba 118, 137-138
Conroy, James P. 218
Constantine, Emperor 36, 109-115
  his plan to unite heathenism and Christianity 109

316

Index

Sunday law of 109-110
Constantinople, transfer of government to 218
Constitution, United States 237, 257-258, 302-303
"Constitutions of the Society of Jesus" 275, 276, 279
Conybeare and Howson 90
Cook, F. C. 71
"Cosmopolitan Magazine" 30, 31
Coughlin, Father 242
Council of, Friaul 117
   Laodicea 85, 116-117, 293
   Nicæa 114
   Trent 19, 20, 24, 161, 196
   on canon law 220
Counter-Reformation 242, 278
Cox. Robert 112, 115, 148
   S.H. 231, 271
Coxe, Wm. 169, 170
"Coxe's House of Austria" 246
Cramp, J. M. 144
Croly, George 56
Crown, pope's, triple, origin of 36
Cruden, A. 238
Cumont, Frantz 99
Cunninghame, Wm. 56
Dachsel, K. A. 81, 188
Dahle, L. 187
Daniel seven 34, 52, 67, 217, 234
D'Aubigne, J. H. M. 139, 140
Day-year principle 226
Deadly wound 60, 210, 234
   healed 299, 311
Declaration of Independence 236-237, 257-258
"Decretalia" 297
De Latti, M. 228
Deliverance for God's people 315
Dellon 156, 157
De Sanctis, Dr. 126
Devens, R. M. 236, 237
Dixon, A. C. 306
Douay Bible 23-25, 35, 203, 219, 296
   on day for year 226
   six hundred sixty-six 219
Dowling, John 20, 21, 26, 66, 99, 171
Dragon, of Revelation twelve 217-218, 239
   speaking like a 239
Draper, J. W. 49, 103
Durham, M. James 233
Ebrard, A. 138
Eck, Dr. 295
Edmonds, I. W. 309
Edwards, Jonathan 303
Elector Frederick's dream 12, 13
Elliott, E. B. 36, 57-58
Ellis, Wm. T. 214
"Encyclopedia Americana" 273, 277
   Britannica 79, 97
England, Catholic aims in 240
Enright, Father 289
Eusebius 112, 115
"Evangelist, The," Sweden 175
Evarts, W. W. 312
Excommunication of rulers 263-265
Fathers, Early Church, estimation of 98, 202
Falsehood, a weapon of the Papacy 132, 224-225, 243
Federal Council of Churches 304-305
Ferraris, F. L. 61, 222

Finlay, George 44, 53
First day of the week in the Bible 88, 92
Fleming, Robert 229
Flick, A. C. 218
"Forum" 20
France, struggle against Rome in 265-269
Frederick, Wm. 100
"Freeman's Journal" 248
Fulop-Miller, Rene 276, 277, 281
Fulton, John 85, 117
Gault, M. A. 303
Geiermann, Peter 69, 293
Gibbon, Edward 40, 46, 47, 54, 113, 115
Gibbons, Cardinal 206, 232, 292
   letter from 232, 292-293
Gieseler, John C. L. 87
Gilly, W. S. 119, 121
Goldastus 124
Gospel of Christ defined 204-205
Gordon, G. A. 307
Graham, H. G. 24
   J. E. 262
Gratian, Decretum of 219, 220
"Great Controversy" 147
Great words, speak 61-62, 199, 297
Green, Thomas S. 197, 235
Gregory I, Pope 117, 122
   VII, Pope 263, 264
      struggle with King Henry IV 263-265
   IX, Pope 65-66
   XIII, Pope 220, 221
Griesinger, Theodor 273, 278, 283-285
Grimelund, Bishop A. 86, 108, 149
Grotius, Hugo 112
Guinness, H. Grattan 210-211, 229
Guppy, Henry 22-23
Gury 282, 283
Hallam, Henry 262
Hamilton, Thomas 71
Hansen, S., and Olsen, P. 176
Hart, Richard 134, 137, 142
Hastings, H. L. 33, 192
"Haydn's Dictionary of Dates" 144, 174
Hays, F. P. C. 218
Heathenism enters the church 98, 102-105, 114, 115
Hefele's "Councils" 131
Heggtveit, H. G. 109
Henderson, E. F. 165
Henry IV, King, struggle with Rome 263-265
Heresy defined 62, 63, 128
Heretics, laws against 131
Heruli 36, 37-40
Heylyn, Peter 84, 92, 95, 116
Higher criticism, fruits of 30-33
   origin of 26, 28-32
Hiscox, Edward T. 177
   on change of the Sabbath 107
"History of King Christian the Third" 179
"History of the Norwegian Church Under Catholicism" 178
Hodgkin, Thomas 37, 39, 45-46, 48
Hoffman, B. 227
Holtzman, J. H. 296
Holy Spirit, Vicar of Christ 198
Hook, W. F. 106
Horn, little 35, 52, 61, 62, 67, 202-203
Horns, ten 35
   three plucked up 36, 52
   two, defined 235

318   *Facts of Faith*

like lamb 234, 235
Huc, M. l'Abbe 153
Huguenots 241, 244
Hull, Moses 308
Humphrey, Wm. 198
Huss, and Hussites 147, 148
   martyred by treachery 130
Infallible rule 9, 26-28, 121-122, 199, 295
Image to the beast 302-315
Immaculate Conception 206
Immorality in Medieval Church 159-162
"Index of Prohibited Books" 11, 16, 17, 253-254
Indulgences, defined 162-164
   sale of 162-172, 244, 246
Innocent III, Pope 62, 126
Inquisition 15-16, 127-130, 156-158, 160, 178, 244
"Inter-Ocean" 304
Inventions, table of 213-214
Ireland, Archbishop 239
Jacobites, Sabbath-keepers in India 154
Jahn, Dr. Johann 19, 21
James, John, martyr for Sabbath 144
Jefferson, Dr. Charles 31
Jerome of Prague 147, 148
Jerome, St. 119
Jesuits 23, 149, 172, 173, 241, 243, 251, 252, 262, 273-287, 296, 310
   abolition of 278-280, 285-286
   bibliography on 287
   danger to United States from 280, 286-287
   dates when expelled 285-286
   falsehood, doctrine of 225, 280-282
   methods of 277-278
   mission of 277
   morality, teachings on 283
   murder, doctrine of 283
   obedience, doctrine of 274-277
   organization and rules of 273-277
   origin 273
   registers of 273-274
   teachings on Antichrist 201, 202
Jones, Wm. 118, 120, 123
"Jubilee of the Norwegian Synod" 183
"Jubilees," source of revenue to Catholic Church 165-167
Justinian, Emperor 36, 40-41, 42, 43, 46-49, 52, 54-56
Keenan, S. 206, 207, 292
Kenny, Michael 254-255
Keyser, R. 178, 179
Kinkead, T. L. 198
Kitto, John 74, 93, 95
Knowledge, increase of 213-214
Labbe, Philippe 223
Lamblike principles of two-horned beast 235-238
Lang, Andrew 138, 140, 141, 143
Lange, J. P. 73
Lattey, C. 220
Law, civil, priests exempt from 159
Law of God, changed by Papacy 68-69, 105-106, 291
Lawrence, Eugene 14, 15
Lea, H. C. 16, 65, 128, 159, 160, 161-162, 166, 169
Lecky, W. E. H. 66
Leech, S. V. 305
Leo XIII, Pope 61, 62, 199, 240, 256-261, 297, 299
Leone, Abbate 274, 281

Lewis. A. H. 110, 111, 112
Ley, John 117
Liberty, Catholic doctrine on 256-262
   civil and religious 235-239
   Rome hates 46
Liberty, *see also* Religious Liberty
Libraries, controlled by Rome 248, 251-252
Liguori, Alphonsus de 62, 206, 207, 208, 282
Limborch, Philippus van 127-130, 166, 313
Llorente, D. J. A. 15, 16
Lombards 49-51
Lord's Day Alliance 303-304
"Lord's Day" of Rev. 1: 10 91-92
Lorimer, J. G. 312
Loyola, Ignatius 273, 277
Lund, Truels 77
Lunt, Wm. E. 164, 165, 166, 167, 168
Luther, Martin 12, 13, 72, 200
   and Reformers, on the Sabbath 295-296
   on Antichrist 199, 200
   theses by 172
Lutheran Church in America, Sabbath reform in 182-185
Machiavelli, N. 38-39, 50
Madison, James, sponsor of Bill of Rights 152
"Make America Catholic" 239-255
Manning, E. H. Cardinal 223
"Manual of Christian Doctrine by a Seminary Professor," 260-261, 287
"Manual of the Catholic Religion" 295
"Mark of his name" 297-298
Mark of the beast 289-299, 312
   not received by innocent Sunday-keepers 290-291
   received by earth 288-289
   in forehead 289-290
   in hand 289
Margaret, Romanized Scottish church 140-143
Mary, Virgin, Catholic praise of 207
   Protestant teaching about 204
   sinlessness of 205-206
Mass, Catholic doctrine of 208-209
Massie, J. W. 154, 155
Matthews, A. H. 262, 263, 264, 265
McCarty, M. J. F. 251, 252
M'Clintock and Strong's Encyclopedia 83
McGinnis, Wm. 248, 249, 250, 251
Mendham, Joseph 15
Merry del Val 11
Milman, H. H. 37, 44, 47, 111, 114, 115
Milner, J. 208, 293-294
"Minneapolis Journal" 269, 271
"Minneapolis Tribune" 270
Miracles, spurious 143
"The Missionary" 240
"Mission Movement in America" 240
Mithraism 97, 99
Moffatt, James C. 138
Moody, D. L. 215
"Monthly Church Tidings" 183-185
Moravians 148-150
Morer, T. H. 78, 85, 100
Morrell and Carey 198
Morton, F. T. 266, 267, 280
Mosheim, J. L. 97, 103, 104, 125
Motley, John L. 67
Muller, M. 208
Murphy, J. G. 73
Murray, Gilbert 100
   John 11

Muston, Alexis 133
Myers, P. V. N. 42, 244
Mysteries, Christian 193
 heathen 97-98, 103-105
Mystery of godliness 193, 194
Mystery of iniquity 195, 208, 310
National Reform Association 302-303
Neander, J. A. W. 114, 135
"Nelson's Encyclopedia" 43
Netherlands, papal persecutions in 67
"New Catholic Dictionary" 62, 232
Newman, John Henry Cardinal 39, 104
Newton, Thomas 35, 36, 147, 233
 Sir Isaac 35
Nielsen, Fr. 147, 148
Norlin, Theodore 181
"North British Review" 79, 101
"Our Sunday Visitor" 223-226
Ostrogoths 44, 45-49
Owen, J. J. 81
Pacelli, Cardinal 242
Pagit, Ephraim 134, 135
Paine, Thomas 31
Palmer, E. R. 14-15
Papacy, believed antichrist, by all ages 200, 201
 by Reformers 199, 200
 supremacy of 52-60, 213, 218
"Parallel Source Problems in Medieval History" 264
Patrick 134-137
Pennington, A. R. 58
Perrin, J. P. 122, 124
Persecution 14-17, 41, 42, 62-67, 126-133, 143, 144, 148, 155, 179, 181, 243, 244, 261-262, 303
 in the United States 151, 312
Phelan, Father 66
Philippines, moral conditions in, under Catholicism 161
Pius X, Pope 262
Plagues, seven last 314
"Plain Talk About the Protestantism of Today" 298
Politics, Rome interferes in 265-272
Poole, W. H. 79
Pope, the, the vicar of Christ 198
Pope's crown, inscription on 223, 227-232
Portuguese in India 155-158
Preus, A. C. 182
Press, daily, controlled by Rome 248-250
Priests, Catholic, power of 206-208
 exaltation of 62
Printing and the Bible 11-12, 14-16
Procopius 41
Procter, J. 163
Prophecy, light on, after 1798 213-214
Prophetic symbols explained 34
 why used 212
Protestants, ceased to protest 204
Purchas, Samuel 154
Purgatory and masses for the dead 162-163
Raymond, Earl of Tholouse 129-131
Reaves, Father 226
"Records of Civilization Sources and Studies," 263
Reformation 12-14, 28, 127, 147, 159-177, 244, 262, 277, 310
 called revolt 244-245
 immorality of church a cause 159-162
 needed 172
 suppression of, resulted in declension 181-182
 to be finished 173
Religious liberty and United States Constitution 151
 defined 151, 235-236
 endangered 302-315
 struggle over, in America 235-237
 under Theodoric 46
"Report of the Second Church Meeting in Copenhagen" 189
Rhyn, Otto Henne an 281, 283
Rickaby, Joseph 58, 299
Robertson, Wm. 171, 275
Robins, Bascom 313
Robinson, J. H 246
Roche, J. T. 163, 266
"Roger de Hoveden's Annals" 143
Rome's challenge to Protestants 292-298
Roosevelt, F. D., and Rome 271
Rordam, Skat 108
Rulers, duty to murder 283-285
 list of murders of 285
Rupp, I. D. 146
Sabbath, among ancient nations 74
 and Sunday, final conflict over 298-299
 and Waldenses 113, 122-123
 an Edenic institution 70
 changed by apostate church 105, 106, 108-109
 in Egypt 77
 change of, claimed by Rome 102-104, 289, 292-297
 counterfeit 291
 hated by Papacy 84
 in Eden 70-74
 in Egypt and wilderness 74
 in New Testament 80-82
 in the early church 83-87, 92-96
 Luther on 72
 moral or typical 75-76
 not changed by apostles 82
  by Christ 76 106-108, 294
 not Jewish 71, 294
 when changed by Rome 293
Sabbath-keepers, boycotted in France and Spain 312-313
 in America 144-146, 150, 151
 in Bohemia 148, 149
 in British Isles 118, 137, 138, 140-146
 in China 118, 153, 190-192
 in India 118, 127, 153-158
 in Scandinavia, origin of 178-180
 under Catholicism 178, 179
Sabbath-keeping in Italy 117
 Pope Gregory I against 117
Sabbath, kept in Constantine's day 112-113, 116
Sabbath reform in America 182-185
 in England 174
 in Scandinavian countries 175-176, 178-189
 supernatural basis for 178, 180, 181
Sacho, Reinerus 120
St. Bartholomew Massacre 17
"St. Paul Pioneer Press" 241
Salvation, Catholic doctrine of 207
Sayce, A. H. 74
Schaff, Dr. Philip 53, 110, 115
"Schaff-Herzog Encyclopedia" 29, 56
Scharling, Dr. 181
Schiorn, Fr. 186-187

Scoles, D. E. 228
Scott, M J. 27, 162, 163, 199
Scovel, S. F. 305
Seal of God 300-301
Second advent, D. L. Moody on 215
 message sent before 217
Sheppard, J. G. 45, 46, 49
"Shepherd of the Valley" 225
Shimeall, R. C. 230-231
Showerman, Grant 99
Simon, Richard 28-29
Sismondi, J. C. S. de 51
Six hundred sixty-six 218-233
Skene, Wm. F. 140
Smiles, Samuel 11, 12, 16, 17
Smith, George 105
 Wm. 92
 and Wace 53
Smyth, J. P. 20
Socrates 83
Sommer, M. A. 176
Spangenberg, A. G. 149, 150
Spiritism, modern 307-311
"Spiritten" 308
Spiritual bank, Catholic doctrine of 163-164
Stanley, A. P. 114
Stennet, Edward, wrote to defend Sabbath 144
Steinmetz, Andrew 64, 225, 287
"Stockholms Posttidning" 57
Strong, James 197
Summerbell, N. 48, 49, 54, 92, 105
Sunday, accepted from heathenism 97-117
 and Mithraism 97, 99
 a working day 68-69, 94-96
 early morning meetings on 94-96
 not found in Bible 88
 origin of name 77-78, 101-103
Sunday-keeping not in the Bible 298
 the mark of the beast 288, 312
 upheld by spurious miracles 143
Sunday law, first 108-111
Sunday laws 312
 in America 303-306
Sun worship 78-79, 97, 99, 100, 101, 111-112
Sverdrup, George 105
"Swedish Church History" 180, 181
"Tablet, The" 267-268
Taft, W. H. 161
Taiping Revolution 190-192
Tanner, Joseph 201
Taylor, Jeremy 85, 95
 W. B. 92
Temporal power of the pope 218, 223, 226, 234
Tertullian 103, 134
"Testimonies" 260, 311
Tetzel, seller of indulgences 170-172
Textbooks Romanized, see Books changed by Catholic Church
Thatcher and McNeal 127
Theodoric 39, 44-46
"Theological Association of the Deans of Drammen" 185-186
"Theological Periodicals for the Evangelical Lutheran Church in Norway" 179
Thomas, Apostle, missionary travels of 153
Thorndike, L. 40
Thurston, Herbert 165-166
Time of the end 212-215
Todd, Dr. 136
Townsend, G. A. 235, 238

Tradition 9, 11, 26-27, 106, 295
Transportation, modern, foretold 214
Trask, John, martyr for Sabbath 144
Trevor, George 59
Tuberville, Henry 292
Turgot 141-142
Twelve hundred sixty years 52-60, 212-215, 226, 299
Two-horned beast, see Beast, two-horned of Revelation 13
United States, Catholic aims in 225, 239-272
 influence of 238-240
 in prophecy 234-242
 in prophecy see also Wesley, John; Horns, two; Beast, two-horned; Religious Liberty, Lamblike principles; Liberty, Declaration of Independence; Constitution, U. S.; Washington, George; Bill of Rights; United States, Catholic aims in; "Make America Catholic"; "Catholic Action"; Coughlin, Father, Pacelli, Cardinal
Union of churches, dangers foreseen in 306-307
Union of Protestant churches 306
Protestantism and Catholicism 304-305, 310-311
Vandals, destroyed 42-44
Vaudois, see Waldenses
Verstegen, Richard 102
Vicar of Christ 297-298
 the Holy Spirit 198
 the pope 198
Vicarius Christi 226, 237
Filii Dei 219, 221-224, 226-233
Villari, P. 38, 39, 42, 43, 46, 47, 52
Vulgate Bible 19-22, 24, 296
Waldo 120, 121
Waldenses 10, 17, 118, 133, 178, 244
 boycotted 133
 crusades against 131-133
 destroyed 126-133
 origin of 118-120, 123-125
 righteousness of 123, 126-128
 Sabbath-keepers 113, 122-125, 128, 137
Warnings, God has always sent 216
Washington, George, letter on religious liberty 151, 237
Watson, Thomas E. 168, 245-246
Webster, Hutton 110
Week, names of days of 77-78
Wesley, John, on Revelation thirteen 234
"Western Watchman" 66, 225, 269
Whalley, G. H. 139, 140
White, Francis 94
Whitmore, Thomas 228
Whittle, D. W. 25
"Why Don't You Keep the Sabbath Day?" 295
Williams, Michael 270
"Woman in the Ephah" 310-311
"Words, Speak Great" 61-62
World War helped Papacy 270
Woywod, S. 164
Wright, C. H. H. 200, 203
Wylie, J. A. 13, 67, 132, 133, 172, 197, 210
Xavier, Francis 156
Yeates, Thomas 153, 154, 156
Zahn, Theodore 86
Zechariah, prophet, foretold exaltation of Papacy 310-311
Zinzendorf, Count, a Sabbath-keeper 149, 150

We invite you to view the complete
selection of titles we publish at:

www.TEACHServices.com

or write or email us your praises,
reactions, or thoughts about this
or any other book we publish at:

TEACH Services, Inc.
P.O. Box 954
Ringgold, GA 30736

info@TEACHServices.com

Finally, if you are interested in seeing
your own book in print, please contact us at

publishing@teachservices.com.

We would be happy to review your manuscript for free.

www.ingramcontent.com/pod-product-compliance
Lightning Source LLC
Chambersburg PA
CBHW071619170426
43195CB00038B/1461